UTAH
Michael R. Kelsey

MOUNTAINEERING
GUIDE And The Best Canyon Hikes

Second Edition

D1558711

Kelsey Publishing Co.
310 East 950 South
Springville, Utah
USA   84663

First Edition February 1983
Second Edition October 1986

Copyright © 1983 Michael R. Kelsey
        All Rights Reserved

Library of Congress Catalog Card Number — 86-082457

ISBN Number 0-9605824-5-2

Climbers, hikers and travelers are requested to send corrections, comments, suggestions, and orders for books to the author at the following address:

Michael R. Kelsey
310 East 950 South
Springville, Utah, USA
84663   Tele. 801-489-6666

Printed by Press Publishing, Ltd.
            1601 West   800 North
            Provo, Utah 84601

All Fotos by the Author

All Maps, Charts, Diagrams, etc., Drawn by the Author

Cover Fotos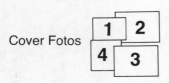

1. Yard Peak and Allsop Lake

2. Kings Peak from Henrys Fork Basin

3. Mineral Gulch of Parunuweap Canyon

4. Cascade Peak, from Northeast Ridge

TABLE OF CONTENTS

MAP SYMBOLS

Town or City	Peak
Buildings or Homes	Peak and Prominent Ridge
Hut or Shelter	River or Stream
Back Country Campsite	Narrows
Campsite	River, Intermittent - Dry
Campgrounds	Lake
Picnic Site	Mine, Quarry
Church	Waterfalls
Ranger Station	Spring or Seep
Guard Station	Spring, Intermittent
Ski lift or Tramway	Glacier or Perpetual Snow
Airport or Landing Strip	Radio Tower
Railway	Pass
Interstate Highway	Natural Arch
U.S. Highway	Steep Escarpment
Utah State Highway	Narrow Canyon
Road-Unsurfaced	Geology Cross Section
Road-4 Wheel Drive	Pictograph
Trails	Petroglyph
Car Park, Trailhead	Indian Ruins
Route, Climbing	

ABBREVIATIONS

Canyon	C. or Can.	Picnic Ground	P.G.
Lake	L.	Reservoir	Res.
River	R.	Ranger Station	R.S.
Creek	CK.	Guard Station	G.S.
Campground	C.G.	4 Wheel Drive	4WD

4

Acknowledgments

It's impossible to recall at this time all the many people who have helped me put this book together. There are countless forest rangers who spent hours going over maps indicating trails or the lack of. Also the BLM rangers and national parks employees who made recommendations as to the best hikes, especially in the southeastern part of Utah. There was also other hikers and climbers who gave information.

But the one person who helped most, the one person who spent hours going over the maps and especially the manuscript, and the one person who just simply put up with me, was my mother, Venetta Kelsey.

The Author

The author experienced his earliest years of life in Eastern Utah's Uinta Basin, namely around the town of Roosevelt. Later the family moved to Provo, where he attended Provo High School, and later Brigham Young University, where he earned a B.S. degree in Sociology. Soon after he discovered that was the wrong subject, so he attended the University of Utah, where he received his Masters of Science degree in Geography, finishing that in June, 1970.

It was then that real life began, for on June 9, 1970, he put a pack on his back and started traveling for the first time. Since then he has traveled to 129 countries and island groups. All this wandering has resulted in several books written and published by the author: *Climbers and Hikers Guide to the Worlds Mountains, 2nd Ed.*; *China on Your Own and the Hiking Guide to China's Nine Sacred Mountains*; *Canyon Hiking Guide to the Colorado Plateau*; and finally *Hiking Utah's San Rafael Swell*.

After having climbed or attempted most of the mountains in the world guide, he then "settled down" to do what he has dreamed about for many years, a mountaineering guide to Utah.

The author and his father take a rest at Trail Rider Pass (3612 meters), not far from Lake Atwood, in the upper Uinta River drainage. The lower slopes of Mt. Emmons seen in the background (50mm lens).

INTRODUCTION

For the most part this book consists of maps of mountains and some canyons and hiking areas within the state of Utah. Each map is accompanied by a page of written information and one fotograph. The written part includes sections on location of mountains or hiking areas, geology, access routes and problems, trail information, time needed for the hike or climb, the best time of year for an outing in each location, and a list of forest service or U.S.G.S. maps available for each area.

All the hikes and climbs in this book are divided into 6 different regions. They include: The Great Basin, located in western Utah, extending from the Nevada border eastward to the Wasatch Mountains and the central Utah Plateaus. Next section is the Greater Wasatch Mountains. This includes all the mountains from Mt. Nebo in the south, north to the Idaho border, along the Wasatch Front. It also includes the Bear River and Wellsville Mountains near the Idaho line. After that is the part including peaks and summits on the High Plateaus of central and southern Utah. The fourth section is of the Uinta Mountains in the northeast part of the state. The detail and coverage of this section has been very much upgraded from the first edition of this book. The next part covers the mountains of the Canyonlands area; and the last section covers the best of Utah's canyon hikes, all of which are located on the Colorado Plateau.

Each of these areas are interesting in their own way and each area has its own unique problems for travel or access, its own vegetation and to some degree its own climate. For example, in the Great Basin, distances are usually long and travel is always partly on gravel roads. However these roads are generally well maintained, and on many driving can be done at or near highway speeds. The Great Basin is also a dry area, so climbers and hikers should take extra amounts of water in the vehicle, as well as extra gasoline in some cases. In most other areas of the state, one can travel on paved roads to very near the intended hike or climb, with only a few exceptions, most of which are in the Canyonlands region. The Canyonlands region is another dry area, and water should always be carried in one's vehicle. The Canyonlands part is another region having some stretches of long dusty roads. All other parts of the state are well watered and have only short lengths of gravel or dirt roads leading to mountains.

Other topics covered in this guide which are of interest to climbers and hikers, are the bristlecone pine trees located in the Great Basin part of Utah. Later on in this book is a map showing locations of this tree, both in Utah and the west. This tree is the oldest living thing on earth, and Utah has a fair number of peaks where the bristlecone pine is found.

Also found in another section of this book is a map showing peaks which were used in the 1880's as Heliograph or triangulation stations. These survey stations were set up on some of the highest and most prominent peaks as the U.S. Coast and Geodetic Survey crossed the state while surveying the USA along the 39th parallel. There is some evidence of these stations on most of the peaks indicated, and in some cases, stone walled houses are still standing. Ibapah and Belknap Peaks have the best ruins.

To help the reader become better acquainted with Utahs weather patterns, and especially those climbers from out-of-state and perhaps even foreign travelers, a group of climographs have been created which show the annual rainfall, elevation, annual temperature range, temperature curve, monthly precipitation and length of growing season, of 19   Utah cities and towns. These charts or climographs show in a graphic way the difference in the weather patterns throughout the state. And there are great differences in rainfall and temperature patterns from one part of the state to another, especially from north to south, and from near the Great Salt Lake to areas away from that lake.

To help the reader understand the processes which have formed the earth and especially those parts of Utah where hiking is of interest, a number of geologic cross sections have been drawn. Several are enlarged, but a number of others are included right on the maps of hiking areas. These smaller cross sections are on maps of the Canyonlands hikes. These cross sections show the different beddings or formations, but not the age of the rock. In many cases they also show Anazasi ruins in relation to overhangs and the sun, and natural bridges. The climber or hiker should find these geologic cross sections both interesting and informative.

Another chart or list in the back of the book compares the highest peaks in the state. There are 15 summits in Utah over 4000 meters (13123 feet), all of which are found in the Uinta Mountains of the northeast. There's another list of peaks over 3600 meters (11810 feet). This is for all peaks outside the Uinta Mountains, namely in the La Sal, the Tushar, and the Deep Creek Ranges. Mt. Timpanogos isn't even in this group, as it's only 3582 meters. All elevations in this book are in meters and all distances are in kilometers. So for the reader who doesn't yet comprehend metrics, there's a chart or conversion table in the book as well.

In several of the canyon hikes covered in this book, mention is made of the ruins and rock art in those areas. So a map and a short piece of information has been prepared shedding light on the Anasazi and Fremont Indian ruins and pictographs and petroglyphs. Nowhere else can one view *outdoor museums,* such as those found in the southeastern corner of Utah.

Also included in the back of this book is a list of BLM (Bureau of Land Management) offices, forest service ranger stations, national parks and park office headquarters, and the locations of places where maps can be found and purchased. Included is an index map showing the states new 1:100,000 scale maps (metric).

This book differs from a lot of other guide books in that there is no advice as to how to climb mountains, or how to get on in the wilderness. It's assumed that the reader will already know most of the basics before getting involved with real mountaineering, or before he or she gets too far into some of the long canyon hikes. But here are some tips concerning equipment. For the Uinta Mountains a good tent with rainsheet is the one most important piece of equipment to be taken. Also, a raincoat or piece of plastic for the hiker is needed because of the frequency of summer showers. In early summer mesquito repellent is a must — again in the Uintas. When hiking in the canyons, which are very dry regions, one can usually get by without a tent, but it's always a more comfortable camp if one is inside away from the insects. The author takes and uses a tent no matter where he's hiking or climbing. Footwear is almost exclusively the leather hiking or climbing boot, either medium or high top. But for the canyon hikes the recently introduced rubber, leather and nylon walking or hiking shoe seems ideal. Up till now the jungle boots have been the most popular footwear used in the canyons, along with the common running shoe. The reason for the change of footwear in the canyons is that in most cases there are no trails and one simply walks in the sandy canyon bottom, and many times in the stream itself.

For those hiking in the canyons of southeastern Utah, water is sometimes a problem. Actually, there's plenty around, but you'll have to know where it is, and plan your campsites accordingly. Before entering any of the canyons mentioned in this book, always stop at the park visitor center, or the nearest BLM office or ranger station, for the latest word on the availability of water and its whereabouts. Be prepared by taking extra water bottles in your car and in your pack. By having the potential to carry water, finding a campsite is made easier, especially if time is a factor.

A hat is an important piece of equipment, although most don't use one. The author has been climbing and hiking around the world since 1970 without a hat, and now is afflicted with "sun spots"; that's stage one on the road to skin cancer. Utah is generally a dry state with lots of sunshine, so the use of a hat or cap of some kind is important.

One should think about the use of a small climbers or backpackers stove. As time goes on, and as climbing and hiking become more popular, some popular camping spots will become wood scarce. This is especially true around some lakes in the High Uintas, in the central Wasatch Mountains, and a few sites in some canyons in the southeast part of the state. The author carries the smallest kerosene stove available in his pack at all times and it is an indispensable part of his camping gear. The new stoves these days weigh almost nothing and take up a very small space in one's pack.

Some writers spend a lot of time lecturing about leaving a clean campsite, carrying out all trash, leaving all ruins undistrubed, not cutting pine boughs for bedding, etc., etc. This book does not, beyond this line. The author has found that people reading books such as this one are almost always considerate of nature and of those who will follow. It appears to be someone else, people who will never see, or least of all, read this book, who are leaving their beer and soda pop cans all about for posterity to view.

The author has spent years hiking and climbing in the state, years dreaming of putting together this book and a couple of years in direct preparation in writing and publishing this book and now hopes each reader can have even more enjoyable moments than the author as a result of the information and maps presented here.

METRIC CONVERSION TABLE

1 Centimeter = .39 Inch	1 Mile = 1.609 Kilometers	1 Quart (US) = .946 Liter
1 Inch = 2.54 Centimeters	100 Miles = 161 Kilometers	1 Gallon (US) = 3.785 Liters
1 Meter = 39.37 Inches	100 Kilometers = 62 Miles	1 Acre = 0.405 Hectare
1 Foot = 0.3048 Meter	1 Liter = 1.056 Quarts (US)	1 Hectare = 2.471 Acres
1 Kilometer = 0.621 Mile		

METERS TO FEET (Meters x 3.2808 = Feet)

100 m = 328 ft.	2500 m = 8202 ft.	5000 m = 16404 ft.	7500 m = 24606 ft.
500 m = 1640 ft.	3000 m = 9842 ft.	5500 m = 18044 ft.	8000 m = 26246 ft.
1000 m = 3281 ft.	3500 m = 11483 ft.	6000 m = 19686 ft.	8500 m = 27887 ft.
1500 m = 4921 ft.	4000 m = 13124 ft.	6500 m = 21325 ft.	9000 m = 29527 ft.
2000 m = 6562 ft.	4500 m = 14764 ft.	7000 m = 22966 ft.	

FEET TO METERS (Feet ÷ 3.2808 = Meters)

1000 ft. = 305 m	9000 ft. = 2743 m	16000 ft. = 4877 m	23000 ft. = 7010 m
2000 ft. = 610 m	10000 ft. = 3048 m	17000 ft. = 5182 m	24000 ft. = 7315 m
3000 ft. = 914 m	11000 ft. = 3353 m	18000 ft. = 5486 m	25000 ft. = 7620 m
4000 ft. = 1219 m	12000 ft. = 3658 m	19000 ft. = 5791 m	26000 ft. = 7925 m
5000 ft. = 1524 m	13000 ft. = 3962 m	20000 ft. = 6096 m	27000 ft. = 8230 m
6000 ft. = 1829 m	14000 ft. = 4268 m	21000 ft. = 6401 m	28000 ft. = 8535 m
7000 ft. = 2134 m	15000 ft. = 4572 m	22000 ft. = 6706 m	29000 ft. = 8839 m
8000 ft. = 2438 m			30000 ft. = 9144 m

CENTIMETERS

INCHES

METERS

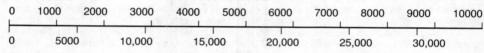

FEET

KILOMETERS

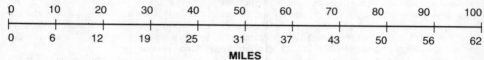

MILES

FAHRENHEIT

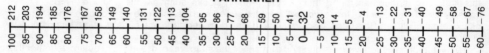

CENTIGRADE

8   This is the trailhead at Henry's Fork Campground, Henry's Fork Creek (50mm lens).

Reference Map

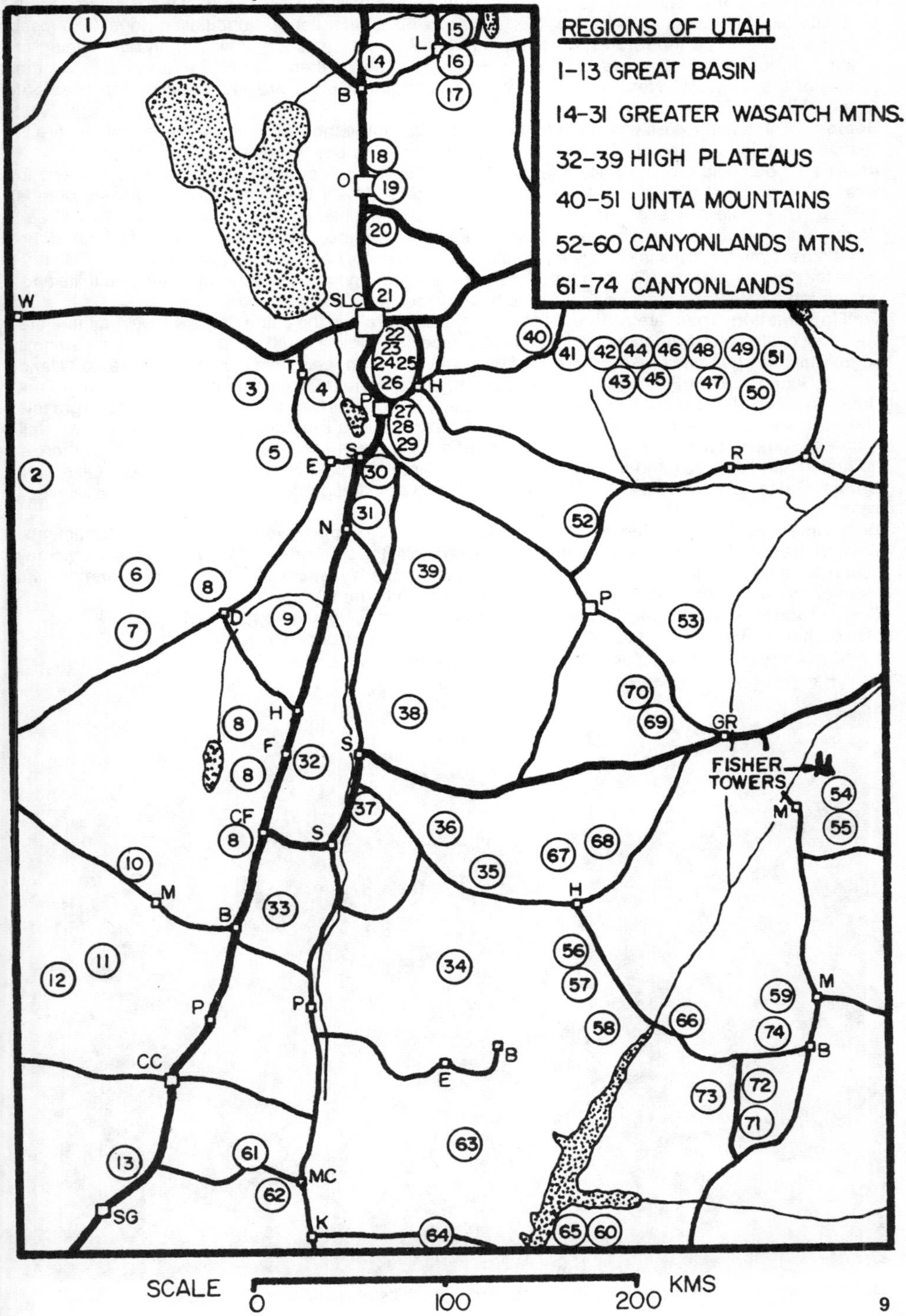

REGIONS OF UTAH

1–13 GREAT BASIN
14–31 GREATER WASATCH MTNS.
32–39 HIGH PLATEAUS
40–51 UINTA MOUNTAINS
52–60 CANYONLANDS MTNS.
61–74 CANYONLANDS

FISHER TOWERS

SCALE

0   100   200 KMS

9

Bull Mountain, Raft River Mountains

Location One of the least known ranges in the state of Utah is the Raft River Mountains in the extreme northwest corner of the state. The range runs east-west, a rare thing in the USA. The highest peak is Bull Mountain, at 3028 meters. It's merely the high point on a long, flat and undulating ridge. The local economy is based on the raising of sheep, cattle, jackrabbits, alfalfa and wheat, and the mining of building stone, namely the green-colored rock, olivine. The northern half of the range is under the control of the Sawtooth National Forest, while the southern parts are managed by the Hereford Association out of Park Valley.

Geology The same forces which made the Uintas also made the Raft Rivers. The mountain core is quartzite, with intrusive bodies on both the north and south slopes (granite).

Access One should drive to Snowville on I-84, then drive west on US Highway 42-30. Proceed to Strevel, Clear Creek and to the Clear Creek Campground — if the all-public-land access route is desired. This route has about 16 kms of dusty, but well-maintained roads (Strevel to Clear Creek Campground). The easiest approach is via Park Valley, but the land between the highway and the mountains is private. This is usually no problem though, simply ask a local rancher for permission to cross the associations land. At the church in Park Valley, turn north and follow the main road to its end, go through a gate, then proceed to the mouth of Fisher Creek Canyon.

Trail Information There are no forest service maintained trails in the entire range. However, there are abundant cattle trails throughout all the canyons, especially on the southern slopes. Along the summit ridge, which is open and grassy, there's a 4WD road. One can reach this summit ridge via Left Hand Fork of Dunn Creek or Fisher Creek on the south, or from Clear Creek Campground and Lake Fork Creek on the north. The canyons are wooded, mostly with douglas fir — the ridges are open and grassy. The best area for rock climbers is in the cirque basin holding Bull Lake. The canyons are all well watered. Some streams even have fish. (The northern approach is the recommended route, as there is no private land to cross and there are many good campsites with water along Clear and Lake Fork Creeks. Get to Lake Fk. Creek by driving through Clear Ck. Campground, then pass through a livestock gate.)

Best Time and Time Needed From Salt Lake City it's a 3-4 hour drive to the Raft River Mountains. Then hikers can reach the higher summits from the north or the south in one day, which means a two day outing for the average hiker. These mountains receive heavy winter snows but little summer rain, therefore mid-June through October are the normal months for hiking.

Campgrounds Clear Creek C.G. is on public land, as is most of the north slope.

Maps Utah Travel Council Map 8 — Northwestern Utah, Sawtooth National Forest, U.S.G.S. maps Grouse Creek (1:100,000), Yost, Park Valley, Kelton Pass (1:62,500)

Bull Mtn. and its north facing cirque basins. From the hills above Clear Ck. CG. (150mm lens).

Map 1, Bull Mountain, Raft River Mtns.

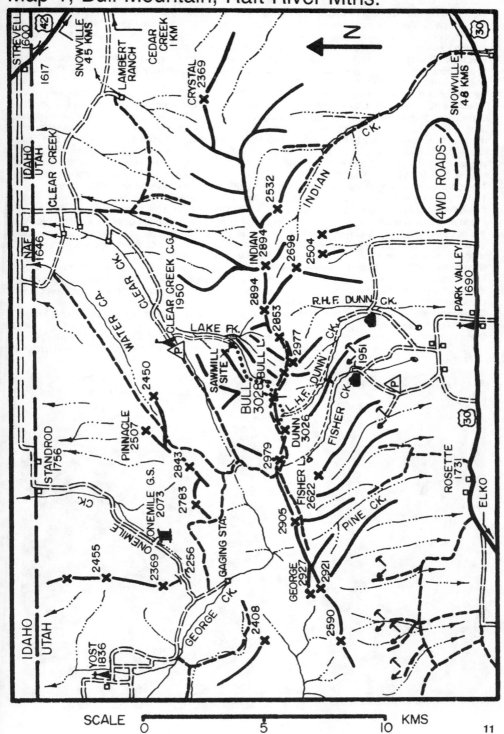

SCALE 0 5 10 KMS

Ibapah Peak, Deep Creek Range

Location The Deep Creek Range, in which Ibapah Peak at 3684 meters is the highest summit, is located in extreme western Utah and about 100 kms south of Wendover. This range is part of the Basin and Range System of mountains which covers all of Nevada and parts of Utah. The Goshute Indian Reservation is located on the western slopes and the range is under the control of the BLM. On top of Ibapah Peak are the remains of an old Heliograph Station dating from the early 1880's.

Geology The north and south ends of the Deep Creeks is made of Precambrian rock, quartzite. But the central core including the highest peaks is composed of a Tertiary intrusive body of granite. The area is pocked with old mines.

Access For Utahns, this is one of the more isolated ranges in the state. The best approach is via Interstate 80 to Wendover, then south on US Highway 93, and finally east to Ibapah and Callao. One can also reach the east side of the range via Dugway or Vernon, and the old stage coach line running to Fish Springs. One can climb on the west side of the range, but most of the better camping spots and most running water seems to be on the eastern slope. The author climbed the peaks via Indian Farm Creek, but it's likely the route up Granite Creek is the better and most direct route to Ibapah Peak. A third access route is from the Delta area and Highway 50-6. From near the Utah-Nevada line, drive north to Gandy, then Trout Creek. Ibapah is the only settlement in the area that has food and gasoline available. Be prepared for a long dusty ride and carry plenty of fuel, food and water for emergencies.

Trail Information Because of its isolation, there are very few people visiting the Deep Creeks — as a result, there are few if any trails. There are some 4WD roads to most of the canyon mouths, but beyond those points, one must usually route-find. On one visit, the author climbed both of the high peaks via Indian Farm Creek, but later found the trail up Granite Creek is the normal route. Cars can't make it far up Granite Canyon, but there is an old trail there to the pass at 3375 meters. From the pass there is a trail to the summit of Ibapah, but you'll likely not find it until you're halfway up.

Best Time and Time Needed It will take most of one day for people in Utah to reach these mountains. From somewhere on Granite Creek it will take one day for the actual hike, then perhaps another day for the return trip. But a fast hiker and driver can make the entire trip from say Salt Lake, in two long days. Climbing season, late June through October.

Campgrounds One BLM campground here, but good campsites exist in the mouths of all major canyons on the east slope.

Maps Utah Travel Council Map 7 — Northwestern Central Utah, U.S.G.S. maps Fish Springs (1:100,000), Trout Creek (1:62,500), Ibapah Peak, Indian Farm Creek, Goshute, Goshute Canyon (1:24,000)

From summit of Ibapah, one can see the second highest peak, Haystack Mt. (50mm lens).

Map 2, Ibapah Peak, Deep Creek Range

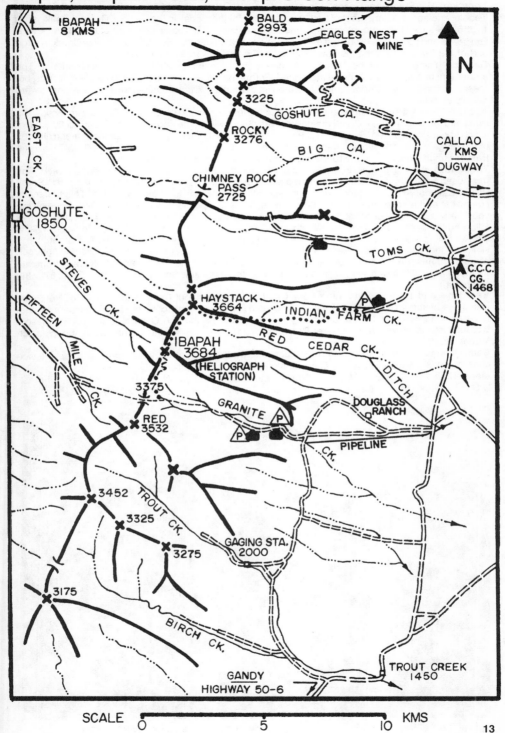

IBAPAH
8 KMS

BALD
2993

EAGLES NEST
MINE

N

3225

GOSHUTE CA.

EAST CK.

ROCKY
3276

BIG   CA.

CALLAO
7 KMS

DUGWAY

CHIMNEY ROCK
PASS
2725

GOSHUTE
1850

TOMS CK.

C.C.C.
CG.
1468

STEVES   CK.

HAYSTACK
3664

INDIAN FARM CK.

P

FIFTEEN   MILE   CK.

IBAPAH
3684
(HELIOGRAPH
STATION)

RED   CEDAR   CK.

DITCH

3375

GRANITE

P

DOUGLASS
RANCH

RED
3532

P

PIPELINE

CK.

3452

TROUT CK.

3325

GAGING STA.
2000

3275

3175

BIRCH   CK.

GANDY
HIGHWAY 50-6

TROUT CREEK
1450

SCALE

0   5   10   KMS

13

Deseret Peak, Stansbury Mountains

Location The Stansbury Range is located in Tooele County about 25 kms due west of the town of Tooele, and about 70 kms west of Salt Lake City. The highest peak in the range is Deseret Peak, rising to 3363 meters. These mountains are almost unknown outside Tooele County, but they have several fine peaks and some nice hiking trails. There are even catchable size fish in South Willow Creek. A large part of the Stansbury Range is now included in the Deseret Peak Wilderness Area.

Geology The geology of the Stansbury Range is similar to that of other Great Basin mountains. The earth's crustal folding has exposed the Oquirrh Formation, mostly limestone, on the eastern slopes, but the highest peaks are composed mostly of the Tintic Quartzite. Cirque basins indicate these peaks were heavily glaciated in the past.

Access The single most important access road is the one running south out of Grantsville. Follow the signs into the South Willow Creek drainage. From Grantsville to the end of the road is about 20 kms, of which about 13 are paved. By parking at the upper end of the Loop Campground, one can reach all parts of the range via the trail leaving that point. Another route of access would be North Willow Creek, and East Hickman Canyon, but the roads into these canyons are less well-maintained.

Trail Information The trails in the Stansbury Range are well-maintained and moderately used. The most used trail is the one running to the top of Deseret Peak. It begins at the end of the road in South Willow Canyon. At the first junction, a sign points the way up Mill Fork and to the top. This trail fades somewhat as it reaches the eastern summit ridge, but at that point the way is easy to find. Once on top you'll have a choice of descent routes. You may return the same way, or better still, return via the trail following the north ridge. This trail eventually joins the main trail running from North to South Willow Creeks. There's plenty of water in the canyons, but on the higher ridges there is none. The vegetation is similar to that in the Wasatch Mountains. The northeastern face of Deseret Peak has some fine rock climbing routes. (In the spring of 1983, there was flooding and the road was cut 3 kms from the trailhead. By 1985, it was still cut, so plan to walk an few extra kms until monies can be found to fix the wash-out.)

Best Time and Time Needed From Loop Campgrounds it's about 7 kms to the top of Deseret Peak, with a rise of about 1000 meters. Fast hikers can do it in a couple of hours, but for most hikers it'll be a half-day hike. From Salt Lake, an all day trip. Mid-June on through October is the hiking season. Because of the elevation of Deseret Peak, precipitation is very similar to that along the Wasatch Mountains.

Campgrounds Campgrounds are small and uncrowded, except on weekends. All forest service campgrounds are in South Willow Canyon, along with a guard station.

Maps Utah Travel Council Map 7 — Northwestern Central Utah, Wasatch-Cache National Forest, U.S.G.S. maps Tooele, Rush Valley (1:100,000), Timpie, Deseret Peak (1:62,500)

Deseret Peak in the Stansbury Range, showing the northeast face (35mm lens).

Map 3, Deseret Peak, Stansbury Mtns.

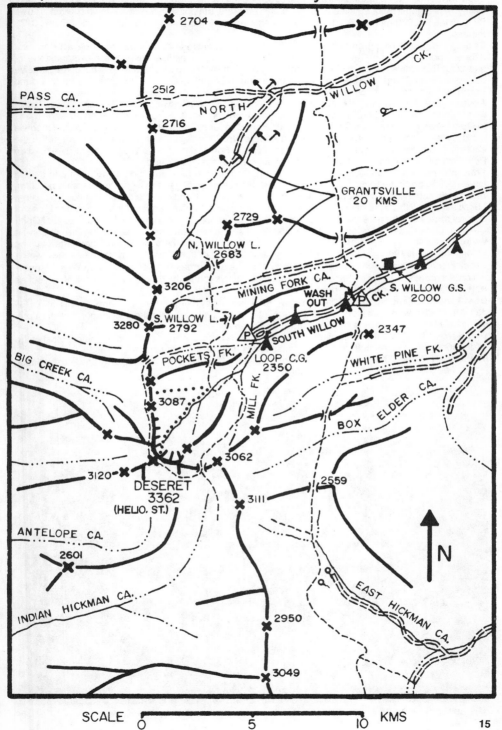

PASS CA.

NORTH WILLOW CK.

2704

2512

2716

GRANTSVILLE 20 KMS

2729

N. WILLOW L. 2683

MINING FORK CA.

WASH OUT

CK. S. WILLOW G.S. 2000

3206

S. WILLOW L. 2792

3280

SOUTH WILLOW

2347

POCKETS FK.

LOOP C.G. 2350

WHITE PINE FK.

BIG CREEK CA.

MILL FK.

BOX ELDER CA.

3087

3062

3120

2559

DESERET 3362 (HELIO. ST.)

3111

N

ANTELOPE CA.

2601

INDIAN HICKMAN CA.

EAST HICKMAN CA.

2950

3049

SCALE   0   5   10   KMS

15

Lowe Peak, Oquirrh Mountains

Location The Oquirrh Mountains are west of Salt Lake City, and form the western side of the Salt Lake Valley. The highest peak is called Flat Top, at 3237 meters, but possibly the best known summit is Lowe Peak rising to 3228 meters. Another familiar name appearing on many maps is Lewiston Peak, 3173 meters.

Geology If you're hiking and climbing on the highest summits in this range, you'll be walking over different portions of the Oquirrh Formation. This is mostly limestone, with layers of sandstone or quartzite. But notice all the mining symbols in the southwestern part of the map. There are intrusive bodies forming Sharp, Bald, and Dry Peaks just north of Ophir, and another intrusive body around Porphyry Hill north of Mercur. Gold and silver have been the primary metals mined here.

Access The route used by the author in reaching and climbing Lewiston, Flat Top and Lowe Peaks, was Highway 73 running between Tooele and Lehi. From this well-traveled road one can drive the 5 kms to Ophir, then on dirt roads to Ophir and South Fork Canyons. The northern peaks can be reached via the dirt road running between Riverton and Tooele, up Butterfield Canyon. Also, one can get to the eastern side by leaving Highway 73 just north of Cedar Fort and driving up West Canyon. The road up Pole Canyon from Cedar Fort would make southern peaks easy to climb.

Trail Information The Oquirrh Mountains are entirely private property, belonging mostly to mining interests and are not a part of any national forest. However, getting to the higher peaks is no problem. Sheep and cattle graze the slopes in summer, thus it's livestock and deer hunter's trails you'll be using. There's a trail to the base of Lowe from the end of the road in Ophir Canyon. Once at the base, one of several routes can then be taken. One may or may not be able to get a vehicle up South Fork of Ophir Canyon, but an easy route can be found up the west ridge of Lewiston, or an old 4WD road can be walked to a cabin just west of Flat Top, then up the west ridge to the summit. An advantage of using Ophir Canyon, is the availability of water, which is lacking in some other canyons mentioned. Ophir Creek is a fine stream above where it is piped out. The author has climbed Lowe from West Canyon, which is a more scenic route, but a longer hike. If taking this route, you'll likely have to park at the locked gate, but hikers are allowed to pass.

Best Time and Time Needed Climbing Lowe Peak is an easy half-day hike for many, but will take a full day from the Provo or Salt Lake Areas. Doing Flat Top and Lewiston will take a bit longer, but still a one day hike. Hiking season is from June 1 through October.

Campgrounds There are no constructed campgrounds here, but one can camp anyplace. Most of the larger springs in canyon bottoms have access roads, so these make fine campsites.

Maps Utah Travel Council Map 7 — Northwestern Central Utah, U.S.G.S. maps Rush Valley (1:100,000), Mercur, Lowe Peak (1:24,000)

The northern ramparts of Lowe Peak, seen from upper West Canyon (55mm lens).

Map 4, Lowe Peak, Oquirrh Mtns.

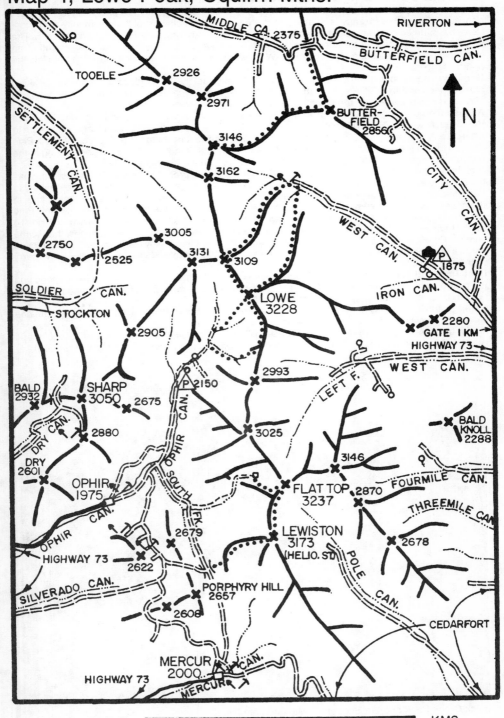

RIVERTON →

MIDDLE CA. 2375
BUTTERFIELD CAN.

TOOELE
2926
2971
3146

BUTTER-
FIELD
2856

CITY CAN.

SETTLEMENT CAN.
3162

WEST CAN.

P 1875

3005
2750
2525
3131
3109

IRON CAN.

LOWE
3228

SOLDIER CAN.
STOCKTON

2905

2280
GATE 1 KM
HIGHWAY 73

WEST CAN.

2993
P 2150

LEFT F.

BALD
2932
SHARP
3050
2675

BALD
KNOLL
2288

2880
3025

OPHIR CAN.
SOUTH FK.

DRY CAN.
DRY
2601

3146

FOURMILE CAN.

OPHIR
1975

FLAT TOP
3237
2870

THREEMILE CAN.

2679

LEWISTON
3173
(HELIO. ST.)

2678

HIGHWAY 73
2622

POLE CAN.

OPHIR CAN.

SILVERADO CAN.

PORPHYRY HILL
2657

2608

CEDARFORT

MERCUR
2000

MERCUR CAN.

HIGHWAY 73
MERCUR →

SCALE 0   4   8 KMS

17

Black Crook Peak, Sheeprock Mountains

Location Few people have heard of the Sheeprock Mountains, but they are practically on our back door step. This compact range is located just to the south and southwest of the community of Vernon. Vernon is situated northwest of Eureka about 35 kms, and 56 kms south of Tooele on Highway 36. The land immediately south of Vernon is flat and has been used as experimental pastures by the Uinta National Forest. On the map are numerous 4WD roads extending from the Benmore Pastures into the nearby canyons.

Geology The geology of the Sheeprock Range is complex, but the exposed rock on the higher peaks is mostly Precambrian in age, with quartzite the dominant rock type (Big Cottonwood Formation). An intrusive body is evident on the south slopes where all the old mines are shown.

Access The only logical approach to the Sheeprock Range is via Vernon and Highway 36. From Vernon drive west on Sharp Road towards Lookout Pass, but turn south on Harker Road. Drive south to where the fenced area terminates, then turn west and southwest heading in the direction of North Pine Canyon just to the left of the highest peak, Black Crook at 2827 meters. There's a good spring in the canyon and many cow trails. This is the best access route to the highest summits.

Trail Information There are few if any trails as such in the Sheeprock Mountains. In the past there has been mining activity here and as a result many roads and trails once existed. But today it's necessary to route-find up to the higher peaks. In most cases it's easier to climb a ridge, but that's not always true. In the case of Black Crook Peak, the best route might be to walk up the right-hand fork of North Pine Canyon beginning not far above the spring and water trough. This involves some bushwhacking. To climb Dutch Peak, 2733 meters, drive or walk up Bennion Creek to some of the old mines, then to the summit. For Pole and Mine Peaks, drive southwest above the Little Valley Campground. Keep in mind this is a dry mountain range. The only running water is in Little Valley and Vernon Creeks. Always carry water in your vehicle.

Best Time and Time Needed The amount of time needed for hiking any of these peaks depends on the type of vehicle one has. With a 4WD, any hike can be done easily in half a day, round trip. Hiking season here is from mid-May through about mid-November.

Campgrounds The only forest service campsite in the range is the Little Valley Campground. But one can camp anywhere. Best campsites are usually around springs.

Maps Utah Travel Council Map 7 — Northwestern Central Utah, Uinta National Forest, U.S.G.S. maps Rush Valley, Lynndyl (1:100,000), Lookout Pass, Vernon, Erickson Knoll, Dutch Peak (1:24,000)

Black Crook Peak and the Sheeprock Mtns. (55mm lens).

Map 5, Black Crook Peak, Sheeprock Mtns.

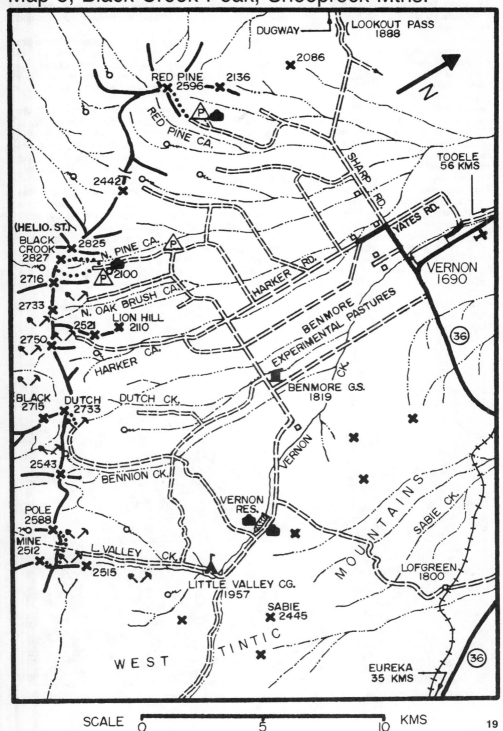

DUGWAY — LOOKOUT PASS 1888

✗ 2086

RED PINE ✗ 2596 ✗ 2136

RED PINE CA.

SHARP RD.

TOOELE 56 KMS

✗ 2442

YATES RD.

(HELIO. ST.)
BLACK ✗ 2825
CROOK
2827 ✗
N. PINE CA.
✗ 2716 ✗ 2100

VERNON 1690

HARKER RD.

36

✗ 2733

N. OAK BRUSH CA.

LION HILL
✗ 2521 ✗ 2110

BENMORE
EXPERIMENTAL PASTURES

✗ 2750

HARKER CA.

HARKER

BENMORE G.S.
1819

BLACK
2715 ✗ DUTCH
✗ 2733

DUTCH CK.

VERNON CK.

✗

✗

✗ 2543

BENNION CK.

✗

M O U N T A I N S

SABIE CK.

POLE
2588 ✗

VERNON
RES.

✗

MINE
2512 ✗

L. VALLEY CK.

✗ 2515

✗

LITTLE VALLEY CG.
1957

LOFGREEN
1800

SABIE
✗ 2445

✗

T I N T I C

W E S T

✗

EUREKA
35 KMS

36

SCALE 0 — 5 — 10 KMS

19

Swasey Peak, House Range

Location The mountains on this map are in Utah's Great Basin. This is the House Range, about 60 kms due west of Delta and directly north of the Sevier Dry Lake Bed. The highest point on this map and the entire range is Swasey Peak at 2947 meters.

Geology The rocks in the northern part of the House Range are almost the same as those to the south around Notch Peak. It's almost all limestone. There's the Swasey Limestone, Marjum Formation and the Tatow Formation. The bedding is tilted to the east, with a fault line running along the western edge of the range. The result is a sharp and nearly vertical escarpment on the western edge of the peaks. Many parts of the escarpment rise from 100 to 200 vertical meters. On top of Swasey is a stand of bristlecone pines, a tree that does well on limestone soils.

Access There are many old roads in the valleys and mountains of the Great Basin, many of which are well-maintained. Some lead to present day mining activity, others are used by ranchers running cattle in the more favorable area. The main road to be used by most Utahns gaining access to Swasey Peak is the one beginning about 19 kms west of Delta and about 8 kms west of Hinckley. This well-used gravel road is well-marked. There's a signpost pointing the way to Antelope Spring and Marjum Pass. One could also reach Swasey Peak from the Notch Peak area. See Notch Peak map for more information. These valley roads can accommodate traffic at highway speeds.

Trail Information There are a few cattle trails in these mountains, but mostly it's 4WD roads. This means some bushwhacking is required to reach the summits or peaks. This is especially true of the southwest ridge of Swasey Peak. The brush there is very thick and difficult to penetrate. It's therefore recommended that one drive or walk along the road leading to the west face of Swasey, then route-find up a western ridge or face not far beyond Sinbad Spring (marked 2400). There is no live or running water in the entire range, so take note on the locations of springs which are usually piped to tanks.

Best Time and Time Needed The road beyond Antelope Spring is steep and rough, so for many that's the place to park. For those driving beyond it's a half-day hike to the summit of Swasey. But from the spring it may take a full day for some. Because of the low elevation and the resultant light amount of snowfall, Swasey can be climbed from May through November.

Campgrounds There are no maintained campgrounds in the House Range, but water has been piped from Antelope Spring down to the Trilobite Quarries with a water tap as shown.

Maps Utah Travel Council Map 6 — Southwestern Central Utah, U.S.G.S. maps Tule Valley (1:100,000), Marjum Pass, Swasey Peak (1:24,000)

Looking at the north end of the House Range, from the top of Swasey Peak (105mm lens).

Map 6, Swasey Peak, House Range

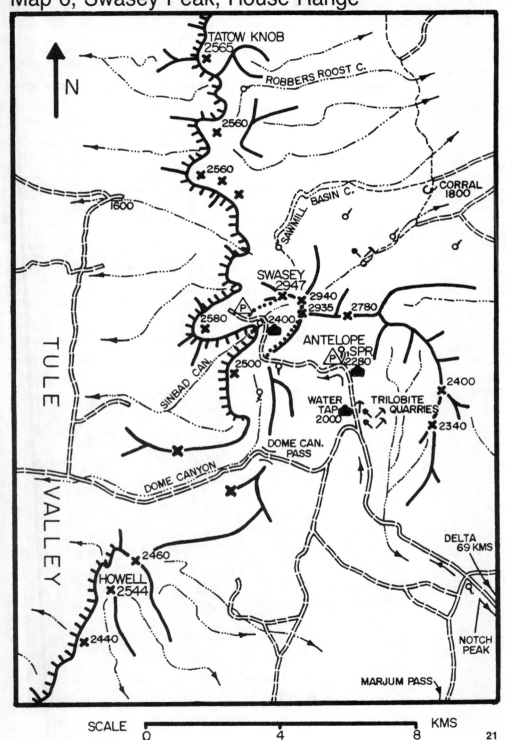

N

TATOW KNOB
2565

ROBBERS ROOST C.

2560

2560

1600

SAWMILL BASIN C.

CORRAL
1800

SWASEY
2947

P

2940
2935

2780

2580

2400

ANTELOPE
SPR
2280

P

2400

2500

2340

SINBAD CAN.

WATER
TAP
2000

TRILOBITE
QUARRIES

DOME CAN.
PASS

DOME CANYON

TULE

VALLEY

DELTA
69 KMS

2460

HOWELL
2544

2440

NOTCH
PEAK

MARJUM PASS

SCALE
0   4   8   KMS

Notch Peak, House Range

Location The mountain range here is the House Range of west central Utah. The House Range runs north-south in Utah's Great Basin. More exactly it's about 60 kms due west of Delta and north of US Highway 50-6 which runs east-west across Utah. The highest peak on this map is Notch Peak at 2943 meters. Notch Peak is perhaps the single best rock climbing peak in Utah. But it's almost unknown due to it's isolated position. The west face of the north-south ridge has a tremendous drop, with the north face of Notch Peak itself being the steepest and highest vertical drop in the state. There's nearly a 400 meter vertical drop on Notches north face, while there's a drop of nearly 1600 meters from the summit to the floor of Tule Valley just 5 kms away.

Geology The entire House Range has been uplifted and tilted slightly to the east. The entire mountain is Notch Peak Limestone, a thick and massive hulk of solid limestone. The mines in the area are at the bottom of the Notch Peak Formation, and mostly in an intrusive body.

Access If approaching from the Utah or east side of the range, drive west out of Delta about 67 kms to a well-signposted road which runs north to Antelope Spring and Swasey Peak. This is on US Highway 50-6. Then drive about 5 kms north on this well-maintained graveled road till a signpost points out the way to Miller Canyon. Drive this road to the stone cabin as shown. The road to Swasey Peak is good enough to drive at highway speeds and the road into Miller and Sawtooth Canyons is in good condition up to the cabin.

Trail Information There are no trails in this range, only a few 4WD type tracks leading into canyons and mining areas. Park at the stone cabin just mentioned, then walk up Sawtooth Canyon which is completely dry. Take all your water. It's walking on a 4WD track at first, then in the dry creek bed. At about the point the 4WD track fades, turn left into the left fork of Sawtooth Canyon. This is only about 3 kms up from the cabin. Once in this canyon it's a straight shot to the summit in a narrow and steep-sided canyon. No difficulties are found on this route. Just east of the summit are two groves of bristlecone pines. Interested rock climbers could try the west canyon route.

Best Time and Time Needed This normal route could be used as early as late April or May, and on through November. Strong climbers can climb the normal route easily in half a day, but most parties will want a full day.

Campgrounds No campground here, but if taking in Swasey Peak in the same trip, camp at Antelope Spring, shown on the Swasey Peak map. Only water here is at Painter Spring — no running water anywhere near.

Maps Utah Travel Council Map 6 — Southwestern Central Utah, U.S.G.S. maps Tule Valley (1:100,000), Notch Peak (1:62,500)

The north and west faces of Notch Peak, seen from near Painter Spring tanks (210mm lens).

Map 7, Notch Peak, House Range

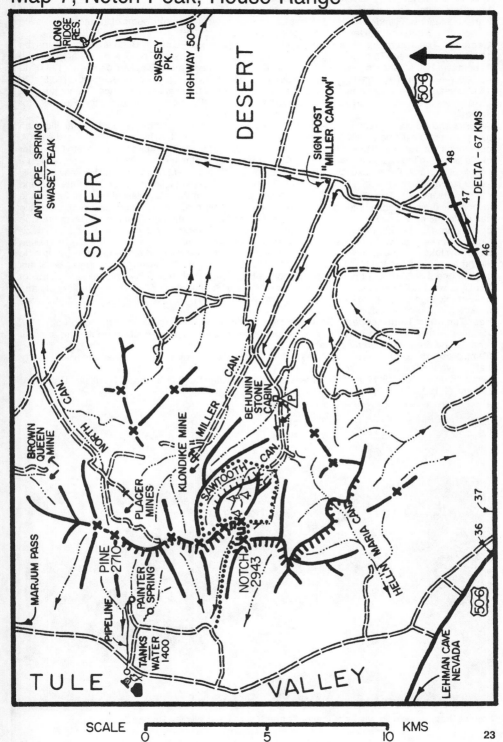

SCALE 0 5 10 KMS

Utah Volcanos, Black Rock Desert

Location   Utah has several locations with volcanic cinder cones and craters, but the area west of Kanosh, Meadow, Fillmore and Holden, has some of the newest, therefore some of the most interesting in the state. Northwest of Delta there is one last old volcano.

Geology   The lava or basalt flows surrounding Twin Peaks and Fumarole Butte are very old, maybe 100,000 years or so. This includes the Deseret Volcanic Field as well as part of the area around Tabernacle Hill. Most of the Pavant and Kanosh V. Fields are from early Lake Bonneville (17,000 to 40,000 years old). Tabernacle Hill Volcanic Field is from the later stages of L. Bonneville (10,000 to 14,000 years old) and Cove Fort and the flows around Miter, Crescent and Terrace Craters are post Lake Bonneville, some as late as 4,000 years ago (4,000 to 7,000 years old). See "Further Reading" for source.

Access and Routes   Reach Fumarole B. by driving north out of Delta and through Sugarville, then turn west; or from the north, and halfway between Lynndyl and Delta, turn west and drive past the I.P.P. operations, then to the west. When you see the black bench, turn north and walk or drive into the center of the flow from the east or the southwest. This is an old plug or the throat of the volcano. Drive west a couple of kms from Clear Lake town site to climb Pot Mtn. (Dunderberg Butte). Pavant B. (known locally as Sugarloaf) can be reached by driving west, then northwest out of Fillmore; or south from Delta and east at Clear Lake. The summit can be reached easiest from the southwest ridge, but be sure to investigate the old windmill site on the southeast corner of this cinder cone. This was an experiment to see if electric power could be generated. It went up sometime in the early 1920's but never became operational. Pavant Butte is perhaps the most interesting of the volcanos. Miter, Crescent and Terrace Craters can be seen by driving west from Fillmore. These rocks are red in color and a mining operation there now takes out the lava ash and cinders. Drive west from Fillmore or Meadow to reach Tabernacle Hill (shaped similar to the Salt Lake Tabernacle). There are lava tube caves on the north side of this cinder cone. Drive west out of Kanosh to find the Black Rock Volcano. Easy access, easy climbing. Continue west from the Black Rock V. to reach North or South Twin Peaks. These are very old and eroded volcanos. Stop on the freeway at the junction of I–70 and I–15, and walk west on a quarry road (locked gate) to climb Cove Fort Crater.

Best Time and Time Needed   On a weekend, it should be possible to climb to the top of all the volcanos on this map. They are all easy to climb. Spring or fall would be the best time to visit this area. All roads in the area are good for all vehicles.

Campgrounds   Camp in the mountains to the east of I–15, or anywhere on public land (BLM). Carry water in your car if camping in the desert.

Maps   Travel Council Map 6--Southwestern Central Utah, U.S.G.S. maps Richfield, Delta and Lynndyl (1:100,000).

Pavant Butte (known locally as Sugarloaf), from Clear Lake Wildlife Refuge (55mm lens).

Map 8, Utah Volcanos, Black Rock Desert

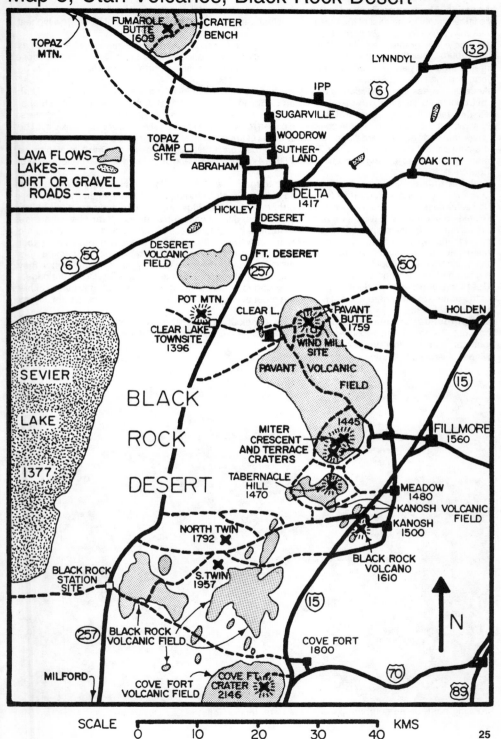

TOPAZ MTN.

FUMAROLE BUTTE 1609

CRATER BENCH

LYNNDYL

132

IPP

6

SUGARVILLE

WOODROW

SUTHER-LAND

OAK CITY

TOPAZ CAMP SITE

LAVA FLOWS
LAKES
DIRT OR GRAVEL ROADS

ABRAHAM

DELTA 1417

HICKLEY

DESERET

6 50

DESERET VOLCANIC FIELD

FT. DESERET

257

50

POT MTN.

CLEAR L.

PAVANT BUTTE 1759

HOLDEN

CLEAR LAKE TOWNSITE 1396

WIND MILL SITE

PAVANT VOLCANIC FIELD

SEVIER

BLACK

LAKE

ROCK

15

1445

1377

DESERT

MITER CRESCENT AND TERRACE CRATERS

FILLMORE 1560

TABERNACLE HILL 1470

MEADOW 1480

KANOSH VOLCANIC FIELD

NORTH TWIN 1792

KANOSH 1500

BLACK ROCK STATION SITE

S. TWIN 1957

BLACK ROCK VOLCANO 1610

N

257

15

BLACK ROCK VOLCANIC FIELD

COVE FORT 1800

MILFORD

COVE FORT VOLCANIC FIELD

COVE FT. CRATER 2146

70

89

SCALE

0   10   20   30   40

KMS

25

Fool Peak, Canyon Range

Location The Canyon Range is a little-known group of mountain peaks located in central Utah. They lie immediately to the east of the small town of Oak City, and a few more kms east of Delta. The highest summit is Fool Peak at 2962 meters.

Geology The greater part of the Canyon Range is composed of Precambrian metasediments, but as one approaches the summit region, the Tertiary Formation, Fool Creek Conglomerate is found. These are for the most part rounded summits, but there are some very steep north and northeast faces to be found on the higher peaks.

Access Access is rather good to this range and it's relatively close to the southern part of the Utah metropolitan area. One can take I-15 south to Scipio, then use gravel and dirt roads to the steeper eastern face. Use the road up Little Oak Creek to gain access to the pass marked 2286 meters. However, the principal route of access is the paved road leading southeast and east out of Oak City. The pavement ends at the guard station and Oak Creek Campgrounds. From there it's a good gravel road up the canyon to the mouth of Lyman Canyon. The road ends just above that point. One can also use a much rougher road leading up Fool Creek. With a 4WD one can reach an altitude of 2500 meters west of Fool Peak.

Trail Information For those wanting to climb to the summit of Fool Peak, drive to the confluence of Lyman Canyon and park (or park in the area of Little Creek Campground). From Lyman Canyon, walk up to the pass on a good trail. From there, route-find up the ridge north to the summit. Or from Little Creek, walk up the 4WD road a ways, then turn east and bushwhack up a canyon. Near where there is a spring marked on the map, is a box canyon. From the end of it, regress 30 meters and climb the western slope to the top, then again use the canyon and cow trails to the summit. These two routes the author used. Later it was found that a real trail goes to the top from the end of North Walker Canyon and from the southern end of Fool Creek Canyon. This is apparently the route used by survey parties when they established an encampment near the summit. The only live running water is in the Oak Creek drainage.

Best Time and Time Needed If the easier west ridge trail is used, this is an easy half-day hike. If either of the other two routes are used, it could take most of one day for most people. Hike here from June 1 through October.

Campgrounds One reason for using the Oak Creek approach is the excellent campgrounds in that canyon. The best one is the Bowens Canyon C.G. situated in a large grove of ponderosa pine trees. But one can camp almost anywhere.

Maps Fishlake National Forest, U.S.G.S. maps Delta (1:100,000), Oak City, Scipio North (1:62,500)

Looking north at the southern part of Fool Peak (50mm lens).

Map 9, Fool Peak, Canyon Range

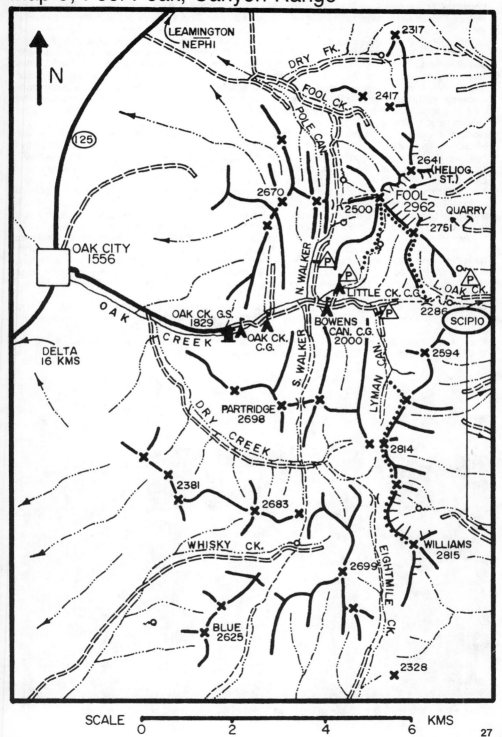

N

LEAMINGTON
NEPHI

DRY FK.

2317 ✕

FOOL CK.

2417 ✕

125

POLE CAN.

2641 ✕ (HELIOG. ST.)

2670 ✕   ✕

2500

FOOL 2962

QUARRY

✕ 2751

OAK CITY 1556

N. WALKER

P

P

LITTLE CK. C.G.

L. OAK CK.

P

2286 ✕

SCIPIO

OAK   CREEK

OAK CK. G.S. 1829

OAK CK. C.G.

BOWENS CAN. C.G. 2000

P

DELTA 16 KMS

DRY   CREEK

S. WALKER

LYMAN CAN.

✕ 2594

PARTRIDGE 2698 ✕   ✕

2814 ✕

✕

2381 ✕   ✕ 2683

WHISKY   CK.

EIGHTMILE CK.

WILLIAMS 2815

2699 ✕

BLUE 2625 ✕

✕

✕ 2328

Frisco Peak, San Francisco Mountains

Location This range is the San Francisco Mountains, with the highest summit Frisco Peak, at 2944 meters. This small range is due west of Milford about 25 kms. The southern end of the range begins at the old Frisco mining town on Highway 21 and runs north. Visiting these mountains can be interesting, especially if one makes the climb to Frisco Peak and in the same trip visits the remains of old Frisco. It was in the late 1800's that mining was most active. By 1885, over 60 million $US worth of zinc, lead, gold and silver had been extracted from the Rich Horn Silver Mine. There was a branch of the Utah Central Railway running there (the old grade can still be seen) which brought water and supplies and returned with the ore. At one time there were 4000 inhabitants living there. By the 1920's it was a ghost town.

Geology If climbing Frisco Peak itself one will be walking over Precambian rocks, mostly metamorphic such as quartzite. But in areas of this map which show the old mines, an intrusive body is found, as is the case in most mining areas.

Access There's only one way to reach Frisco and that's on Highway 21 running west out of Beaver, Minersville and Milford. If visiting the ghost town most of the ruins can be seen within 1 km of this highway. But if climbing the peak, one must turn north where the old railway grade crosses the highway, then drive up Carbonate Gulch on a rough road. There's a 4WD road to the summit with telecommunications facilities, but there's a nice hike too.

Trail Information There are no trails in these mountains, only 4WD roads to old mines and to most springs. To reach the summit on foot, drive up Carbonate Gulch to the two large kilns. Passenger cars should be parked here as the way is very rough beyond. Then walk along the power lines, then the power cables lying on the ground, past Morehouse Spring and to the summit over a boulder field, still following the cable. On top one can witness bristlecone pines, and have a good view of the Great Basin. One could hike up the ridge crestline from the highway but that's a long hike with some bushwhacking.

Best Time and Time Needed Strong hikers can walk from the kilns to the top and back in half a day, but a full day is recommended for the climb and the Frisco town visit. Hikes can be made here from about May through November. No running water in the whole range, so take your own. Only a few springs around.

Campgrounds No campgrounds here but there are countless campsites everywhere. Good campsites around the kilns. Carry water up the mountain, as Morehouse Spring has a very small discharge.

Maps Utah Travel Council Map 6 — Southwestern Central Utah, U.S.G.S. maps Wah Wah Mts. North, Wah Wah Mts. South (1:100,000), Frisco, Frisco Peak (1:62,500)

Frisco Peak rises behind a couple of kilns, remnants of the old mining era (35mm lens).

Map 10, Frisco Peak, San Francisco Mtns.

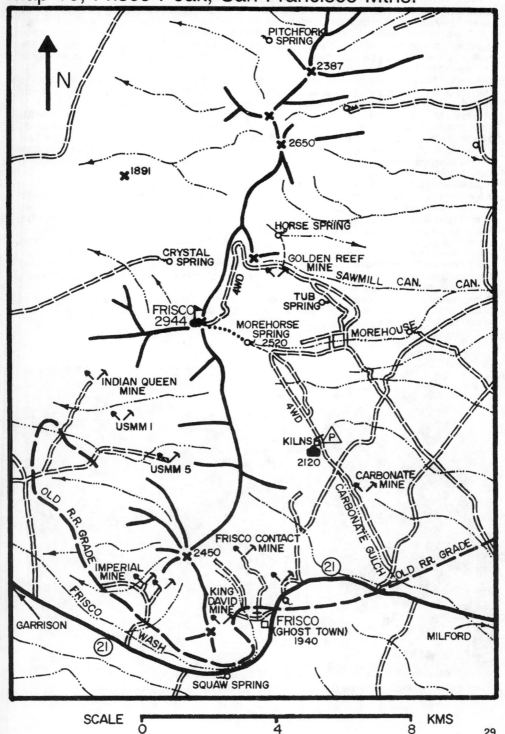

N

PITCHFORK SPRING
2387

2650

×1891

HORSE SPRING

CRYSTAL SPRING

GOLDEN REEF MINE

SAWMILL CAN.   CAN.

4WD

TUB SPRING

FRISCO 2944

MOREHORSE SPRING 2520

MOREHOUSE

INDIAN QUEEN MINE

USMM I

4WD

KILNS 2120

P

CARBONATE MINE

USMM 5

OLD R.R. GRADE

CARBONATE GULCH

OLD RR GRADE

FRISCO CONTACT MINE

2450

21

FRISCO

IMPERIAL MINE

KING DAVID MINE

FRISCO (GHOST TOWN) 1940

GARRISON

21   WASH

MILFORD

SQUAW SPRING

SCALE

0   4   8   KMS

29

Wah Wah Peak, Wah Wah Mountains

Location   The Wah Wah Mountains are located in southwestern Utah, about halfway between Milford and the Nevada line. The range runs north-south, with the highest portion being to the south of Highway 21. The peak featured here is Wah Wah Peak, which rises to 2863 meters. This is one of the higher summits in that part of the Great Basin. Because of the altitude, there's even a small stream or two. The higher summits also have a good stand of bristlecone pines. In 1984, there were some active mines in the area of the highest peaks.

Geology   The extreme western slopes of the Wah Wahs have very old quartzite rocks, but in closer to the center, and including the highest summits, the rocks are middle and upper Cambrian, and made up of various formations, but are composed mostly of limestone.

Access   Most Utahns will arrive in the Wah Wahs via Milford. From Milford, drive west on Highway 21. After about 25 kms you'll pass the ruins of the old Frisco mining town. This is worth a stop. About 30–35 kms west of Frisco, and just beyond Wah Wah Summit or Pass, turn south and follow the signs to Pine Grove Reservoir and the canyon above. In 1984, this road was in very good condition and well used by mining interests. The road to the pass marked 2440 meters is good, but on the eastern slope it deteriorates. From or near the pass, you can park or camp and begin hiking.

Trail Information   There are no trails in the Wah Wahs, other than those used by game, but there are a few old mine exploration tracks around. Just south of Pass 2440 are several of these but marked with the trail symbol. Just before the pass, and on the west slope, is an old track you can use to gain access to the higher slopes to the north. Use this, then ridge-walk north to the top of the highest summit, Wah Wah Peak. If you continue north along this high ridge, you'll pass through several stands of bristlecone pines. These pines are very likely spread out all along this long north-south ridge, where there's an abundance of limestone.

Best Time and Time Needed   Climbing or hiking season here would be from about June 1 on through the end of October, but May or November may also be possible depending on the year. Round-trip from the pass to Wah Wah Peak is an easy half day, unless you want to explore.

Campgrounds   Plan to camp somewhere along Pine Grove Creek, which is a perennial stream.

Maps   Utah Travel Council Map 6, Southwestern Central Utah, U.S.G.S. maps Wah Wah Mtns. South (1:100,000), Sewing Machine Pass, Lamerdorf Peak (1:24,000).

Typical scene along lower Pine Grove Creek with ponderosa pines (55mm lens).

Map 11, Wah Wah Peak, Wah Wah Mtns.

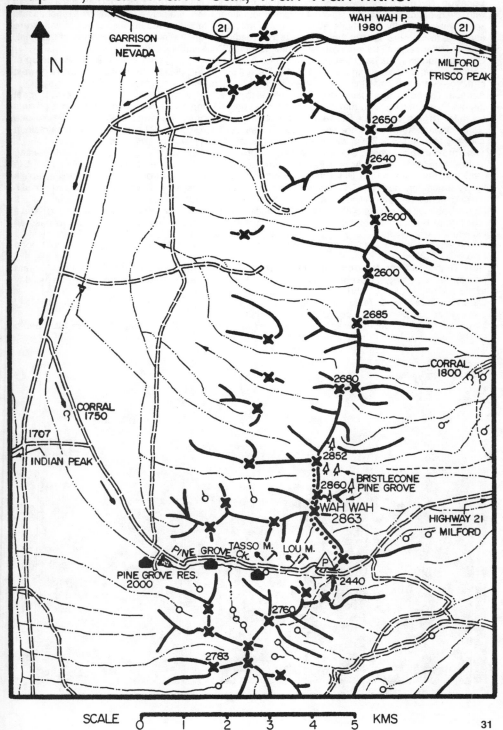

SCALE 0 1 2 3 4 5 KMS

Indian Peak, Needle Range

Location Not much is known of or written about mountains in the Great Basin of Utah. It's a dry area with few rivers or streams, thus almost void of population. There are only a few scattered ranches and some mining activity and that's about it. But there are interesting mountains, some of which are attractive to climbers. One of these areas is the Needle Range. It's in the southwest part of the state, west of Milford about 80 kms. Highest summit is Indian Peak, 2984 meters.

Geology Indian Peak has the appearance of a volcanic cone, but is not. However, it is made up of Tertiary volcanic rocks of various kinds — rhyolite, tuff and basalt. Just to the south and to the northwest of the peak are two small intrusive bodies which explain the existence of former mining activity.

Access The best way of getting to Indian Peak is to drive west out of Milford on State Highway 21 past the old Frisco mining town ruins to between mile posts 41 and 42. There a good graveled road runs south for 18 kms to where a BLM sign points out the road running southwest to the Indian Peak State Game Management Area. The graveled road running between Highway 21 and Lund is well-maintained allowing cars to pass at highway speeds. Go prepared with plenty of fuel, food and water.

Trail Information There are no trails in the area, only 4WD tracks and the few improved roads leading to the Game Management Area. This state game area was bought by the Utah Fish and Game Dept. in 1957 from the Piute Indians. Since then the Fish and Game Dept. has introduced and maintained an elk herd surrounding the peak. The only live or running water here is Indian Creek, which flows for about 6 kms. To get to the peak follow the arrows on the map. At the junction near the house, one can make a loop on the road running east of the peak. The best route, with the least amount of bushwhacking, is up a small canyon southeast of the summit. Walk up a 4WD road, then use game trails which pass an excellent spring, eventually curving to the north. Follow the fence north to the summit. There must be bristlecone pines here, but the author failed to see any on this route. A northeast ridge route looks good also.

Best Time and Time Needed One could climb Indian Peak as early as the beginning of May and perhaps as late as early November. If a vehicle is taken to the very base of the peak, then it's a half day to the summit, a full day if the car is left near the house.

Campgrounds There are no campgrounds here, but many good campsites along Indian Creek. Many cattle graze the area, so the best drinking water is higher up in the creek.

Maps Utah Travel Council Map 5 — Southwestern Utah, U.S.G.S. maps Wah Wah Mts. South (1:100,000), Buckhorn Spring, Pinto Spring (1:24,000)

Indian Peak as seen from the Pine Valley Road. It's 8 kms to the peak (35mm lens).

Map 12, Indian Peak, Needle Range

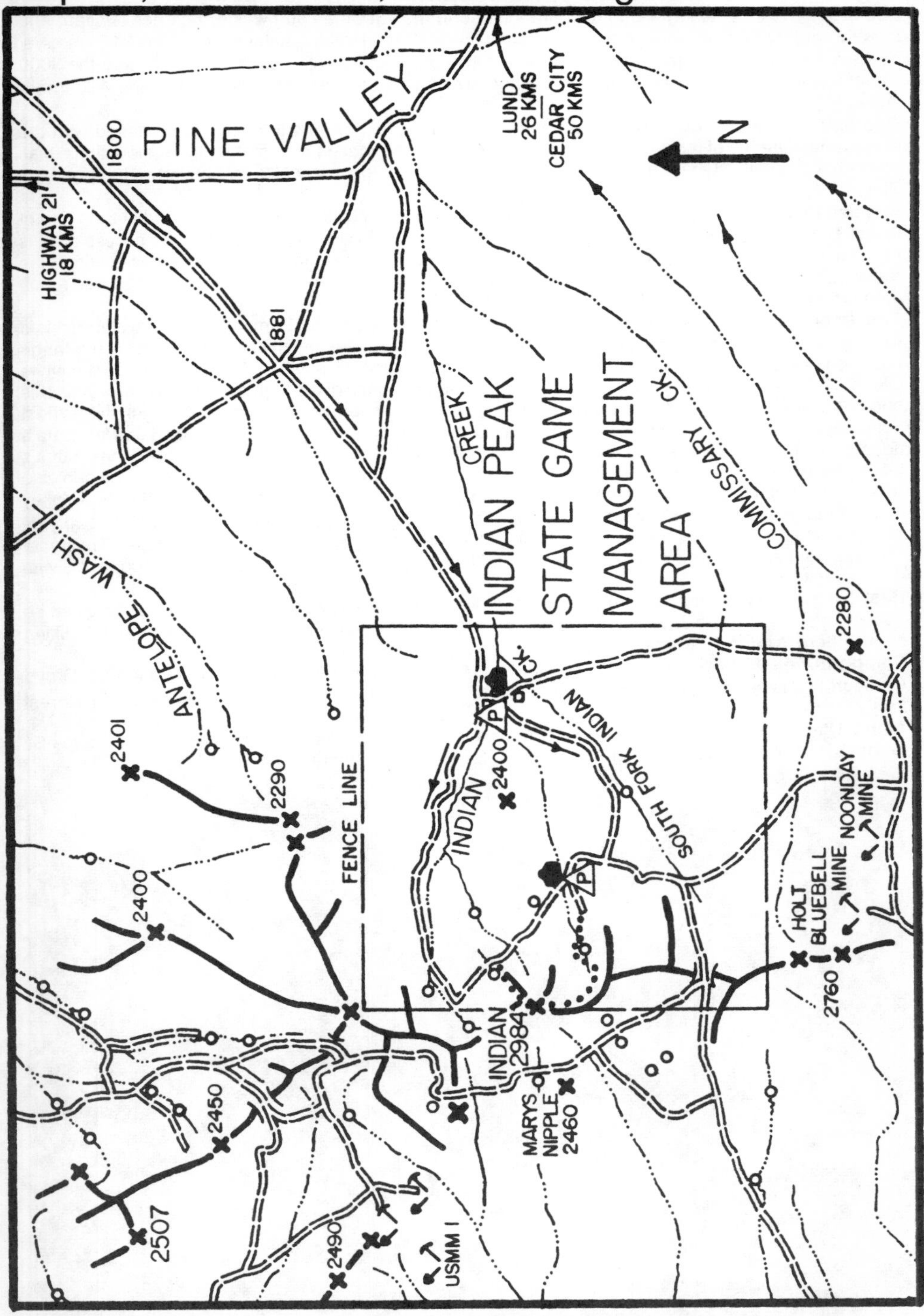

PINE VALLEY

1800

HIGHWAY 21
18 KMS

LUND
26 KMS
CEDAR CITY
50 KMS

N

1881

INDIAN PEAK STATE GAME MANAGEMENT AREA

COMMISSARY CK.

CREEK

ANTELOPE WASH

FENCE LINE

INDIAN

✕ 2401

✕ 2290

✕ 2400

✕ 2400

✕ 2280

SOUTH FORK

INDIAN CK.

HOLT ✕
BLUEBELL
2760

NOONDAY
MINE
BLUEBELL ➤ MINE
➤ MINE

✕ 2450

✕ 2507

✕ 2490

INDIAN
2984 ✕

MARYS
NIPPLE ✕
2460

USMM I

SCALE

0   4   8   KMS

33

Signal Peak, Pine Valley Mountains

Location The Pine Valley Mountains are located in the extreme southwestern corner of Utah, and directly north of St. George. The highest summit here is Signal Peak reaching a height of 3159 meters. There are many other summits very near this elevation, and the entire summit ridge is near the 3000 meter level. The higher elevations of this range are now part of the Pine Valley Mountains Wilderness Area.

Geology The map shows an escarpment on the east side, but this is not to be confused with the sandstone plateaus of most of Southern Utah. Most of the exposed rock at the higher elevations is an intrusive body called Quartze Monzonite. In a way it's similar to the laccolith mountains on the Colorado Plateau.

Access By exiting Interstate 15 at Leeds one can proceed to Oak Grove Campground at the head of Leeds Creek. This is the best road and access point on the east side. The other main access road is from the west. This road leads north out of St. George passing through Central and a place called Pine Valley. It's paved all the way to the Pine Valley Campground, at the end of the road. One can also reach the northern areas by using I-15 and exiting at New Harmony.

Trail Information There are two main trails here. One known as the Summit Trail is a well-used trail running from north to southwest making a half-moon arch. It runs along the highest portion of the range and is on the summit ridge almost all the way. This is the main trail that most hikers will encounter while hiking. There's also a trail system running along the eastern base of the high escarpment; however, this one is at a low elevation and is extra warm during the summer season. If you're out to reach the highest point, Signal Peak, then begin hiking at the Oak Grove Campground. A good, well-used trail leads up a ridge to the top and connects with the Summit Trail. There's no trail to the top of Signal Peak, but it's easy to reach after you pass a spring called Further Water (near the last "R" on Burger). One can also reach the summit ridge by using the Forsyth Creek Trail or a trail beginning just west of the Pine Valley Campground. This trail is known as the Browns Point Trail. It heads up the ridge east of Nay Canyon, and is well used. At the extreme eastern end of the Pine Valley CG., is the Whipple Valley Trailhead. The trail from this point runs to the northeast and to Whipple Valley. In Whipple Valley it connects with the Summit Trail.

Best Time and Time Needed From either campground, Oak Grove or Pine Valley, this climb can be done in one day, but two day trips are common. Be aware of a lack of water on the Summit Trail. Hiking season here is June 1 through October.

Campgrounds Both campgrounds mentioned are improved and open most of the year. Oak Grove Campground is free for usage and likely the least crowded of the two. (In 1986, it was burned in a forest fire).

Maps Utah Travel Council Map 5 — Southwestern Utah, Dixie National Forest, U.S.G.S. maps St. George (1:100,000), New Harmony (1:62,500), Saddle Mtn., Central East (1:24,000)

Somewhere along the Summit Trail in the Pine Valley Mountains (28mm lens).

Map 13, Signal Peak, Pine Valley Mtns.

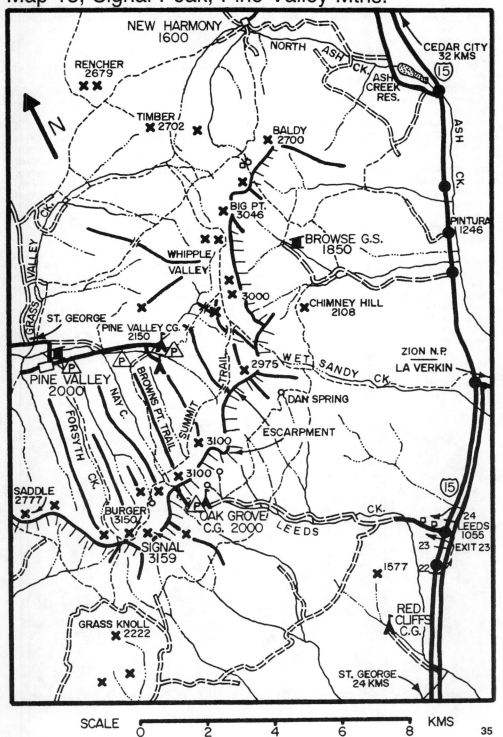

NEW HARMONY 1600

NORTH ASH CK.

CEDAR CITY 32 KMS

(15)

ASH CREEK RES.

RENCHER 2679
✗ ✗

N

TIMBER
✗ 2702   ✗

BALDY
✗ 2700

ASH CK.

PINTURA 1246

✗

BIG PT. 3046
✗

BROWSE G.S. 1850

WHIPPLE VALLEY
✗ ✗

GRASS VALLEY CK.

✗

✗ 3000

CHIMNEY HILL 2108
✗

ST. GEORGE
PINE VALLEY CG. 2150

PINE VALLEY 2000

P P

ZION N.P.
LA VERKIN

WET SANDY CK.

NAY C.

BROWNS PT. TRAIL

SUMMIT TRAIL

✗ 2975

DAN SPRING

FORSYTH CK.

ESCARPMENT

✗ 3100

SADDLE 2777
✗   ✗

BURGER 3150

✗ 3100

(15)

✗
✗

P

OAK GROVE C.G. 2000

LEEDS CK.

P P
24
LEEDS 1055
23
EXIT 23

SIGNAL 3159
✗

22

✗ 1577

GRASS KNOLL
✗ 2222

RED CLIFFS C.G.

✗   ✗

ST. GEORGE 24 KMS

SCALE
0   2   4   6   8   KMS

35

Box Elder Peak, Wellsville Mountains

Location The Wellsville Mountains are a small, compact and relatively unknown mountain range in northern Utah. These are the mountains lying due north of Brigham City and directly west of the small Cache Valley town of Wellsville. The highest summit is Box Elder Peak at 2857 meters. Immediately north of this summit is another high peak, Wellsville Cone, 2852 meters. This range is no more than one long ridge running north-south, but it receives heavy winter snows and has an impressive eastern face.

Even though the elevation is not great, the highest summits are above timberline. The higher portion of this range is now an official wilderness area.

Geology The Wellsville Mountains have been thrust upwards by a number of faults. Exposed on the eastern slopes are parts of the Wells Formation, which is almost entirely limestone. Around the highest summit is the Lodgepole Limestone.

Access Because it's a north-south ridge, there are three main access routes. First from the west. If driving north on I-84 north of Brigham City, exit at Honeyville and drive through town to the east side, to the large power station. From there take the gravel road north for about 2 kms, then look for one of several rough roads heading east to the mouth of the canyon. The road ends at a livestock water tank. But a route on the east slopes has the best trails and is more scenic, so drive to the town of Wellsville, then north to Mendon. From north Mendon one can drive west on 3rd North Street to the mouth of Deep Canyon; or drive in a southwesterly direction from the south end of Mendon, and follow the signs to "Forest Service Lands." This last road is moderately good for all vehicles, and it ends at a watering trough and spring.

Trail Information From the Honeyville side and the water tanks, there's a trail running east up the canyon, but it gradually peters out and may be impossible to find. If, or when you lose it, simply route-find to the main ridge and the summit trail. On the east side the trails are more often used and easier to locate. The Deep Canyon trail is easy to follow as it winds its way up the canyon to a pass near Mendon Peak. The Coldwater Lake Trail is also well-used. They meet on the ridge at Stewart Pass. From Stewart Pass walk south along the trail to Youngs Cabin and spring, or simply walk along the summit ridge to the highest peaks. Always carry water as there's none on the ridge.

Best Time and Time Needed The climb of Box Elder Peak is an all day affair from any route, but the easiest and shortest is via the Coldwater Lake Trail. Mid-June through October is the hiking season.

Campgrounds There are no forest service campgrounds in the area, but there are good campsites at each trailhead, especially at Coldwater Lake Trailhead.

Maps Wasatch-Cache National Forest, U.S.G.S. maps Logan, Tremonton (1:100,000), Honeyville, Wellsville (1:24,000)

Foto taken from near Stewart Pass, looking towards Wellsville Cone (35mm lens).

Map 14, Box Elder Peak, Wellsville Mtns.

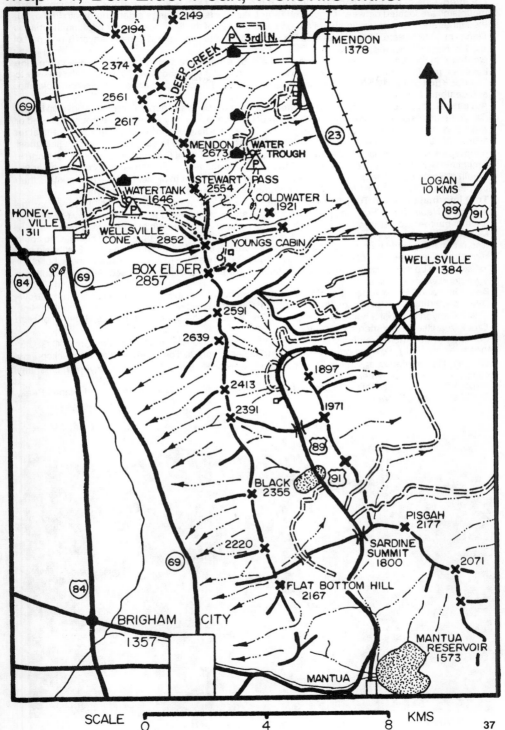

2149

2194

3rd N.

MENDON
1378

2374

DEEP CREEK

2561

69

2617

23

MENDON
2673

WATER
TROUGH

LOGAN
10 KMS

STEWART
2554

PASS

89

91

WATER TANK
1646

COLDWATER L.
1921

HONEY-
VILLE
1311

WELLSVILLE
CONE   2852

YOUNGS CABIN

WELLSVILLE
1384

84

BOX ELDER
2857

69

2591

2639

1897

2413

2391

1971

89

91

BLACK
2355

PISGAH
2177

2071

2220

SARDINE
SUMMIT
1800

69

FLAT BOTTOM HILL
2167

84

MANTUA
RESERVOIR
1573

BRIGHAM   CITY

1357

MANTUA

SCALE   0   4   8   KMS

37

Mt. Naomi, Bear River Mountains

Location One of the most northerly ranges in the state of Utah is the Bear River Mountains. These mountains are located between Logan and Bear Lake. Parts of the range extend north into Idaho, but the higher and more interesting parts are on the Utah side of the line. The highest peak on the map is Naomi at 3042 meters. Much of the area between the Utah-Idaho line and Logan Canyon is now part of the Mt. Naomi Wilderness area.

Geology In the area of the highest summits the rock is limestone and in the basin above White Pine Lake, a type of Karst topography exists, complete with sink holes and caves. This is Utahs answer to Floridas Karst country. The limestone in question is part of the Lodgepole Limestone, Hyrum Dolomite, and Leatham Formations.

Access There are several roads into this area, but the most used and popular route is to drive up Logan Canyon east of Logan, heading in the direction of Bear Lake. At Tony Grove Campground, turn left or west, and drive up the paved road to Tony Grove Lake. This lake is in the area of high peaks and at an altitude of 2553 meters. Camping is not allowed at the lake, but there is a parking lot, and it's here most people park when they hike into White Pine Lake. For the Smithfield C. route, drive east on 1st North in Smithfield (which later is called Canyon Road). Drive northeast to where the road is closed, near the mouth of South Fork. The High Creek route is popular too. Drive north of Richmond to mile post 42, then turn east and drive 13 kms to the road's end, at the junction of north and south forks.

Trail Information From Tony Grove Lake one can walk northwest on a good trail to very near the summit of Naomi Peak. From the pass, simply walk south along the ridge. Also from Tony Grove Lake another much-used trail heads over the pass to the north and leads to White Pine Lake. From this lake, Magog and Gog can be climbed. The easiest route up Magog is a walk-up from the south. One could also reach this central part by walking up the trail from the end of either of the roads in Smithfield and High Creek Canyons. One could also walk up Cherry and White Pine Creeks as well as others, but other trails may not be as easy to locate. Most trails shown on the map are fairly well-used. All canyon bottoms have good water supplies.

Best Time and Time Needed For most it's a two hour hike to the top of Naomi Peak from Tony Grove Lake and perhaps less for Magog (from the south). Climbing Doubletop from the end of the road in High Creek Canyon is about a half-day hike. Cherry Creek Pk. can be climbed from Tony Grove L. or High Creek in a little longer than half a day.

Campgrounds There are plenty of campgrounds in Logan Canyon, including Tony Grove C.G., but these are generally crowded on weekends. One cannot camp at Tony Grove Lake, but backcountry camping is permitted everywhere. The upper ends of both High and Smithfield Canyons have many campsites, with good water.

Maps Wasatch-Cache National Forest, U.S.G.S. maps Logan (1:100,000), Richmond, Naomi Peak, Smithfield, Mount Elmer (1:24,000)

White Pine Lake with Magog Peak in the background (35mm lens).

Map 15, Mt. Naomi, Bear River Mtns.

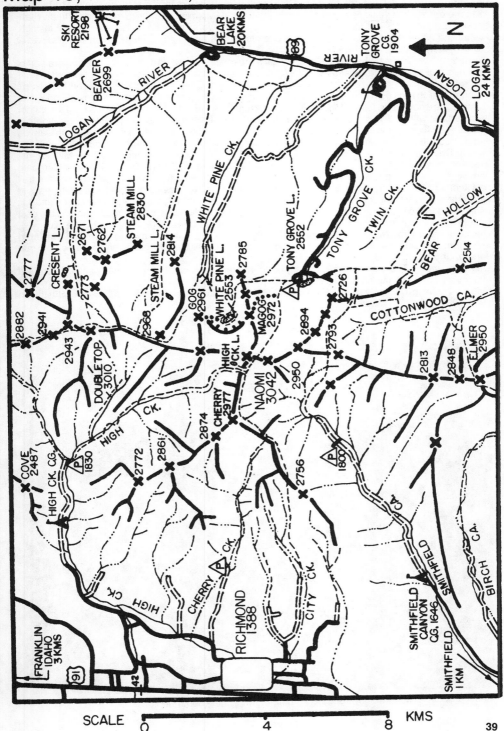

SCALE 0   4   8 KMS

Elmer and Jardine, Bear River Mountains

Location   The peaks featured here are Mt. Elmer, at 2950 meters, and just to the south, Mt. Jardine, 2916 meters. Both of these fine summits are located in the Bear River Range in extreme northern Utah, between Logan and Bear Lake, and just north of Logan Canyon. These peaks are also just south of Mt. Naomi and White Pine Lake. Most of the higher parts of the area north of Logan Canyon are now part of the Mt. Naomi Wilderness Area.

Geology   Most of the higher parts of these peaks are made of limestone and dolomite, and are part of the Lodgepole Limestone, Leatham and Water Canyon Formations, and the Hyrum Dolomite.

Access   Possibly the best access road is the one running up Green Canyon. Drive east on 1800 North in Logan, which runs right into this canyon. The road ends at the junction of the main canyon and Water Canyon. It's a good road for all vehicles. There's another road, then trail, into Dry Canyon, but the author is unfamiliar with it. Birch Canyon is another possibility. Reach it by driving east on 1st North in Smithfield, which later is called Canyon Road. At the mouth of the canyon turn right onto Birch Canyon Road. You'll find a gate after a km, but you can pass OK; just leave the gate as you find it, open or closed. Drive as far as you can and park. You could also walk south on the ridge from Mt. Naomi.

Trail Information   There's a good and well used trail running up Green Canyon. It runs underneath Jardine, and right next to the summit of Elmer. There's one good spring (with trough) right on the trail and another coming from a side canyon; otherwise it's a dry hike. The author hasn't walked the trails in either Birch or Dry Canyons, but has seen the trail from the summit of Jardine, so it does exist, and it is used some. From just north of the spring and trough east of Jardine, you can walk west and up the east face to the summit of Jardine. You can then ridge-walk north to Elmer, and return by the trail.

Best Time and Time Needed   To climb both of these peaks will take the average person all day from any route. Winter snows stay in these mountains till very late, so the hiking season would be from late June on through October.

Campgrounds   There's no official campground in Green Canyon, but many campsites. There are many very crowded campgrounds in Logan Canyon.

Maps   Wasatch-Cache National Forest, U.S.G.S. maps Logan (1:100,000), Mt. Elmer, Smithfield (1:24,000).

Looking south at Mt. Jardine, from the summit of Mt. Elmer (50mm lens).

Map 16, Elmer and Jardine, Bear River Mtns.

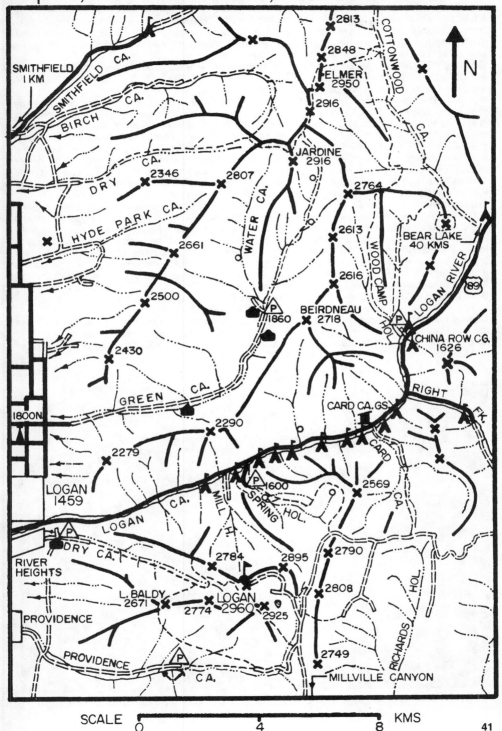

SMITHFIELD
1 KM

SMITHFIELD CA.

BIRCH CA.

DRY CA.

HYDE PARK CA.

2346

2807

2661

2500

2430

GREEN CA.

2290

2279

1800N

LOGAN
1459

2813

2848

ELMER
2950

2916

COTTONWOOD CA.

JARDINE
2916

2764

2613

2616

BEIRDNEAU
2718

P
1860

WATER CA.

WOOD CAMP HOL.

BEAR LAKE
40 KMS

LOGAN RIVER

89

P

CHINA ROW C.G.
1626

RIGHT FK.

CARD CA. G.S.

CARD CA.

2569

P
1600

MILL H.

SPRING HOL.

LOGAN CA.

RIVER
HEIGHTS

DRY CA.

PROVIDENCE

P

L. BALDY
2671

2774

LOGAN
2960

2925

2784

2895

2790

2808

2749

RICHARDS HOL.

PROVIDENCE CA.

P

MILLVILLE CANYON

N

SCALE

0   4   8   KMS

41

Mt. Logan, Bear River Mountains

Location   This is the third of three maps covering the Bear River Mountains of extreme northern Utah. Mt. Logan, which rises to 2960 meters, is located due east of Logan and the small town of Providence, and just south of Logan Canyon. This whole area is between Logan in Cache Valley, and Bear Lake. While there is a 4WD road to the summit, and a small solar-powered radio transmitter on top, there are also at least two trails, making it a fine hike none-the-less.

Geology   The whole of Mt. Logan, at least the highest portion, is made up of limestone rock, largely of the Lodgepole Limestone Formation. At the very summit, the Round Valley Limestone Formation appears. Logan Canyon cuts deep into the Hyrum Dolomite.

Access   Through the middle of this region runs US Highway 89, up Logan Canyon. This good highway divides the Bear River Range and offers a good access road. One good route is up Spring Hollow. This is about 8 kms into the Logan Canyon, and just east of the small diversion pond. A sign points out the canyon and there's a good paved road running to a picnic site half a km off the highway. This is the best place to park to climb the mountain from the north and from Logan Canyon. Possibly the best hike on the mountain is the route up Dry Canyon. Get to the mouth of this canyon by driving east through the center of the Logan suburb of River Heights and to the east bench beyond. Drive as far as you can, and park. There's also a trail up Card Canyon further up Logan Canyon, and a trail beginning at the upper end of Providence Canyon, but the author is unfamiliar with either of these.

Trail Information   In Dry Canyon there's a rough old road for a ways above where you'll have to park, but that changes into a regular trail after only a km or so. When you finally arrive in the basin at the head of the canyon, the trail fades; but remember, it turns to your left and heads northwest. After walking through sagebrush a ways, it again turns and heads east, to the top. The last part of the trail is easy to follow. (This canyon is totally dry.) In Spring Hollow, one trail heads up past the spring (no water beyond this spring) in the bottom of the canyon; another heads up the ridge to the west of the picnic grounds, then up-canyon. The two join after about two kms. This trail fades near the top, but comes out near Peak 2790. You then walk old 4WD roads to the summit.

Best Time and Time Needed   Both hikes here are all-day hikes. Generally the hiking season is from mid or late June on through the deer hunt, or late October.

Campgrounds   Many are in Logan Canyon, but very crowded. You could likely drop a tent at the mouth of Dry Canyon, but not on weekend nights (which are party nights in the canyon).

Maps   Wasatch-Cache National Forest, U.S.G.S. maps Logan (1:100,000), Logan Peak, Logan (1:24,000).

The eastern slopes of Mt. Logan, seen from near the top of Spring Hollow Trail (28mm lens).

Map 17, Mt. Logan, Bear River Mtns.

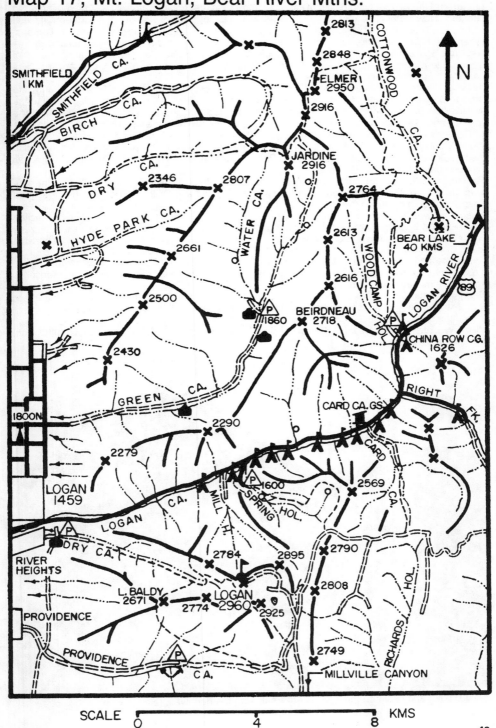

SCALE

0   4   8   KMS

Ben Lomond, Wasatch Mountains

Location The two mountain peaks of interest on this map are Willard Peak, at 2977 meters and Ben Lomond, a few meters lower, at 2961. These peaks lie directly north of Ogden in the northern Wasatch Mountains. There's a road to near the top of Willard Peak, so emphasis is placed more on Ben Lomond. What Timp is to Utah Valley and Provo, Ben Lomond is to Ogden and surrounding communities.

Geology The very steep and rugged western faces of Willard and Ben Lomond Peaks are the result of a part of the Wasatch Fault. The highest portions of these peaks are made up mostly of quartzite rock of both Cambrian and Precambrian ages.

Access For those interested in Willard Peak, and not much of a hike, then the easiest access route is to drive to Brigham City and Mantua, then go up Box Elder Creek to the south. This road leads to the Willard Basin just north of the peak. From the campground and small lake, a trail leads to the summit and to Ben Lomond. For those interested in a good hike, the normal route to the top of Ben Lomond is to drive up Ogden or North Ogden Canyon to the Ogden Valley and turn north. Continue north past Liberty to the Weber County North Fork Park and Campground. From the area of the horse corrals begins the trail to the top. One could also begin at North Ogden Pass, 1885 meters, and walk north along the Skyline Trail to Ben Lomond and Willard Peak.

Trail Information For the most part, the one major trail on this map is the Skyline Trail. This trail runs from the Willard Basin Campground south over Ben Lomond and Chilly Peaks and to North Ogden Pass, then south to Ogden Canyon, due east of Ogden. This is a very good trail and well-used. At the time of this writing, motorcycles were allowed on this trail. The other main trail is the one connecting North Fork Campground with the Skyline Trail and Ben Lomond. From the campground the trail zig zags up the slope, passing the ruins of Bailey Cabin where a small spring is located. There's also a short trail to the Cutler Spring located at the head of Cutler Creek. Carry water along the Skyline Trail.

Best Time and Time Needed The hike from North Fork Park to Ben Lomond is most of one day for most people. From North Ogden Pass to Willard Basin is generally an entire day's hike. Hiking season is from about mid-June through October.

Campgrounds Campgrounds in the area include two near Mantua, North Fork Park, and perhaps the best at Willard Basin. Lots of backcountry campsites, but you'll have to carry water, or camp at one of the springs.

Maps Wasatch-Cache National Forest, U.S.G.S. maps Ogden (1:100,000), Mantua, North Ogden, Huntsville (1:24,000)

Willard Lake and basin on the left. Willard Peak from the northwest (28mm lens).

Map 18, Ben Lomond, Wasatch Mtns.

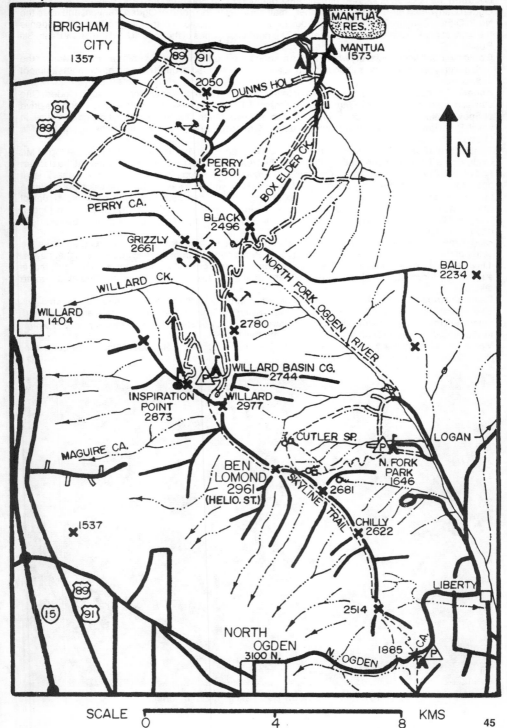

BRIGHAM CITY 1357

MANTUA RES.

MANTUA 1573

89 91

2050 ✗

DUNNS HOL

91
89

BOX ELDER CK.

PERRY 2501 ✗

PERRY CA.

BLACK 2496 ✗

GRIZZLY 2661 ✗

BALD 2234 ✗

WILLARD CK.

NORTH FORK OGDEN RIVER

WILLARD 1404

2780 ✗

WILLARD BASIN CG. 2744

INSPIRATION POINT 2873 ✗

WILLARD 2977

LOGAN

MAGUIRE CA.

CUTLER SP.

N. FORK PARK 1646

BEN LOMOND 2961 (HELIO. ST.) ✗

SKYLINE TRAIL

2681 ✗

✗ 1537

CHILLY 2622 ✗

89

15 91

LIBERTY

2514 ✗

NORTH OGDEN 3100 N.

N. OGDEN

1885

CA.

P

SCALE 0 — 4 — 8 KMS

N

Mt. Ogden, Wasatch Mountains

Location Mt. Ogden is located directly east of Ogden and South Ogden, and between Weber and Ogden Canyons. This map covers another small area just to the north of Ogden Canyon, and up to the North Ogden Canyon. This section includes Lewis Peak and portions of the Skyline Trail. Mt. Ogden is the highest peak in the area at 2918 meters. The northeast slopes of this massif hold the Snow Basin Ski Resort.

Geology Fault lines run everywhere in this mapped area, especially in the northern parts. Most of the rock making up Mt. Ogden is Precambrian in age and composed of quartzite and other metasediment rocks.

Access There are several access points into this area from the cities of Ogden and North Ogden. One can also drive east up Ogden Canyon to the Pineview Reservoir, then turn southwest and end the drive at Snow Basin; or drive east out of North Ogden and over North Ogden Pass into the Ogden Valley, in which Pineview Reservoir is the central attraction. One can also enter some parts of the massif from Mt. Green.

Trail Information For those interested in a good hike and exercise, the logical route to the top of Mt. Ogden is via Taylor Canyon, Malans Peak and the west face of the peak. This trail begins at the eastern end of 27th Street. It enters Taylor Canyon, and zigzags up the slope to the top of Malans Peak. Then it goes down to the stream in the upper part of Waterfall Canyon. The trail gradually dies out, but continue up the gully and to the top via the west face of Mt. Ogden. One can also reach the top via the ski runs of Snow Basin. An interesting ridge hike is the Skyline Trail extending from Ogden to North Ogden Canyons. Carry water on this route, as much of the trail is on a ridge. This is a very popular trail and is in good condition.

Best Time and Time Needed For the average hiker, the Malans Peak Trail up Mt. Ogden takes the better part of one day. If one were to drive to Snow Basin and hike from there to any of the higher peaks, it is a very easy half-day hike. If hiking from Ogden to North Ogden Canyon on the Skyline Trail, that is one full day for most. The hiking season is from early June through October, depending on the route taken.

Campgrounds The only designated forest service campsite in the area of this map is located in Snow Basin called Maples Campground. If one is using the Malans Peak Trail, there are many good campsites in the Upper Malans Basin at the head waters of Waterfall Creek. There's plenty of water in Waterfall Canyon, except higher up where the trail fades.

Maps Wasatch-Cache National Forest, U.S.G.S. maps Ogden (1:100,000), Ogden, Snow Basin, North Ogden, Huntsville (1:24,000)

East face of Mt. Ogden, viewed from Snow Basin ski lifts (28mm lens).

Map 19, Mt. Ogden, Wasatch Mtns.

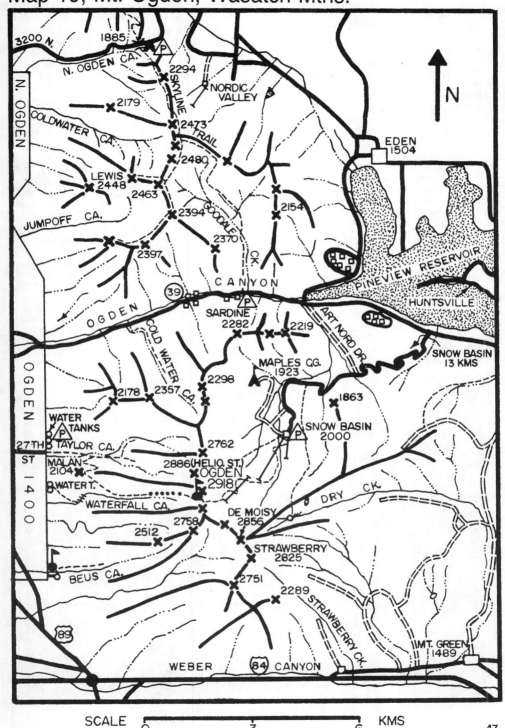

SCALE 0 3 6 KMS

North Francis Peak, Wasatch Mountains

Location The region covered by this map is that part of the Wasatch Mountains between Farmington and Weber River Canyon. At this point the range consists of a single north-south ridge. The highest point on this ridge is what the author calls North Francis Peak, 2959 meters. This is not to be confused with Francis Peak, at 2911 meters, which lies further to the south on the same ridge and which has a road to the summit.

Geology The rock seen in these peaks is a mixture of quartzite and other metamorphic rock Precambrian in age. It's the Big Cottonwood and Farmington Canyon Formations here.

Access While one can drive to the summit of Francis Peak, it's also possible to hike up to this ridge from the west and Highway 89. If using the Francis Peak Road and the Skyline Drive, one must begin at the north end of Farmington, or possibly east of Bountiful on 1300 East Street. If climbing North Francis from the valley floor is anticipated, then one should get off the freeway at Lagoon, travel north on US Highway 89 and use one of the trails in the canyons between Fruit Heights and the Hill Field Road. One problem you may encounter in hiking here is the growing number of new roads and homes east of the highway. Any detailed information given here will surely change quickly.

Trail Information To climb North Francis, drive to where Highway 89 and Hill Field Road meet. On the east side of the road locate an abandoned building (1986), and park where the "No Trespassing" sign is located. (Landowner Mel West has given the author permission to state you can walk past the sign and onto his land, as long as there are no ORV's or guns along.) From the sign walk up the hill to the gravel pit, then veer south and use the fire road atop the Bonneville shoreline for about one km, then locate the trail to the left. It's a dry hike except for water at two springs. Once at the cabin, route-find to the summit. Baer Creek also has a trail. Drive along Mountain Drive into Fruit Heights to where the road crosses the creek, then locate a road to the water pond. From there a trail first goes along the north side of the creek, then it crosses and re-crosses the creek. Farther up, where you'll likely lose the trail, merely bushwhack to the north to the open top ridge, then east to the main ridge and peaks. The trail up Adams Canyon begins at a gravel pit at 2925 E., East Side Drive, between mile posts 340 and 341. This trail runs up-canyon to a waterfall and not much beyond, then fades.

Best Time and Time Needed For the average person, a hike to the top of one or several of these ridge peaks is an all day affair. Strong hikers who know the access routes can do it in half a day. Carry water on all trails as the lower portions are usually warm while the ridge tops are always dry.

Campgrounds Bountiful Peak and Sunset Campgrounds are open, but crowded.

Maps Wasatch-Cache National Forest, U.S.G.S. maps Ogden (1:100,000), Kaysville, Peterson (1:24,000)

The northern part of North Francis cirque basin and Peak 2918 (50mm lens).

Map 20, North Francis Peak, Wasatch Mtns.

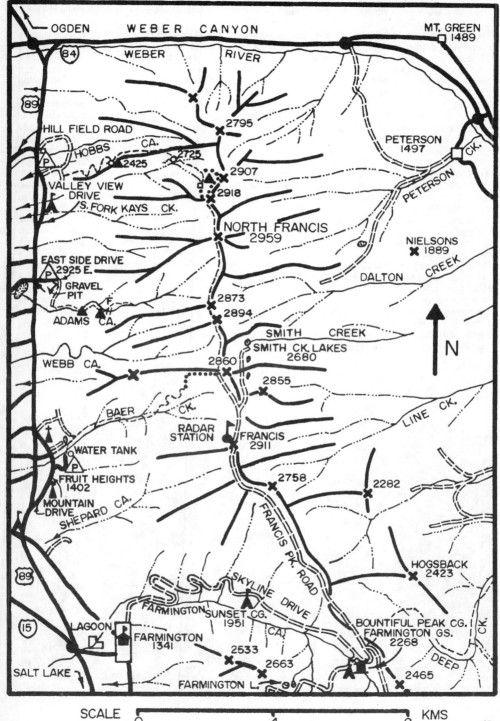

OGDEN   WEBER   CANYON   MT. GREEN
1489

84   WEBER   RIVER

89

HILL FIELD ROAD   CA.   PETERSON
1497

✕ 2795

✕ 2795   2725

HOBBS   2907   PETERSON CK.

2425   2918

VALLEY VIEW DRIVE   NORTH FRANCIS
2959   NIELSONS
1889

S. FORK KAYS CK.   DALTON   CREEK

EAST SIDE DRIVE
2925 E.   2873

GRAVEL PIT   2894

ADAMS CA.   SMITH   CREEK

WEBB CA.   2860   SMITH CK. LAKES
2680

2855

BAER   CK.   LINE CK.

RADAR STATION   FRANCIS
2911

WATER TANK   2758   2282

FRUIT HEIGHTS
1402

MOUNTAIN DRIVE   SHEPARD CA.   FRANCIS PK. ROAD   HOGSBACK
2423

89   SKYLINE DRIVE

15   SUNSET CG.
1951   CA.   BOUNTIFUL PEAK CG.
FARMINGTON GS.
2268   CK.

LAGOON   FARMINGTON
1341   2533   DEEP

SALT LAKE   2663   2465

FARMINGTON L.

N

SCALE   0   4   8   KMS

49

Grandview Peak, Wasatch Mountains

Location This map includes some of the lesser known hiking areas in the Wasatch Mountains east of the Salt Lake Metropolitan area. The highest summit here is Grandview Peak at 2869 meters. These peaks are due east of Bountiful and North Salt Lake.

Geology Most of the rock formations here have been upturned and are now nearly vertical, at least in City Creek Canyon. Beginning in City Creek Canyon one sees these different formations: Maxfield Limestone, Tintic Quartzite, Ophir Formation and the Deseret Limestone. Right on top of Grandview and other summits of the Sessions Mountains one can observe parts of the Wasatch Formation, a mixture of limestone and quartzite and other rocks. Beneath the northern parts of this map lie the Pre-Cambrian Big Cottonwood Formation.

Access The easiest access road to Grandview Peak is up City Creek Canyon, but keep in mind this canyon is closed to camping, dogs and horses, and is closed at night. One must have reservations to enter the canyon. Call the Salt Lake City Dept. of Public Utilities for the latest restrictions and entry requirements. Because of the problems in City Creek, other routes are suggested, one being Mueller Park southeast of Bountiful. To reach these picnic sites drive east up 1800 South Street in Bountiful which ends at Mueller Park. Another less congested entry point would be North Canyon.

Trail Information If using City Creek Canyon, walk northeast along the creek until Cottonwood Gulch, then walk due north to the summit on an unmaintained trail. Perhaps some bushwhacking is needed here. If beginning at Mueller Park, cross the creek at the beginning of the park or use the second trail at the locked gate higher up. These trails meet higher up and take hikers to the ridge top above City Creek. From there one can walk down North Canyon, or continue northeast along the ridge to Grandview Peak. There's supposed to be a trail from Mueller Park to the Sessions Mountains Ridge, but the author failed to locate that trailhead. All of the trails on this map are well-used and usually maintained by the Wasatch National Forest.

Best Time and Time Needed One can hike in the canyon bottoms from April through November, but to climb the higher peaks without a lot of snow, hike from about June 1 through October. All hikes here are day hikes.

Campgrounds There is no camping allowed in City Creek Canyon or in any of the canyon bottoms near the metropolitan area. Backcounty camping is allowed only in areas in the eastern portions on this map. Plan on day hikes only.

Maps Wasatch-Cache National Forest, U.S.G.S. maps Salt Lake City (1:100,000), Mountain Dell, Porterville, Bountiful Peak, Fort Douglas (1:24,000)

The northern face and ridges of Grandview Peak, from across upper Mill Ck. (55mm lens).

Map 21, Grandview Peak, Wasatch Mtns.

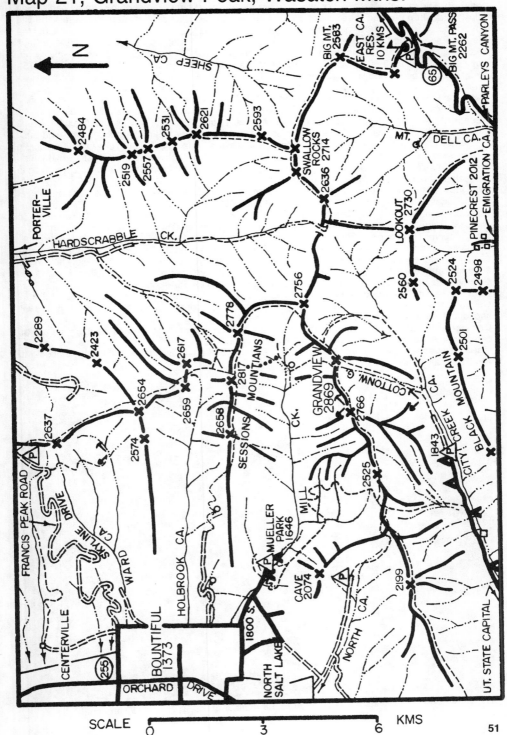

SCALE

0   3   6   KMS

Olympus, Raymond, Gobblers Knob, Wasatch Mtns.

Location The mountains shown on this map are those almost directly east of the central part of Salt Lake Valley. In particular, most of the peaks here are those which lie between Mill Creek and Big Cottonwood Canyons. The peaks here are not as high as those to the south near the ski resorts, but the area has some good, well-used paths which make for good hiking right on Salt Lake City's back doorstep. The highest peak in the group is Gobblers Knob, at 3124 meters, followed closely by Mt. Raymond at 3122 meters. However, the most famous mountain in this area is Mt. Olympus, only 2752 meters. These peaks and summits between the two canyons are now the Mount Olympus Wilderness Area.

Geology On the south slopes of Raymond and Gobblers Knob the Big Cottonwood Formation is exposed while the summits are often Tintic Quartzite. Lots of rugged cliffs on Mt. Olympus.

Access Access to this region is fast and easy. The main approach road is the one running up Mill Creek Canyon. Almost all peaks on this map can be reached from some point along this paved and busy highway. But for the two highest peaks, the fastest way to the top is probably from one of the trails in Big Cottonwood Canyon. One can also reach Mt. Aire from Interstate Highway 80 in Parley's Canyon, then south up Mt. Aire Canyon. Some hikes can be started in Lambs Canyon, but very few. Mt. Olympus can be scaled by parking on Wasatch Boulevard at the mouth of Tolcats Canyon.

Trail Information As just mentioned, the way to the top of Mt. Olympus is via Tolcats Canyon. Park at the sign indicating the beginning of the trail on about 6300 South Wasatch Boulevard. It's a good trail and well-used. One may find water along the way, but that depends on the time of year. Carry water. To climb Mt. Raymond, the best starting point is beside Hidden Falls, not far up Big Cottonwood at the top of the "S" curve. This good trail cuts across the head of Elbow Fork, then along the south side of the peak. The last part of the route is likely easiest up the south face of the peak. One could continue along this same path and eventually end up at the pass west of Gobblers Knob. From there it's an easy hike to the summit from the west. Gobblers Knob can also be scaled from the trail going up Butlers Fork. Climb Grandeur Peak from Church Fork in Mill Creek Canyon, and Mt. Aire from Mt. Aire Canyon.

Best Time and Time Needed From the Salt Lake Valley most mountain climbs here are one full day. Carry water when walking on ridge routes. Hike here from early June through October, although one will find lots of snow on the higher peaks early in the season.

Campgrounds In recent years campgrounds have been changed to picnic sites, so there's really no camping in either of these canyons except in the backcountry.

Maps Wasatch-Cache National Forest, U.S.G.S. maps Salt Lake City (1:100,000), Sugarhouse, Mt. Aire (1:24,000)

The west ridge of Gobblers Knob, seen from the summit of Mt. Raymond (50mm lens).

Map 22, Olympus, Raymond, Gobblers Knob

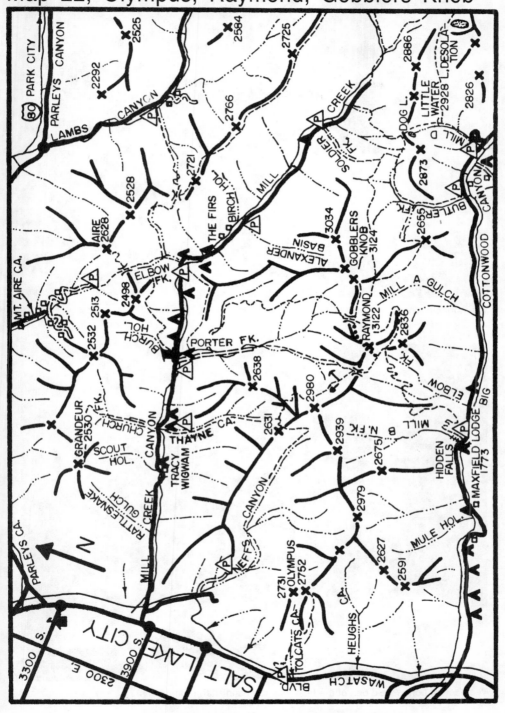

SCALE 0   4   8   KMS

The northern slopes of the Little Matterhorn (Pfeiferhorn) (200mm lens).

West face of Lone Peak, one of the best rock climbs in Utah (50mm lens).

Dromedary Peaks to the left, Twins Peaks to the right (early summer foto) (50mm lens).

Another look at Lone Peak, from the southwest slopes (50mm lens).

Dromedary and Twin Peaks, Wasatch Mountains

Location The area covered by this map is that portion of the Wasatch lying due east of Sandy and Midvale in the Salt Lake Valley. It's also the high area between Big and Little Cottonwood Canyons, and is just west of Utah's major ski resorts. The highest summit on this map is Twin Peaks, with the highest peak to the east at 3454 meters. Probably the best known summit is Dromedary Peak at 3386 meters, just east of Twin Peaks. Other well-known summits are Superior, Millicent and Kessler.   These mountains are now part of the Twin Peaks Wilderness Area.

Geology This is an old mining area with lots of mine shafts about. The rocks you'll be walking on are mostly quartzite, shale, slates, etc., mostly from the Big Cottonwood Formation. Some granite is exposed on the Little Cottonwood Canyon side.

Access There are two major highways providing access to this group of peaks. One is the highway up Big Cottonwood Canyon. This road ends at the Brighton Ski Resort (except for a dirt road going over Guardsman Pass to Park City). The other is the road up Little Cottonwood Canyon. This highway ends at Snowbird and Alta Ski Resorts. Both are good highways and kept open year-round.

Trail Information None of the peaks shown on this map have trails all the way to their summits. However, as time goes on and climbing becomes popular, trails are emerging. Two routes can be taken to the summit of Twin Peaks. One is to walk from the Mill B Picnic Grounds and up Broads Fork. The trail fades out about half-way up, but when that happens, route-find to the saddle east of the peaks, then walk west along the ridge. Twins can also be climbed from the south and one of several gullies on the south face. Dromedary Peak can be scaled from Mill B South Fork and Lake Blanche. Begin this climb at the Mill B Picnic Grounds and take the good trail southeast. From Lake Blanche, walk southwest to a saddle east of the peak, then up the ridge to the summit. If one were to either walk up the old 4WD road in Mill D South Fork, or the prominent trail leading up and to the northwest out of Alta, one could reach the pass and climb Superior to the west, or Flagstaff to the east, by walking along the ridge. There are many trails around the high area between Brighton and Alta, so one of these can be taken when climbing such peaks as Millicent and Sunset.

Best Time and Time Needed All hikes in this region are of the one day variety, with a few being half-day hikes. Hike from late June through October.

Campgrounds One can camp anywhere in the back country, or at the Brighton, Spruces, Tanner Flat or the Albion Basin Campgrounds. All are especially crowded on weekends.

Maps Uinta, Wasatch-Cache National Forest, U.S.G.S. maps Salt Lake City (1:00,000), Brighton, Dromedary, Mt. Aire (1:24,000)

Winter climbing on Dromedary, left, and Twin Peaks, right (55mm lens).

Map 23, Dromedary and Twin Peaks, Wasatch Mtns.

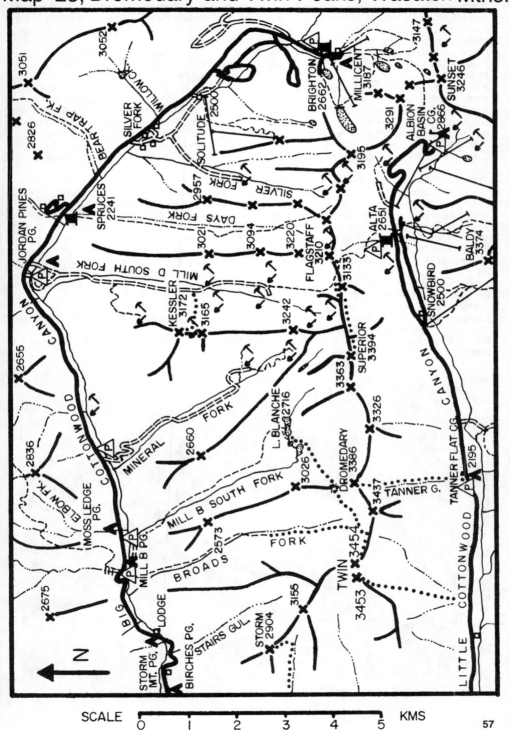

SCALE

0   1   2   3   4   5   KMS

57

Lone Peak and Little Matterhorn, Wasatch Mountains

Location   Both of these peaks are located in the Lone Peak Wilderness Area, which is southeast of Salt Lake City and east of Draper in the south end of the Salt Lake Valley, and north of Alpine in the northern part of Utah Valley. The peaks featured here are Lone Peak at 3430 meters, and the Little Matterhorn (sometimes called Pfeiferhorn), 3453 meters.

Geology   The area covered by parts of Little Cottonwood Canyon, Lone Peak, and the L. Matterhorn, is granite, as a result of an igneous intrusion known as the Cottonwood Stock. Old mines mark the edge of the stock.

Access   For Lone Peak, one has three route possibilities. First you can park on State Road 209 (an extension of 9400 South), just north of the Bell Canyon terminal moraine and due east of Granite. Or you can exit I-70 at 12300 South and drive east through Draper and end up on the gravel and dirt road heading to Corner Canyon and Alpine (Draper Ridge Route). The third possibility is to drive to Alpine, then head north and out of town on 2nd East Street. At the end of that road is a car-park. One can climb the L. Matterhorn from the Alpine or Bell Canyon routes just mentioned, or drive up Little Cottonwood Canyon and park about one km above Tanner Flat Campground and just above the White Canyon Slide Area.

Trail Information   From the mouth of Bell Canyon, you may have to bushwhack over the glacial moraine to Lower Bell C. Res., but then you can easily find the trail which heads for Upper Bell Lake. From this lake, route-find south, then to the west and up to the north ridge, thence the summit of Lone Peak. There are several different beginning points on the Draper Ridge route. Visually pick the route you want, as they all converge near the peak marked 2842. From there follow the trail or cairns to the summit. From the car-park above Alpine, walk west crossing three creek beds, then head up. From the Second Hamongog, route-find to the summit of Lone P., or continue to Lake Hardy, and beyond to the L. Matterhorn. The L. Matterhorn can be climbed from upper Bell Canyon by ridge-walking above L. Hardy, or use the White Pine and Red Pine Canyon Trails (see next map) to the ridge above Red Pine Lakes, then route-find along the ridge to the west.

Best Time and Time Needed   Regardless of the route taken, it's an all-day hike to climb Lone P. or the L. Matterhorn. Take a lunch and get an early start. Climb from about mid-June through October.

Campgrounds   Campgrounds are in upper L. Cottonwood and American Fork Canyons, but these climbs are considered to be day-hikes, not over-nighters.

Maps   Uinta, Wasatch-Cache National Forests, U.S.G.S. maps Provo, Salt Lake (1:100,000), Draper, Dromedary Peak, Lehi (1:24,000).

The west face of Lone Peak, seen from midway up Draper Ridge Route (55mm lens).

Map 24, Lone Peak and L. Matterhorn, Wasatch Mtns.

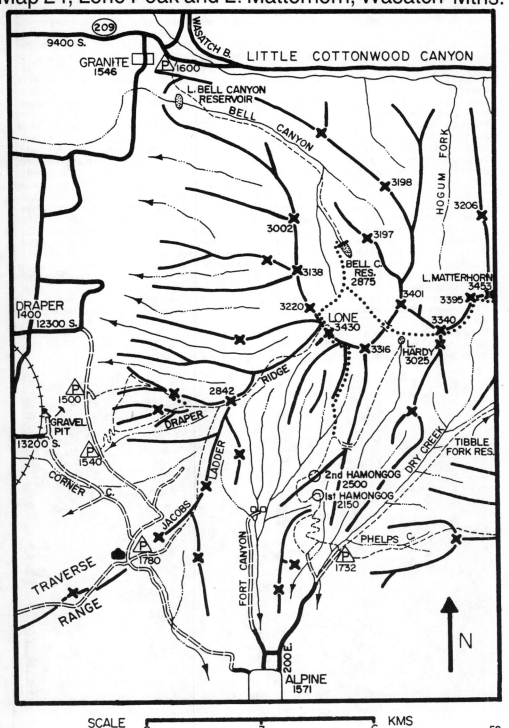

209
9400 S.
GRANITE 1546
P 1600
WASATCH B.
LITTLE COTTONWOOD CANYON
L. BELL CANYON RESERVOIR
BELL CANYON
HOGUM FORK
3198
3206
3002
3197
BELL C. RES. 2875
L. MATTERHORN 3453
3138
3401
3395
DRAPER 1400
12300 S.
3220
LONE 3430
3340
3316
L. HARDY 3025
P 1500
2842
RIDGE
GRAVEL PIT
DRAPER
TIBBLE FORK RES.
13200 S.
P 1540
LADDER
DRY CREEK
CORNER C.
2nd HAMONGOG 2500
1st HAMONGOG 2150
JACOBS
PHELPS C.
P 1780
FORT CANYON
P 1732
TRAVERSE
RANGE
200 E.
N
ALPINE 1571

SCALE   0   3   6   KMS

Box Elder and American Fork Twins, Wasatch Mountains

Location   The peaks on this map are located between Little Cottonwood and American Fork Canyons. Also, they're just north of Timp and east of Lone Peak. Since they are both near areas of high populaton, both canyons are heavily used, but the hiking, climbing and sight-seeing are superb.

Geology   The northern part of the mapped area is granite rock and part of the Cottonwood Stock. The mining symbols on the map are generally along the contact point between the granite and the sedimentary rocks overlaying the stock.

Access   The two access roads are the ones running up Little Cottonwood and American Fork Canyons. In A. F. Canyon, you can drive cars to as far as Granite Flat CG., Silver Lake Flat Reservoir, and to Dutchman Flat; all of which are above Tibble Fork Res. The road in L. Cottonwood ends just beyond the ski resorts of Snowbird and Alta.

Trail Information   To climb a high peak that is little known, Box Elder at 3384 meters, park at Granite Flat CG., and locate the trail near the bridge, then walk up-canyon to the pass, just north of the peak. From the pass, ridge-walk south to the summit. It can also be climbed from Alpine (see Lone Peak map). This map better shows the Red Pine Lake route to L. Matterhorn. Park at the mouth of White Pine Canyon and start on that trail, then continue west and around the mountain into Red Pine C. Walk to the ridge, and turn west and ridge-walk to the summit. American Fork Twins can be climbed easiest from the Snowbird parking lot. From Snowbird look for or ask about the beginning of a trail to the upper slopes. There are several. Any of them will get you to some higher places where you can then route-find to the summits. From the A.F. side, you can park at Silver Lake Flats Res., and walk north on the trail and ridge leading to the A.F. Twins. You could also walk up Mary Ellen Gulch, on first an old mine road, then trail, beginning at Dutchman Flat. Two of the famous peaks above Alta are Baldy and Sugarloaf. They can be climbed right from the Alta parking lot and by using the maintenance roads and trails leading up the mountain alongside the ski lifts. A better hike of it, would be to drive to and start walking from Dutchman Flat. Head for Mineral Basin, then the peaks. There are more peaks here than have been discussed.

Best Time and Time Needed   Trails and campsites are generally wet until about July 1, so from then until about mid or late October is the hiking season (unless winter climbing). All hikes on this map are day-hikes.

Campgrounds   Campgrounds are in both canyons, but they're crammed and noisy most of the time.

Maps   Uinta, Wasatch-Cache National Forests, U.S.G.S. maps Salt Lake, Provo (1:100,000), Dromedary Peak, Brighton, Timpanogos Cave, Aspen Grove (1:24,000).

This campsite is located near Red Pine Lake in Little Cottonwood Canyon (50mm lens).

Map 25, Box Elder and A.F. Twins, Wasatch Mtns.

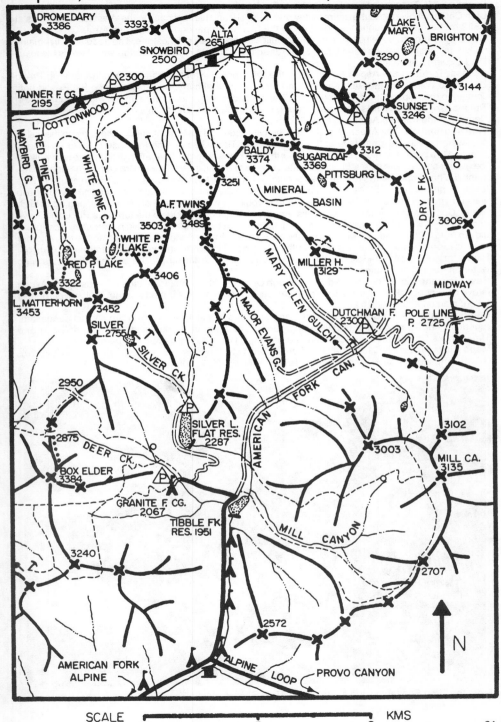

DROMEDARY 3386
3393
ALTA 2651
SNOWBIRD 2500
LAKE MARY
BRIGHTON
3290
3144
TANNER F. CG. 2195
2300
L. COTTONWOOD C.
SUNSET 3246
MAYBIRD G.
L. RED PINE C.
WHITE PINE C.
BALDY 3374
SUGARLOAF 3369
PITTSBURG L.
3312
DRY FK.
3251
A.F. TWINS
3503 3489
WHITE P. LAKE
MINERAL BASIN
3006
RED P. LAKE
3322
MILLER H. 3129
MARY ELLEN GULCH
MIDWAY
L. MATTERHORN 3453
3452
3406
SILVER L. 2755
SILVER CK.
MAJOR EVANS G.
DUTCHMAN F. 2300
POLE LINE P. 2725
2950
AMERICAN FORK CAN.
2875
DEER CK.
SILVER L. FLAT RES. 2287
3102
BOX ELDER 3384
3003
MILL CA. 3135
GRANITE F. CG. 2067
TIBBLE FK. RES. 1951
MILL CANYON
3240
2707
2572
N
AMERICAN FORK ALPINE
ALPINE
LOOP
PROVO CANYON

SCALE   KMS
0   3   6

Mt. Timpanogos, Wasatch Mountains

Location Mt. Timpanogos, or *Timp* as it's called locally, is the dominating mountain at the north end of Utah County. It overlooks the entire valley and is the second highest peak in the Wasatch Mountains at 3582 meters. This mountain is now part of the Mount Timpanogos Wilderness Area.

Geology Timp is a huge hulk of a mountain built almost entirely of limestone. The bedding still remains horizontal, despite having been thrust upwards so high. The dominant formation seen here is the fossil filled Oquirrh Formation.

Access To reach the Aspen Grove Trail, the most popular route on the mountain, drive up Provo Canyon to Wildwood, turn left or north, and proceed up that canyon past Sundance Ski Resort until coming to the Aspen Grove Campground. The second most popular route up the mountain is via the Timpooneke Trail which is on the north end of the mountain. Get to this trailhead via either Provo Canyon or the road up American Fork Canyon.

Trail Information The Aspen Grove Trail is heavily used and well-maintained. It zig zags up the valley past waterfalls to the small lake at the bottom of the Timp Glacier. The trail then goes in a westerly direction to a pass, and along the face and north ridge to the summit. A variation of this route is to walk up the glacier south of the lake and Timp Shelter, to a pass or col, then follow the trail along the ridge to the summit. The Timpooneke Trail is just as scenic, but is about 13 kms long as compared to about 11 kms for the Aspen Grove Trail. These two trails meet high on the mountain. A recommended hike would be to walk up one trail and down the other — but this would take a car shuttle of some kind, or a bit of hitch hiking. Good water supplies on both trails. Another more rugged route to the top is via Pleasant Grove and that city's water tanks just east of town. It begins as a trail up Battle Creek, but crosses a couple of old dirt roads. Then, without trail, one must walk up one of the avalanche gullies right to the top. Another route is to drive to the east end of either 20th or 16th North in Orem, and walk up the trail in Dry Canyon. Higher up when the trail fades, one can then walk up one of the canyons to the summit ridge. Little or no water on the last two routes.

Best Time and Time Needed Mid-July through October is the climbing season when using the Aspen Grove or Timpooneke Trails, but the southwest face routes can be climbed in June. Whichever route is taken, plan on a full day's hike.

Campgrounds Provo Canyon has no campgrounds, only picnic sites which are always congested. American Fork Canyon has many campgrounds, but it too is a popular place. Aspen Grove and Timpooneke Campground are best, but are often full. Backcountry camping is permitted.

Maps Uinta, Wasatch-Cache National Forest, U.S.G.S. maps Provo (1:100,000), Orem (1:62,500), Orem, Timpanogos Cave, Aspen Grove, Bridal Veil Falls (1:24,000)

From the Timp Shelter looking south up the Timp Glacier. Best hike in Utah (50mm lens).

Map 26, Mt. Timpanogos, Wasatch Mtns.

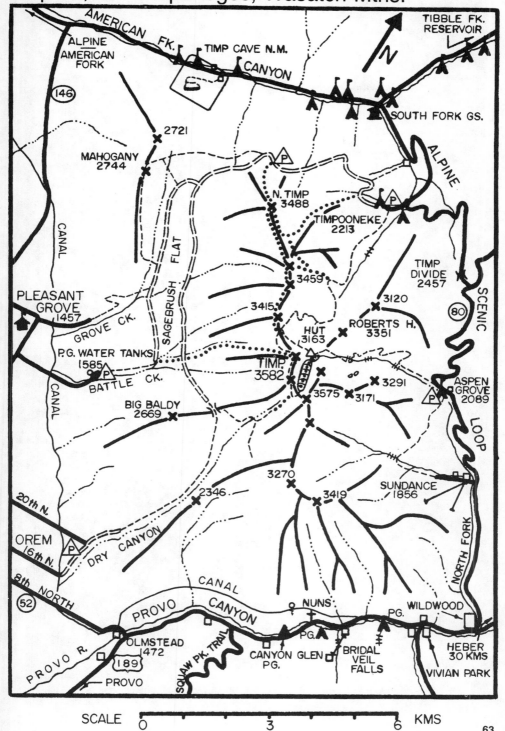

TIBBLE FK. RESERVOIR

AMERICAN FK.

ALPINE
AMERICAN
FORK

TIMP CAVE N.M.

CANYON

SOUTH FORK GS.

ALPINE

146

× 2721

MAHOGANY
2744 ×

N. TIMP
3488

TIMPOONEKE
2213

TIMP
DIVIDE
2457

80

SCENIC

CANAL

SAGEBRUSH FLAT

× 3459

3415 ×

× 3120

ROBERTS H.
3351

PLEASANT
GROVE
1457

GROVE CK.

HUT
3163

P.G. WATER TANKS
1585

BATTLE CK.

TIMP
3582

× 3575 × 3171

× 3291

ASPEN
GROVE
2089

LOOP

CANAL

BIG BALDY
2669 ×

3270
×

3419
×

SUNDANCE
1856

20th N.

2346 ×

DRY CANYON

NORTH FORK

OREM
16th N.

8th NORTH

52

PROVO CANYON

CANAL

NUNS

P.G.

WILDWOOD

PG.

HEBER
30 KMS

OLMSTEAD
1472

SQUAW PK. TRAIL

CANYON GLEN
P.G.

BRIDAL
VEIL
FALLS

VIVIAN PARK

189

PROVO R.

PROVO

SCALE   0   3   6   KMS

Nearing the summit of Timp during a mid-winter climb. Summit to the left (50mm lens).

With good weather, winter climbs on Timp can have a happy ending at the summit. (50mm lens).

October Scene. North face of Timp's North Peak (50mm lens).

Southwest face of Timp in October. Seen from upper west face of Y Mtn. (55mm lens).

Cascade Peak, Wasatch Mountains

Location Cascade Peak lies directly east of Orem and northeast of Provo. This is the mountain with a large western face and high cliffs. It's also the birthplace of Bridal Veil (Creek) Falls, which can be seen from Provo Canyon. The mountain has several peaks over the 3000 meter level with the highest being 3326 meters.

Geology The entire mountain known as Cascade Peak is made up of the Oquirrh Formation. By far the most dominant rock seen here is limestone, but with small amounts of chert, shale and quartzite. The big west face is solid limestone.

Access The two main ways of reaching Cascade Peak are both from Provo Canyon. Drive up the canyon and about 1 km before reaching Springdell, turn right or south, and follow the Pole Canyon road (Squaw Peak Trail) past Hope Campground and to near a quarry at the bend of the road as shown. For the second access road, drive further up Provo Canyon and turn right or south at Vivian Park. This is the South Fork of Provo River. Stop at the picnic grounds near where Bunnells Fork meets South Fork. Park and walk past the Giles Ranch sign into the canyon. This is now open to public access. The mouth of Big Spring Hollow is private land, but one can park at the entrance to Trefoil Girl Scout Camp, and walk up the trail on a dugway to the northwest of the parking lot to gain access to Big Spring Hollow.

Trail Information Probably the most scenic route to Cascade Peak is via Bunnells Fork. It's first a road, then a trail. Halfway up, the trail heads right or northwest and fades near the northeast ridge. Follow that ridge to the summit. Or, one might try the Trefoil–Big Spring Hollow–East Face route, but it may require some bushwhacking in the upper right fork. The shortest walk to the top is via the quarry marked 2296 meters on the southwest corner of the mountain. From that spot, bushwhack up the slopes to the summit ridge, then walk north to the highest point. One can also ride the lift to the top of Bridal Veil Falls where a trail-of-sorts is being developed for hikers. For rock climbers, this may be one of the better climbs in the state, especially on the west and north faces. Also the big gully on the south face has some interesting routes as well. The author once dragged a buckskin down that canyon, and remembers it well.

Best Time and Time Needed Most climbers or hikers can do this peak in one long day by using the Bunnells Fork route, or about half a day for the Bridal Veil Falls or the southwest corner routes. Mid-June through October is the climbing season.

Campgrounds The only forest service campgrounds in the area are the Hope and Rock Canyon Campgrounds. However, one can camp in many places along the Squaw Peak Trail. Much of South Fork along the paved road is private land.

Maps Uinta National Forest, U.S.G.S. maps Provo (1:100,000), Bridal Veil Falls (1:24,000)

From the top of Lion Head Mt., one can see both Timp and south face of Cascade Peak (35mm lens).

Map 27, Cascade Peak, Wasatch Mtns.

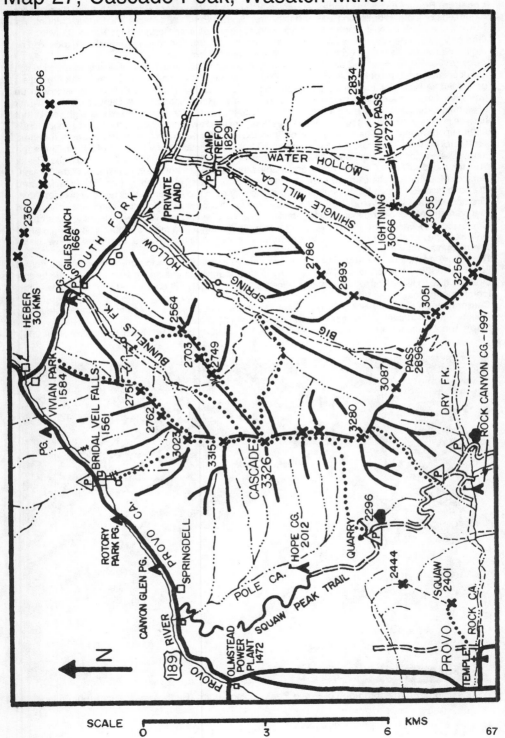

2506

2360

P.G. GILES RANCH 1666

HEBER 30 KMS

SOUTH FORK

PRIVATE LAND

P.G. CAMP TREFOIL 1829

WATER HOLLOW

WINDY PASS

2834

2723

SHINGLE MILL CA.

LIGHTNING 3066

3055

3256

HOLLOW

SPRING

2786

2893

3051

3087

BIG

PASS 2896

2564

BUNNELLS FK.

2703

2749

3280

DRY FK.

ROCK CANYON CG.—1997

VIVIAN PARK 1584

P.G.

2751

2762

3023

3315

CASCADE 3326

QUARRY

2296

BRIDAL VEIL FALLS 1561

HOPE CG. 2012

POLE CA.

SQUAW PEAK TRAIL

2444

SQUAW 2401

ROTARY PARK PG.

SPRINGDELL

CANYON GLEN PG.

PROVO CA.

PROVO RIVER

OLMSTEAD POWER PLANT 1472

189

PROVO

ROCK CA.

TEMPLE

N

SCALE 0   3   6   KMS

Provo Peak, Wasatch Mountains

Location Provo Peak is the highest summit which rises to the east of Provo. There are four smaller mountains or foothills to Provo Peak and they are: Squaw Peak, "Y", Maple and Buckley Mountains. Provo Peak is the highest point along a ridge which stretches from Springville to Provo Canyon.

Geology Provo Peak is a limestone mountain with the Oquirrh Formation prominently exposed. The foothill peaks are also mostly limestone, but from different formations.

Access For Provo Peak and all of its subsidiary peaks, the best means of access is the road which connects the Left Fork of Hobble Creek and Provo Canyon. This is called the Squaw Peak Trail. It's a good road and open for about 4 months each year. For the four foothill peaks, it's usually best to walk up from one of many streets in downtown Provo, and up either Rock, Slide or Slate Canyons. The Left Fork of Hobble Creek would normally be a fine access point, but the land near the paved highway in that canyon is all private and one must have permission from land owners to pass to the forest service lands further up the mountain. Therefore, it's recommended that all climbing be done from the western slopes.

Trail Information There are good and well-used trails in the major canyons east of Provo. There are many hikers in the area, but none of the peaks actually have trails to their summits. Climb Squaw Peak from the mouth of Rock Canyon, and Y and Maple Mountains both from along the trail in Slide Canyon. Buckley Mountain can be climbed easiest from the Squaw Peak Trail Road, or from Slate Canyon and the north face. For Provo Peak, one can walk all the way from Provo, but that's a two day hike for most. The easiest way is to drive on the Squaw Peak Trail to where the west ridge intersects the road. From that point there's an old track up the mountain. After a ways, simply follow the west ridge to the summit. One could also walk up Burnt Hollow, a northern route. A longer and more strenuous hike would be to walk from the mouth of Spring Canyon near Springville, along the prominent south ridge. This would be a very long and dry climb.

Best Time and Time Needed If one drives to the base of the west ridge of Provo Peak, it's only a couple of hours' walk to the top. To climb any of the "foothill mountains", it's an all day walk for the average hiker. Hiking season is from mid-June through October, but earlier and later, for hikes in the foothill mountains.

Campgrounds Only the Rock Canyon Campground is a designated campsite, but there are many places in which to camp. There are also many springs in the canyons.

Maps Uinta National Forest, U.S.G.S. maps Provo (1:100,000), Bridal Veil Falls, Springville (1:24,000)

A June 1 foto. From south ridge of Provo Peak, looking north (Bartholomew Face) (50mm lens).

Map 28, Provo Peak, Wasatch Mtns.

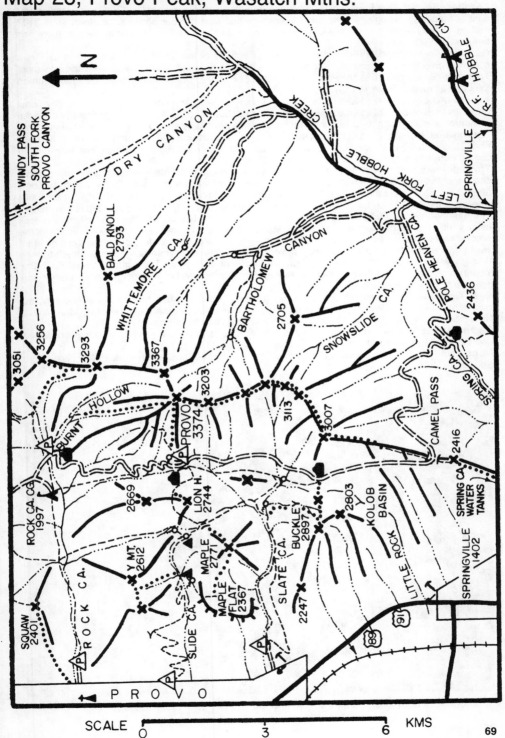

WINDY PASS
SOUTH FORK PROVO CANYON

DRY CANYON

CREEK

LEFT FORK HOBBLE

HOBBLE CK

SPRINGVILLE
R.R.

BALD KNOLL 2793

WHITTEMORE CA.

BARTHOLOMEW CANYON

2705

SNOWSLIDE CA.

POLE HEAVEN CA.

2436

3051

3256

3293

3367

3203

PROVO 3374

3113

3007

CAMEL PASS

SPRING CA.

2416

BURNT HOLLOW

ROCK CA. CG 1997

2669

LION H. 2744

SLATE CA.

KOLOB BASIN

2803

SPRING CA.
WATER TANKS

Y MT. 2612

MAPLE 2771

BUCKLEY 2897

LITTLE ROCK

SPRINGVILLE 1402

SQUAW 2401

ROCK CA.

SLIDE CA.

MAPLE FLAT 2367

2247

91

89

PROVO

SCALE   0   3   6   KMS

69

Spanish Fork Peak, Wasatch Mountains

Location Spanish Fork Peak is one of the more prominent peaks seen in Utah Valley. It's located just east of Mapleton, which is just south of Springville and east of Spanish Fork. Its elevation is 3107 meters. Some people in Mapleton know the mountain as Monument Peak, and in the past there has been an annual hike to the summit.

Geology Spanish Fork Peak is made up almost entirely of the Oquirrh Formation. The rock is a combination of limestone and quartzite for the most part. Notice the flat bench lying along the west face. That's the highest shoreline deposits left from Lake Bonneville. These shoreline features are common to nearly all mountains in western Utah.

Access Access to the normal route to Spanish Fork Peak is via Mapleton. From Mapleton, drive east on 1200 North Street. This paved road heads up Maple Canyon to the Whiting Campground. Above the campground it's a rough road, but one which can be negotiated by any car, up to as far as the Dibbles Canyon area. If one is using the Pace Hollow route on the east side of the mountain, drive up Spanish Fork Canyon to the Diamond Fork Road. Then turn northeast to the Palmyra Campgrounds. From the campgrounds turn northwest 'till the road ends.

Trail Information The normal route is via Maple Canyon and the Right Fork of Maple Canyon. Most cars should be parked on the north side of Maple Creek, then walk south up a 4WD road which lasts only about 1 km. From there the well-used trail heads south up the canyon. Higher up is a large cirque basin where the Maple Canyon Lake lies. This is a good area for camping if an overnight trip is anticipated. The trail then zig zags up the slope to the west until the ridge is reached, then the trail more or less follows the ridge to the summit. Plenty of water available on the trail below the ridge. Perhaps the second best route, and one which always affords a good view of Utah Valley, is to climb the prominent west ridge immediately north of Crowd Canyon. There's only a short section with oak brush to walk through, which makes it an easy walk. There's no water on this route. The author has climbed the mountain on the moderately good trail up Sterling Hollow, which isn't used much except during the deer hunt. Take water on this trail, as it's a dry hike.

Best Time and Time Needed Any route on Spanish Fork Peak can be climbed in one day, but overnight hikes are enjoyable in Maple Canyon. The west ridge route could be climbed in May or November, but the Maple Canyon Trail is open from mid-June to October.

Campgrounds National forest campgrounds are Whiting in Maple Canyon (but it's always crowded) and Palmyra and Diamond Fork Campgrounds on Diamond Fork.

Maps Uinta National Forest, U.S.G.S. maps Provo (1:100,000), Spanish Fork Peak, Billies Mtn., Springville (1:24,000)

The north face of Spanish Fork Peak. From Maple Canyon Lake (55mm lens).

Map 29, Spanish Fork Peak, Wasatch Mtns.

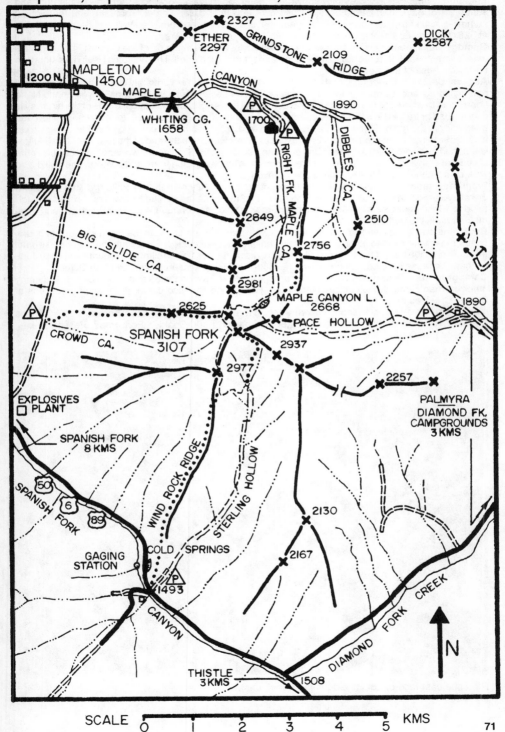

ETHER 2297
2327
GRINDSTONE RIDGE
DICK 2587
2109
MAPLETON 1450
1200 N.
MAPLE CANYON
WHITING GG. 1658
1700
P
P
1890
DIBBLES CA.
RIGHT FK. MAPLE CA.
2849
2510
2756
BIG SLIDE CA.
2981
MAPLE CANYON L. 2668
2625
P
PACE HOLLOW
1890
P
CROWD CA.
SPANISH FORK 3107
2937
2977
2257
EXPLOSIVES PLANT
PALMYRA DIAMOND FK. CAMPGROUNDS 3 KMS
SPANISH FORK 8 KMS
WIND ROCK RIDGE
STERLING HOLLOW
50
6
89
SPANISH FORK
2130
GAGING STATION
COLD SPRINGS
2167
P
1493
CANYON
DIAMOND FORK CREEK
N
THISTLE 3 KMS
1508

SCALE 0 1 2 3 4 5 KMS

Santaquin Pk., Loafer Mtn., Wasatch Mtns.

Location Santaquin Peak, usually known as Loafer Mountain, is located south of Spanish Fork and southeast of Payson in Utah County. This entire massif is called Loafer Mountain, and the highest summit is also known as Loafer. But the peak that is actually seen from Utah Valley is Santaquin Peak, at 3257 meters. Loafer Peak is just one meter higher at 3258 meters.

Geology Santaquin Peak and the whole of Loafer Mountain is made up of the Oquirrh Formation. It's mostly limestone, with some sandstone, chert and quartzite included. The Wasatch Fault runs along the northwest base of the mountain.

Access Because the northern and eastern parts of the mountain are privately owned lands, the only all national forest access route is from the area of Payson Lakes. Drive up Payson Canyon on the Nebo Loop Road to where the first road to the Payson Lakes turns right. On the opposite side of the highway is a 4WD road or trail. Follow this to the corral at the first pass, then go down a bit, then up Mud Hollow and eventually to the top of Santaquin Peak. One can also approach the mountain on a public access road west of Birdseye. A dirt road follows Bennie Creek. Walk west from the end of the road until Mud Hollow is reached, then proceed to the top. One can also use the Cutoff Trail as shown. Another possible route is up Bear Canyon, but that trail may be overgrown. With permission from land owners, one could also walk up from the end of the road in Loafer Canyon.

Trail Information Because much of the mountain is privately owned, the trails are little used and therefore sometimes difficult to locate. However, the Payson Lakes — Mud Hollow Trail is used enough to be self-maintained, and the trail up Bennie Creek is also used enough, especially by deer hunters, to make it a visible path.

Best Time and Time Needed A fast hiker can walk from Payson Lakes to the top in a couple of hours, but for most it turns out to be an all-day affair if driving time is included. Take water on the hike, as most trails are on ridge tops. If the Payson Lakes Trail is used, it's possible to climb the mountain in early June — that's because it's a southern ridge route. So the climbing season is June through October.

Campgrounds There are forest service campgrounds at Payson Lakes and Maple Bench and many other off road campsites along the Nebo Loop Road. One can also camp on the higher sections of Bennie Creek as that's national forest land.

Maps Utah Travel Council Map 7 — Northwestern Central Utah, Uinta National Forest, U.S.G.S. maps Nephi (1:100,000), Santaquin Peak (1:62,500), Spanish Fork, Spanish Fork Peak, Payson Lakes, Birdseye (1:24,000)

The southeast face of Loafer Mountain (28mm lens).

Map 30, Santaquin Pk., Loafer Mtn., Wasatch Mtns.

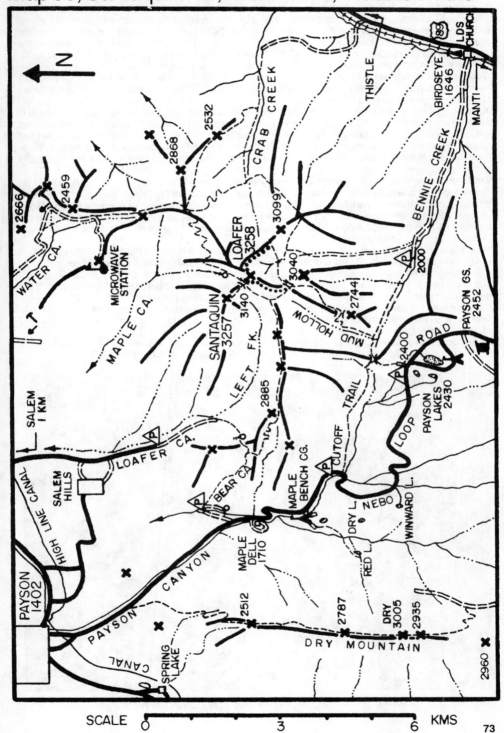

SCALE 0   3   6   KMS

Mt. Nebo, Wasatch Mountains

Location Mt. Nebo is the most southerly of the Wasatch Mountain peaks and is located just to the east of Mona, and northeast of Nephi in Juab County. The mountain has three main summits running in a north-south direction. The highest is the North Peak, at 3637 meters. However, the two trails on the mountain stop at the southern peak, which is 3621 meters. On the south face of South Peak are the remains of the old Heliograph or Trigenometric Station dating back to the early 1880's.   Nebo is the highest peak in the Wasatch Mountains. Its summit rises well above timberline.

Geology Mt. Nebo has many of the same characteristics as other high peaks in Utah County. Nearly the entire mountain is made up of the Oquirrh Formation which is mostly limestone. There are different formations exposed on Bald Mountain.

Access There are two main access routes (and trails) to the south summit. The most convenient is from the west and Mona, and up Willow Creek. From the end of Willow Creek Road a trail circles around the huge amphitheater and eventually reaches the south ridge. The other route is from the east and Salt Creek. Drive from Nephi east on Highway 132. Turn north at the KOA Campground and drive to the sign indicating the Nebo Trail and Andrews Creek. A 4WD road runs west for 1½ kms where the trail begins at the creek.

Trail Information Both trails mentioned are in good condition, but are not used as much as trails on Timpanogos for example. At the beginning of each trail, on Willow and Andrews Creeks, there is water available, but for the most part, nowhere else on the mountain. In early summer there are usually plenty of snow banks and some water at 2920 meters on the east face, as marked. For those preferring a trail-less hike, try the Cedar Ridge, or walk north on the Nebo Basin Trail, then climb direct to the summit on one of the high east face ridges.

Best Time and Time Needed The average hiker will need 4 to 6 hours for the climb to the summit on either trail — in other words, it's an all day hike. For those living in Utah Valley, it's an entire day's trip. For those living further from the mountain, camping at the mountain base might be best. Because the last part of the hike is on the south ridge, Mt. Nebo could be climbed from about the middle of June or July 1 through October in most years without the need for snow climbing equipment.

Campgrounds There are camping sites on Willow Creek which are less crowded than on Salt Creek. There are several national forest campgrounds on Salt Creek, and some very good undeveloped campsites on Andres Creek near the trailhead.

Maps Utah Travel Council Map 7 — Northwestern Central Utah, Uinta National Forest, U.S.G.S. maps Nephi (1:100,000), Santaquin, Santaquin Peak (1:62,500), Nebo, Nebo Basin (1:24,000)

South ridge of Mt. Nebo. South Peak, left; North Peak, right (50mm lens).

Map 31, Mt. Nebo, Wasatch Mtns.

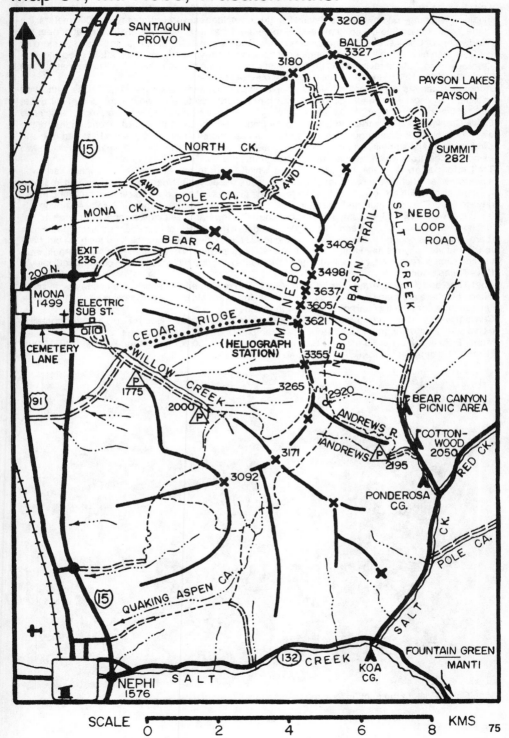

Mine Camp Peak, Pavant Range

Location The mountains included on this map are all located directly east of the central Utah town of Fillmore. The range is known as the Pavant Range and includes several summits over 3000 meters, the highest of which is Mine Camp Peak at 3116 meters. All the higher summits are located at or near the headwaters of Chalk Creek. The mountains in this range are rounded summits, and are used more by 4WDers than hikers, but there are a number of trails in the canyon bottoms which afford good hiking.

Geology Most of the rocks in this area are a mixture of quartzite and limestone. The formations are Tintic Quartzite, North Horn Formation and the Maxfield Limestone.

Access Access is good, for both 4WD people and hikers with passenger cars. Those with 4WD vehicles can use a reasonably good road which runs northeast to southwest along one major ridge, most of which is at or near 3000 meters. This is used mainly by hunters. However, most traffic is up Chalk Creek to several recreation areas, mostly picnic sites. This road is paved for one quarter of the way to Pistol Rock Campground, then it's rough but passable to all cars. By using this road one can climb all the major summits on the map. There's also a reasonably good road up Meadow Creek to two campgrounds, from which begins a trail to the summit road.

Trail Information All trails, or at least those which begin in the Chalk Creek drainage, are well sign-posted and fairly well-maintained. These trails are used by cattlemen, boy scout groups and deer hunters, all of which are local people. As a result the place is not crowded. To climb Mine Camp Peak, drive to Pistol Rock Campground and park. Then follow the creek trail and signs to Paradise Canyon (it's the upper west fork of Bear Canyon). One can then use the Paradise Canyon route or turn left at that junction and eventually reach and follow a 4WD road up a ridge 'till an old service road is reached. From there walk cross country to the northwest to the top of Mine Camp. All these high ridges have old 4WD roads, but the canyons have trails only and are relatively pristine. To hike to the Catherine Peak area, use the Chalk Creek road, but look for one of two trailheads; one half-way up, the other near Copley's Cove Campground.

Best Time and Time Needed The hike up Mine Camp or Catherine can be done in one day by most hikers, but there are many excellent campsites, making overnight trips worthwhile. Hiking in this range can be done from the first part of June through October.

Campgrounds There are four listed campgrounds in Chalk Creek's South Fork, but are more like picnic sites than campgrounds. There are two campgrounds on Meadow Creek.

Maps Fishlake National Forest, U.S.G.S. maps Richfield (1:100,000), Fillmore, Richfield (1:62,500), Fillmore, Holden, Coffee Peak, Mt. Catherine (1:24,000)

Mine Camp Peak to the right, is forested to the summit (35mm lens).

Map 32, Mine Camp Peak, Pavant Range

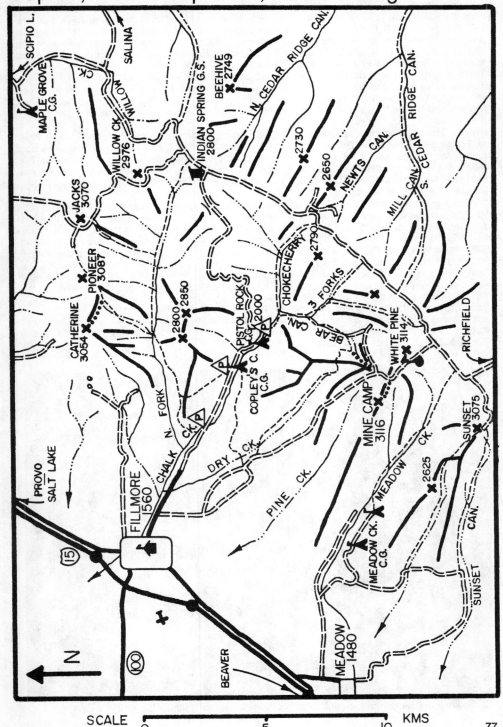

SCALE

0   5   10   KMS

Baldy, Belknap and Delano, Tuschar Mountains

Location The Tushar Mountains are a group of peaks among the highest in the state of Utah. They're in southwestern Utah just east of Interstate Highway 15 and Beaver. The highest summit is Mt. Delano at 3709 meters, but Mt. Belknap at 3699 meters is perhaps the most interesting peak to climb because of its steeper nature and the remains of an old Heliograph Station on its summit. These relics are among the best preserved of any seen by the author in the western USA. This map pretty well covers the entire range, from Signal Peak in the north to Circleville Mountain in the south.

Geology Almost all the rocks included on this map are volcanic in origin. Part of the area is Mt. Belknap Rhyolite, while in the southern part of the map around Birch Creek Peak, one finds the Muddy Creek Formation. There are many old mines in the northern part of the range especially around Copper Belt, Brigham and Bullion Peaks. Lots of old roads to scar the surface are in this area too. This is not a plateau, but true mountains.

Access The one major access route is the paved highway running between Beaver and the Mt. Holly Ski Resort and Puffer Lake. This road is used year-round. One can also get to this high country from Junction on the east side of the range on the same road, but the east side is steep, unpaved, and has hairpin turns even though it's well-maintained. There's also a road up from Marysvale, but it too is steep and bad at times making it a 4WD road. Ask about the latest condition of this road at the Beaver Ranger Station in Beaver, before driving it.

Trail Information Few trails here, but there is one to the summit of Belknap on its southeastern side. Mt. Baldy can be reached from either Blue Lake or Mt. Belknap. There are many easy routes up the southwestern face of Delano. Just head that way from Big John Flat and route-find to the summit. There's an old 4WD track being made into a hiking trail from Big Flat Guard Station to City Creek Peak and Mt. Holly, and ending near Big John Flat. No trails to Circleville Mt., but it's easy to climb by route-finding from one of several locations to the north or west of the peak, and from the area of La Baron Lake.

Best Time and Time Needed The author climbed Delano, Belknap and Baldy in one long day, but most people may feel happy to do one or two in one day. This isn't really a back-packing area, just day hiking for the most part. Hike from mid-June through October.

Campgrounds There are several campgrounds along the Beaver River, but they require a fee. All other campgrounds shown are more primitive but free for usage. Good campsites everywhere.

Maps Fishlake National Forest, U.S.G.S. maps Beaver (1:100,000), Delano Peak (1:62,500), Circleville Mtn., Circleville (1:24,000)

Mt. Belknap, as seen from the southwest and from the summit of Mt. Baldy (50mm lens).

Map 33, Baldy, Belknap and Delano, Tushar Mtns.

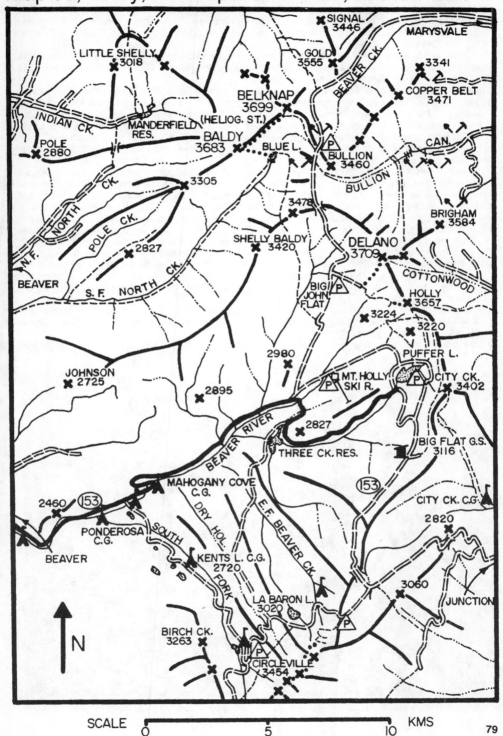

SCALE 0   5   10 KMS

Bluebell Knoll, Boulder Mountains

Location The area covered by this map is known as the Boulder Mountains, the highest part of which is the Boulder Top. The Boulder Top is just west of the central part of the Capitol Reef National Park and south of Loa, Bicknell and Torrey in south-central Utah. The highest point on the Boulder is Bluebell Knoll at 3453 meters.

Geology The Boulder Top has been eroded away on all sides leaving an escarpment as shown on the map. The top or rim of the plateau is about 3250 meters and has a drop of from 150 to 200 meters. The Top is made up of volcanic rock of Tertiary age.

Access The north slope of the Boulder Top can really only be reached from the north and the Fremont River Valley. Use Highway 24 which runs from Richfield to Loa, Hanksville, and on to Green River. From Teasdale or Torrey drive south on the paved road running to Boulder and Escalante, but turn right about 3 kms before Grover. By taking the Fish Creek Road, one is in the best position to hike, climb or fish in some of the best hiking and fishing areas of the Boulder. There's another road running up Pine Creek, passing the Aquarius Guard Station, and eventually ending at Chokecherry Point, but this is often rough and there's not a lot to see on top anyway.

Trail Information Since the Boulder Mountain is a very flat-topped plateau, it has not been used to a great extent for hiking or climbing. This is simply 4WD country and there are numerous 4WD type roads and tracks all over the top. As a result of the physical makeup of the land, hiking and most fishing has been confined to lakes and streams under the Rim. That's where most of the fishing lakes and maintained trails are found. In recent years with more interest in hiking, some 4WD tracks have been blocked off and trails built and maintained — especially between Lost Lake and Chokecherry Point. This is now a good hiking region, with many places where climbers can reach the rim top. The trails from Fish Creek to Beef Meadows and Chokecherry Point are the least used of all trails and hard to find.

Best Time and Time Needed Most of the lakes are around the 3100 meter level, while Boulter Top is between 3300 and 3400 meters. This means it's normally open by about mid-June and through October. Almost any hike in this area can be done in one day, but local scout groups enjoy overnight hikes and fishing trips.

Campgrounds There are several maintained campgrounds on Highway 12 between Torrey and Boulder, but none in this best hiking area. There is a fine camping site as shown on Spring Creek. Below the Rim there are springs and streams everywhere.

Maps Utah Travel Council Map 1 — Southeastern Utah, Dixie National Forest, U.S.G.S. maps Loa (1:100,000), Torrey, Grover (1:62,500), Loa 1 SE, Loa 4 NE (1:24,000)

Fish Creek Lake, with the Boulder Top Rim in the background (35mm lens).

Map 34, Bluebell Knoll, Boulder Mtns.

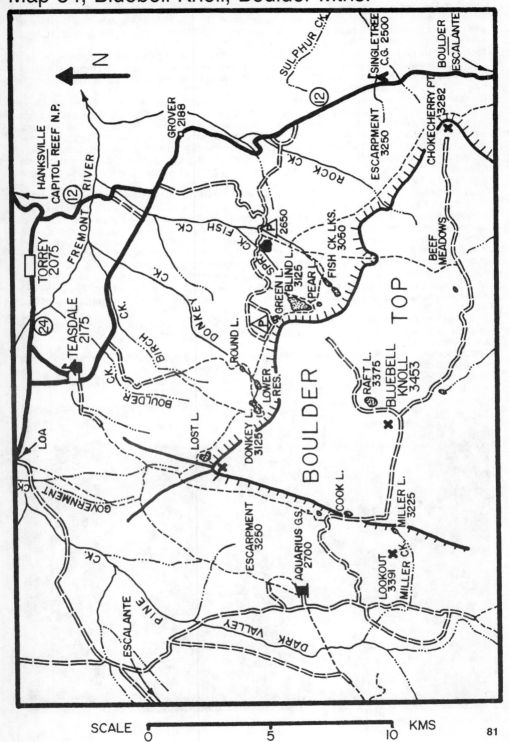

SCALE

0   5   10   KMS

Flat Top, Thousand Lake Mountain

Location Located in south-central Utah's high plateau country is an isolated mesa or plateau among the highest in the state. This is a flat top highland known as Thousand Lake Mountain. The highest part is 3446 meters, and on most maps this is known as the Flat Top. This area is immediately west of Capitol Reef National Park, north of Bicknell and east of Loa.

Geology The part of Thousand Lake Mountain known as the Flat Top (which is all that remains of a larger high plateau) has been eroded away on all sides leaving an escarpment. The height of this rim varies from 75 to 100 meters, but does not present a major obstacle to climbers. The very top is composed of volcanic rock of Tertiary age.

Access One can approach the area from the east and Hanksville, or from the north or west from Richfield and Cedar City. The highway running from Loa to Torrey in the Fremont River Valley, south and west of the mountain, is US Highway 24. This is the same access as to Capitol Reef National Park. For longer hikes, hikers can use dirt roads running into canyons from the areas of Fremont, Lyman, Bicknell, or Torrey. But the one and only road that takes people high on the mountain and to the Elkhorn Campground is the one running east from State Road 72 and passing Heart Lake. This is a typical mountain road, rough in places, but generally maintained. This road reaches above 3000 meters and is open to traffic for only three or four months a year.

Trail Information If one is interested in getting to the top of Flat Top, but has little time, then drive to the Elkhorn C.G. If you have a passenger car it may be best to park there. The road going to Big Lake and beyond is, for the most part, a 4WD track. From the campground walk along the track for about 3 kms till you see a sign pointing out the Deep Creek—Flat Top Trail. Walk south on this trail about 200 meters. Watch carefully, because there's a trail junction at that point. Turn right and walk west upon the Flat Top, or walk south to Big Lake. If you're going south you might as well stay on the road, because the road ends at Big Lake anyway. From Big Lake you can walk south through a logged-over area, finally arriving at an unnamed lake. From there another trail heads northwest to the F. Top. You'll likely lose the trail on top, but there are some cairns as you walk through the open meadows of the Flat Top. The place isn't that big, so you can't get lost for long. Take a compass on cloudy days. There's a spring just east of Neff Res.

Best Time and Time Needed The hike from Elkhorn is a full day hike if you walk all the way and if you make the loop as suggested. If you drive on to Big Lake, you might do the same loop-hike in about half a day. Hike from mid–June through October.

Campgrounds You could camp at Sunglow Campground near Bicknell, but the Elkhorn CG. is much nicer. There are also many campsites on the road to Big Lake.

Maps Utah Travel Council Map 2 — Southeastern Central Utah, Fish Lake National Forest, U.S.G.S. maps Loa (1:100,000), Torrey (1:62,500), Loa 1 NE and SE (1:24,000)

The western escarpment of the Flat Top of Thousand Lake Mountain (28mm lens).

Map 35, Flat Top, Thousand Lake Mtn.

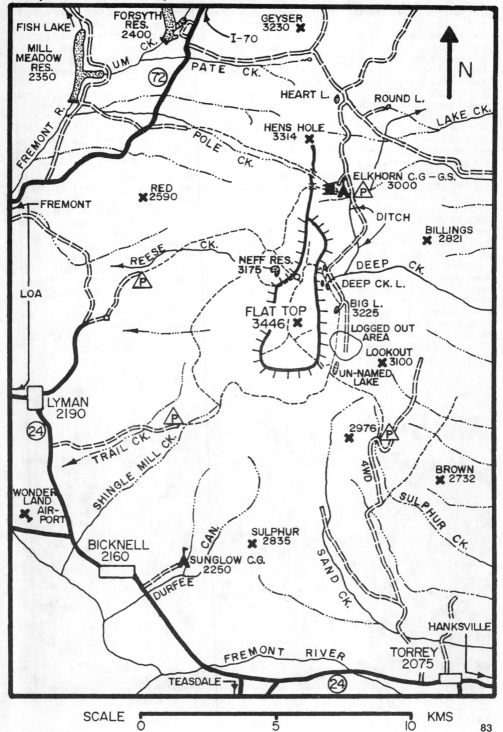

SCALE
0   5   10   KMS

Fish Lake, Marvine, Terrill and Hilgard

Location There are four major peaks or summits on this map, the highest of which is Fish Lake Hightop at 3546 meters. This is the big hulk of a mountain immediately to the northwest of Fish Lake, located north of Loa and southeast of Richfield in south-central Utah. The other three mountains are: Mt. Marvine, 3539 meters, by far the sharpest and most interesting peak to climb; Mt. Terrill, 3520 meters and just north of Marvine, which has a small solar-powered radio tower at the summit; and Mt. Hilgard, 3515 meters, the site of one of the minor Heliograph Stations dating from the 1880's.

Geology The most famous landmark of this area is Fish Lake. This Lake is actually in a graben, or down-faulted block, sandwiched inbetween Fish Lake Hightop and Mytoge Mountain. At one time the lake drained to the south, but later tilting caused it to drain northeast to Johnson Valley Reservoir and the Fremont River. The rocks are part of the Moroni Volcanic Series. Pelican Creek drainage is the path of a former glacier.

Access First head for Fish Lake. Get there from Highway 24 from south of the lake, or from Loa and the road along the Fremont R. You can climb Fish L. Hightop or Mytoge from   or near Fish Lake. Drive up Sevenmile Creek to reach Marvine and Terrill, and leave State Road 72 and drive west to the Clear Ck. G.S. to climb Hilgard.

Trail Information Here are the normal routes to each summit. Climb Fish Lake Hightop by driving or walking to Pelican Overlook, then use a popular and well-used trail running up Pelican Creek. Higher up, this trail turns into a 4WD track at times, and passes Tasha Spring. Then one can return by following Tasha Creek down to the water gauging station located on Sevenmile Creek. This is the best hike in the area. Mt. Marvine can be climbed from the west and Sevenmile Creek Road. No trail, just route-find up the west face. For Terrill, drive further up Sevenmile Creek and park near the guard station, then walk east on an old 4WD track along the fence line as shown. Further along, route-find to the summit. One could climb both Marvine and Terrill from UM Pass as well. From near the Clear Creek G.S., walk southwest on a trail towards Willies Flat Res., then route-find north to the summit of Hilgard.

Best Time and Time Needed Each of the peaks can be climbed easily in one day, but Fish Lake Hightop can be made into an overnight hike. The hiking season is from about mid or late June through October in most years.

Campgrounds There are several campgrounds on the Fremont River and at Fish Lake. But Fish Lake is crowded, and it costs to camp. Drive to out of the way places for better camps.

Maps Utah Travel Council Map 6 — Southwestern Central Utah, Fishlake National Forest. U.S.G.S. maps Salina (1:100,000), Fish Lake, Mt. Terrill, Hilgard Mtn., Forsyth Reservoir (1:24,000)

Foto is from the top of Mt. Terrill, looking south at Mt. Marvine (105mm lens).

84

Map 36, Fish Lake, Marvine, Terrill, and Hilgard

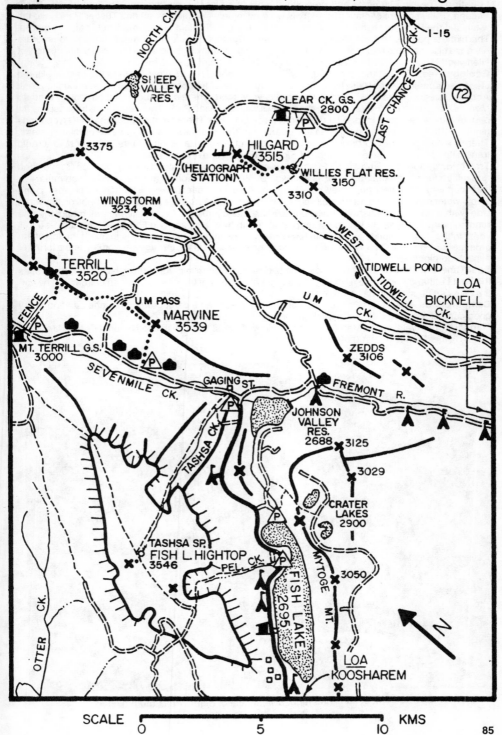

NORTH CK.

I-15

72

SHEEP VALLEY RES.

CLEAR CK. G.S. 2800

P

X 3375

HILGARD 3515

(HELIOGRAPH STATION)

WILLIES FLAT RES. 3150

X 3310

WINDSTORM 3234

X

WEST

TIDWELL POND

TIDWELL

LOA

BICKNELL CK.

TERRILL 3520

U M PASS

MARVINE 3539

U M

CK.

FENCE

P

MT. TERRILL G.S. 3000

P

SEVENMILE CK.

GAGING ST.

P

ZEDDS 3106

X

FREMONT R.

JOHNSON VALLEY RES. 2688

X 3125

TASHSA CK.

X

X

P

3029

CRATER LAKES 2900

X

TASHSA SP.

FISH L. HIGHTOP 3546

PEL CK.

P

MYTOGE MT.

3050

X

OTTER CK.

FISH LAKE 2695

N

LOA

KOOSHAREM

X

SCALE 0 — 5 — 10 KMS

Signal Peak, Sevier Plateau

Location The high summits and precipitous west faces shown on this map are part of the Sevier Plateau. This segment of plateau country is wedged in between the Pavant and Tushar Ranges to the west, and the Fishlake Hightop Mountain. It's due south of Richfield, and immediately east of Monroe. The highest point is Monroe Peak at 3422 meters. But this mountain will hardly be mentioned here because of a road and radio tower on top. The most interesting climb here is a fine hike to the summit of Glenwood Mountain, in which Signal Peak is the highest point at 3421 meters.

Geology Keep in mind this is a plateau with flat lying beds, but it's tilted down to the east, making a steep escarpment on the west face. The rock is tuff, ryolite, and basalt — all volcanic in origin.

Access Access to the main hiking area here is very good. There's a rather poor, but paved road up Monroe Canyon to a small recreation area known as Monrovian Park. This affords the best access for people with passenger cars and for those interested in hiking. There are many dirt and 4WD type roads higher on the plateau and on the eastern parts, but these places are not considered hiking areas. There's also a dirt or 4WD road from near the town of Annabella running to the southeast to a radio transmitter on the lower western ridge of Signal Peak, as shown on the map.

Trail Information To climb Signal Peak, this is probably the best route. Drive up Monroe Canyon and turn left up First Lefthand Fork. This is a steep, rough road, but high clearance vehicles can make it at least part way. After parking somewhere along the road, walk past the small hunters cabin, then along an old water pipeline to where the trail veers to the right. It then zig zags up the canyon wall on the south side, with many deer and sheep trails to make the way confusing. Eventually the trail meets the one running north-south as shown on the map. Walk north here crossing two fine streams. Later, the trail veers to the west and ends at the radio tower. Keep in mind the first objective is to reach the top of the prominent west ridge. Once one is on it, it's a scramble to the summit, through sagebrush and a forest of aspen and pines.

Best Time and Time Needed The best time to hike here is from mid-June through October. If one uses the First Lefthand Fork route, expect to take most of one day. If the radio tower can be reached by car, the hike can be made in half a day.

Campgrounds Monrovian Park is more of a picnic area than a campground, but one can find many good campsites along First Lefthand Fork, with good running water.

Maps Utah Travel Council Map 6 — Southwestern Central Utah, Fishlake National Forest, U.S.G.S. maps Salina, Richfield (1:100,000), Monroe (1:62,500)

Foto shows Glenwood Mountains and rugged west face of Signal Peak (50mm lens).

Map 37, Signal Peak, Sevier Plateau

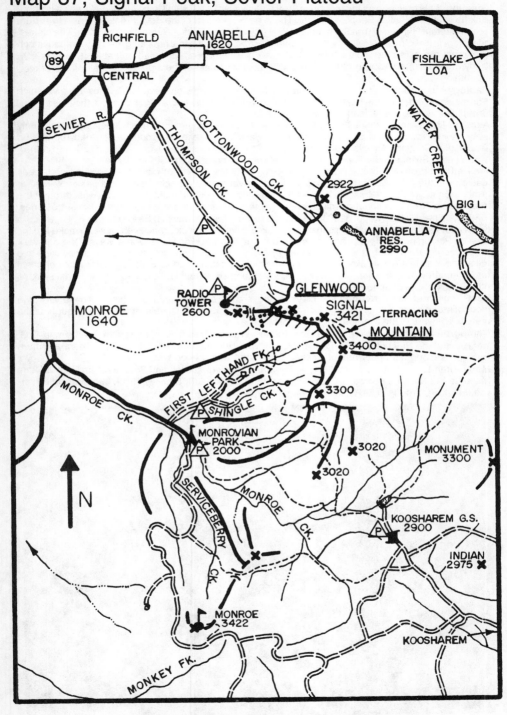

RICHFIELD

ANNABELLA
1620

FISHLAKE
LOA

US 89

CENTRAL

WATER CREEK

SEVIER R.

THOMPSON CK.

COTTONWOOD CK.

2922

BIG L.

ANNABELLA
RES.
2990

P

RADIO
TOWER
2600

P

GLENWOOD

SIGNAL
3421

TERRACING

MONROE
1640

MOUNTAIN

3400

FIRST LEFTHAND FK.

MONROE CK.

P SHINGLE CK.

3300

N

P
MONROVIAN
PARK
2000

3020

3020

MONUMENT
3300

SERVICEBERRY CK.

MONROE CK.

KOOSHAREM G.S.
2900

P

INDIAN
2975

MONROE
3422

KOOSHAREM

MONKEY FK.

SCALE 0   4   8 KMS

Musinia Peak (Mollys Nipple), Sevier Plateau

Location This map covers the mountain area directly east of the small town of Mayfield which is about 20 kms south of Manti in Sanpete County. These peaks are part of the Sevier Plateau which runs from near Interstate Highway 70 on the south to US Highway 6 and Soldier Summit on the north. The highest peak here is Heliotrope Mountain at 3393 meters. However, this is merely a long, flat ridge without much to interest climbers. The most interesting summit on the map is Musinia Peak at 3348 meters. (On many maps this peak is referred to as Mollys Nipple, because of the nipple–like peak on top of the mountain.)

Geology This portion of the Sevier Plateau has three formations exposed. They are: Wasatch Formation on top, then the North Horn Formation, and generally at the lower levels, is the Mesa Verde Group. Rocks are mostly limestone or sandstone.

Access There are dirt roads and 4WD tracks leading into this region from all directions, but the only easy way of reaching all of these summits is via Mayfield and the good gravel road running up Twelvemile Canyon. An alternative route would be to drive east out of Sterling (12 kms north of Mayfield) up Sixmile Canyon and into the area from the north on the Skyline Drive.

Trail Information Not many trails here, mostly 4WD tracks and of course some improved roads leading into the area. So it's likely you'll be walking over old 4WD tracks to near the peak you want to climb, then make the final ascent by simply route-finding. Keep in mind it's easy to walk through the forests here, with or without a trail. And the higher you climb, the more open the forest becomes. Timberline here is from about 3250 to 3350 meters. For Musinia, drive up Beaver Creek Road, which in times of storms and wet weather, can be too slick to drive. Higher clearance vehicles can make it to the area of Porcupine Knoll, but cars will have to be parked back down canyon a ways. One can walk cross-country from where the road crosses upper Beaver Ck. and turns west, or continue west and follow the road to the west side of the summit peak. One can also arrive at the peak from the northeast ridge. Regardless of the approach route, the final steep pitch must be climbed from the east side. All other sides of the peak form a cliff.

Best Time and Time Needed All hikes in the area are considered day hikes. These are high mountains, so it's mid-June through October as the hiking season. There's lots of water throughout the area, but beware of the clay soil in the area of Musinia.

Campgrounds: There are several campgrounds around Ferron Reservoir with Twelvemile C.G. nearby and the Pinchot C.G. in Twelvemile Canyon. But one can camp anywhere. There are many campsites along the upper half of Beaver Creek, and with a good water supply.

Maps Utah Travel Council Maps 6 and 2, Southeastern Central Utah and Southwestern Central Utah, Manti-La Sal National Forest, U.S.G.S. maps, Manti (1:100,000), Sterling, Black Mtn., Ferron Reservoir, Mayfield, Woods Lake, Heliotrope Mtn. (1:24,000)

A close-up view of Mollys Nipple of Musinia Peak, from the northeast ridge (50mm lens).

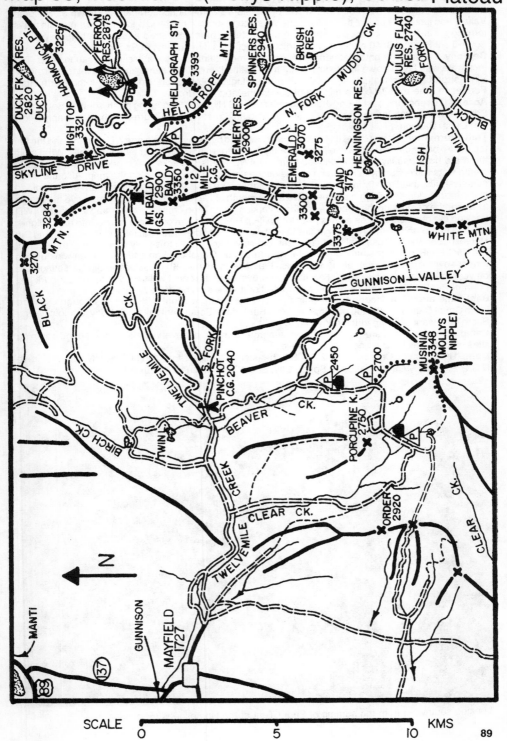

SCALE

0   5   IO   KMS

South Tent Peak, Sevier Plateau

Location In the very heart of Utah, is one of the state's prime agricultural areas known as Sanpete Valley. And just to the east of this valley is the Wasatch Plateau, a high and wild hulk of a mountain mass forming a barrier to storm clouds, thus one of the state's best watershed areas. The highest point is South Tent Peak at 3440 meters. This particular section is directly east of Spring City.

Geology This area is not what geologists call true mountains, but is a massive plateau instead. The rock here was layed down in shallow seas, then uplifted, but at the same time remaining horizontal. Highest parts of the plateau are made up of the Flagstaff Formation. Under that is the North Horn Formation. The rock type is a mixture of sandstone and limestone.

Access To reach the best hiking area one must use US Highway 89 running north-south in Sevier and Sanpete Valleys. At Spring City, drive east on 4th South Street to where it turns south, then simply follow it to Canal Canyon.

Trail Information Beware that this country is considered by many Utahn's as 4WD country, and the flat top nature of the plateau lends itself to that catagory. So there are very few maintained trails. What trails there are have usually been developed from old 4WD roads or tracks which originally were used to create water diversion systems, such as the ditches and one tunnel seen on the map. Also there are hunters' trails, used mostly in September and October. The trails shown on this map are unmaintained and difficult to locate in higher places. Drive to the mouth of Canal Canyon and to just above the bridge to where the cement ditches begin — at the diversion dam. Then cross the creek and locate the 4WD track on the other side. Once on this road follow it up Hell Hole Canyon where it turns into a trail higher up. This trail or one of the branching trails, takes hikers up to some cirque basins known as Little and Big Horseshoes. Again, these trails fade near the top so you may have to simply route-find to the rim top. For Tent Peak, north or south, drive as far as you can up Canal Canyon and park. Then walk up this former sawmill road. Further along don't miss the faintly marked path crossing the Big Horseshoe Ck. on your left. If you can find and follow this overgrown sawmill road it will take you to the car-park just north of Peak 3300. From there you can route-find to the summit of both peaks.

Best Time and Time Needed The hiking season here is from about mid-June on through October. From Canal Canyon to the top of Sanpete, West Sanpete or South Tent will take all day for most hikers. Some may want to camp in the canyon one night.

Campgrounds There are no developed campgrounds here, but everywhere is found good camping sites most of which have good water supplies.

Maps Utah Travel Council Map 2 — Southeastern Central Utah,Manti-La Sal National Forest, U.S.G.S. maps Manti (1:100,000), Spring City, South Tent Mtn. (1:24,000)

Looking southwest from the summit of South Tent at the Horseshoes (50mm lens).

Map 39, South Tent Peak, Sevier Plateau

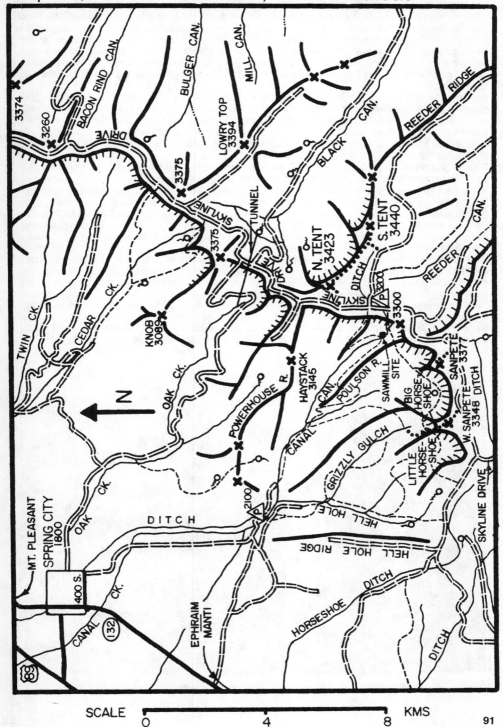

Bald, Reids and Notch Peaks, Uinta Mountains

Location These three peaks, Bald Mountain, 3641 meters; Reids, 3569; and Notch Peak, 3433 meters, are all clustered close together in the extreme west end of the Uinta Mountains, and in the Mirror Lake region. These mountains aren't high, by Uinta Mountain standards, but the access is easy as is the climbing. Thus, it's a good place for the beginning hiker or for those with little time at hand.

Geology The Uintas are an east-west tending range, the only one in the USA to do so. In the Uintas, the oldest rocks are found in the center, while along the outer edges of the range are found younger stata. The older rocks are Precambrian quartzite, while the younger ones are various sedimentary types.

Access Access is easy. Most people approach these peaks from the west and Kamas on State Highway 150. This same road runs north from Mirror Lake to Evanston, Wyoming. Thus you can come in from the north as well. This highway is paved all the way, but is only open from around the 4th of July until the snow flies, usually late October. To climb Bald Mountain and Reids Peak, the best starting point is likely to be from the car-park on Bald Mountain Pass (3255 meters). To get to Notch Peak, or perhaps Mt. Watson, drive to Trial Lake and look for the trailhead.

Trail Information From Bald Mountain Trailhead, there's a trail to the top of Bald Mtn. which makes that hike very easy. Use the same trailhead to get to Reids, but this peak can either be climbed from along the ridge connecting Reids with Bald, or from a second trail leaving Bald Mtn. Trailhead heading in the direction of Dean and Notch Lakes. From this trail and at a convenient location, strike out to the northeast to Reids summit. One could also climb either peak from the car-park at Pass Lake. From the trailhead near the dam on Trial Lake, walk north to Wall Lake, then to the famous notch in Notch Mtn. From the Notch one can easily climb to either peak of Notch Mountain. You can also climb Mt. Watson from the area around Wall Lake.

Best Time and Time Needed Winter snows stay well into summer here, so the climbing season is from about July 4 on, and into September. Early October sometimes brings good weather, but nights are very cold then, and you'll need cold weather type bedding and clothing. Each peak takes about half a day to climb. Bald Mtn. takes only a couple of hours.

Campgrounds The area has many forest service campgrounds, but it's a crowded place, especially on weekends. You could also camp in some less crowded area, and come to this place for day hikes.

Maps Utah Travel Council Map 3--Northeastern Central Utah, Ashley and Wasatch National Forests, U.S.G.S. map Kings Peak (1:100,000), or High Uintas Primitive Area (1:75,000).

From Hayden Peak: Highway 150, Mirror Lake, Bald Mt., Reids Peak (50mm lens).

Map 40, Bald, Reids and Notch Peaks, Uinta Mtns.

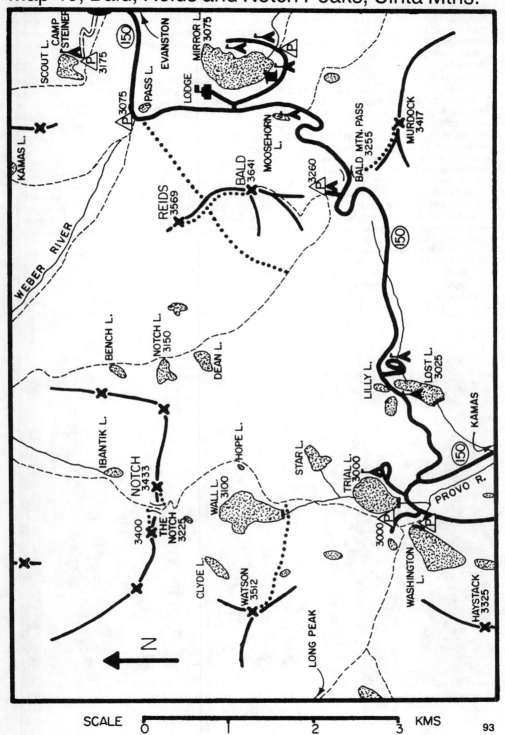

SCALE

0   1   2   3   KMS

93

Agassiz, Hayden, and A-1 Peaks, Uinta Mountains

Location The three peaks discussed here, Mt. Agassiz, 3788 meters; Hayden Peak, 3804; and A-1 Peak, 3773 meters, are all located in the western portion of the Uinta Mountains, just to the east and northeast of Mirror Lake. They lie along one very long ridge, but each is a mountain and a climb in itself.

Geology These peaks are all made up of Precambrian quartzite, with the valleys filled up with Quaternary glacial deposits.

Access These peaks have very easy access. The road to use is Utah State Highway 150, which runs between Kamas, Utah, and Evanston, Wyoming. This road is snow-bound except from about the 4th of July until the first heavy snows of winter arrive, which is usually about late October. This is snowmobile country in winter. There are four trailheads you may use in reaching these peaks. First is at Mirror Lake, which gives access to Agassiz; next is at Hayden Pass, which can be used to reach Mt. Hayden and Kletting Peak; the trailhead which is used to arrive at Hell Hole Lake along Main Fork; and for access to the wilder eastern side, use the trail and trailhead at Christmas Meadows on Stillwater Fork (of the Bear River). This last trailhead is best to use when trying to climb A-1 Peak.

Trail Information If parking at Mirror Lake, take the heavily used trail north, then east and southeast, which eventually runs along the western base of Agassiz. At a convenient spot, leave the trail and climb the western slopes. Agassiz can also be climbed from Jordan L. to the east, or from Ryder L. to the north. There's no trail to Hayden, but you can route-find from the Hayden Pass Trailhead. It can also be climbed from the east and from McPheters or Kermsuh Lakes and Stillwater Fork. This latter route is definitely longer, but it adds wilderness character to the climb. Kletting Peak can be climbed from the same trailheads as when climbing Hayden. The easiest route to A-1 Peak is to park on Stillwater Fork, and use the trail running to Kermsuh L., then route-find north to the summit.

Best Time and Time Needed The very best time is from August 1 to mid-September. July is OK except for wet grounds, some snow early on, and mosquitos. After mid-September, cold sets in, especially at night. Better plan on most of one day for each climb.

Campgrounds Campgrounds and campsites are everywhere, but it's crowded along Highway 150.

Maps Utah Travel Council Map 3--Northeastern Central Utah, Ashley and Wasatch National Forests, U.S.G.S. map Kings Peak (1:100,000), or High Uintas Primitive Area (1:75,000).

A scene viewed by many: Elkhorn Lake, and to the east, Mt. Agassiz (50mm lens).

94

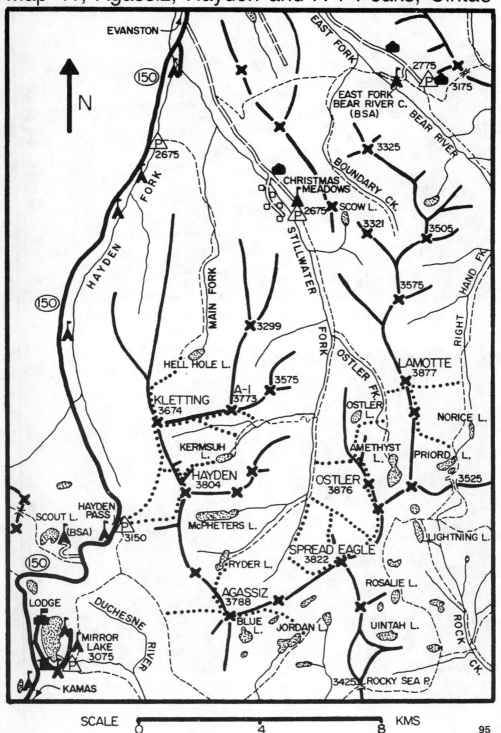

EVANSTON

150

N

EAST FORK

BEAR RIVER

2775
3175

EAST FORK
BEAR RIVER C.
(BSA)

P
2675

HAYDEN FORK

3325

CHRISTMAS
MEADOWS

BOUNDARY CK.

2675

SCOW L.

3321

3505

150

MAIN FORK

STILLWATER

3575

RIGHT HAND FK.

3299

FORK

OSTLER FK.

HELL HOLE L.

3575

LAMOTTE
3877

KLETTING
3674

A-1
3773

OSTLER
L.

NORICE L.

KERMSUH
L.

AMETHYST
L.

PRIORD L.

HAYDEN
3804

OSTLER
3876

3525

HAYDEN
PASS

P
3150

McPHETERS L.

LIGHTNING L.

SCOUT L.
(BSA)

150

RYDER L.

SPREAD EAGLE
3822

LODGE

DUCHESNE RIVER

AGASSIZ
3788

ROSALIE L.

ROCK CK.

BLUE
L.

JORDAN L.

UINTAH L.

MIRROR
LAKE
3075

P

KAMAS

3425 ROCKY SEA P.

SCALE
0   4   8   KMS

95

From the summit of Lamotte Peak, one has a good view of Ostler Peak (28mm lens).

From the summit of Spread Eagle, looking west at northeast face of Mt. Agassiz (50mm lens).

Lamotte Peak. From the trail and pass above Priord Lake (28mm lens).

Base camp in the Left Hand Fork of Bear River. The Cathedral on the right (50mm lens).

Lamotte, Ostler and Spread Eagle Peaks, Uinta Mountains

Location   These three peaks of Lamotte, 3877 meters; Ostler, 3876; and Spread Eagle, at 3822 meters, are all near each other and located on the western end of the Uinta Mountains. The three are not far east of Mirror Lake.

Geology   All of the peaks are composed of Precambrain quartzite and are part of the Uinta Mountain Group, which are about one billion years old. The valley floors are composed of Quaternary glacial deposits.

Access   The one main access road is Utah State Highway 150, which runs between Kamas, Utah, and Evanston, Wyoming. This road is open from around the 4th of July on through about late October. From this good paved road, one must turn east and drive into either the Stillwater Fork and to Christmas Meadows, or to the East Fork of Bear River and the trailhead at the end of that good gravel road.

Trail Information   All these peaks can be approached from Mirror Lake, via the Highline Trail, Rocky Sea Pass and the head of Rock Creek, but the very best approach is via Christmas Meadows on Stillwater Fork. From the trailhead, walk up-canyon on a very good maintained trail into upper Stillwater or into Ostler Fork. From this one trailhead you can climb all three peaks. Spread Eagle can be climbed from its northeast, southwest or north ridge. Ostler can be climbed easiest from Ostler Lake, but also from the ridge separating it from Spread Eagle. One can ascend any one of several routes along the broad western face of Lamotte, or drive to the East Fork of Bear River Trailhead, and use the trail leading to Priord Lake. From this trail, one can use one of several routes on the east face or the south ridge. Another alternative on Lamotte, is to approach it from the north ridge and Boundary Creek. This last route possibility (up Lamotte) means walking a long distance above timberline.

Best Time and Time Needed   The very best time to hike and climb here is in August and early September. July often brings good weather, but meadows are wet and there are mosquitos. After about mid-September, the weather becomes too cold for many, especially at night. Most people can climb all three peaks on a three day week-end.

Campgrounds   There are many campgrounds along Highway 150, but they are always crowded. And there are many campsites along the gravel roads leading to the trailheads, as well as at the trailheads themselves.

Maps   Utah Travel Council Map 3--Northeastern Central Utah, Ashley and Wasatch National Forests, U.S.G.S. map Kings Peak (1:100,000) or High Uintas Primitive Area (1:75,000).

Spread Eagle Peak, as viewed from the slopes of Ostler Peak (50mm lens).

Map 42, Lamotte, Ostler, Spread Eagle, Uintas

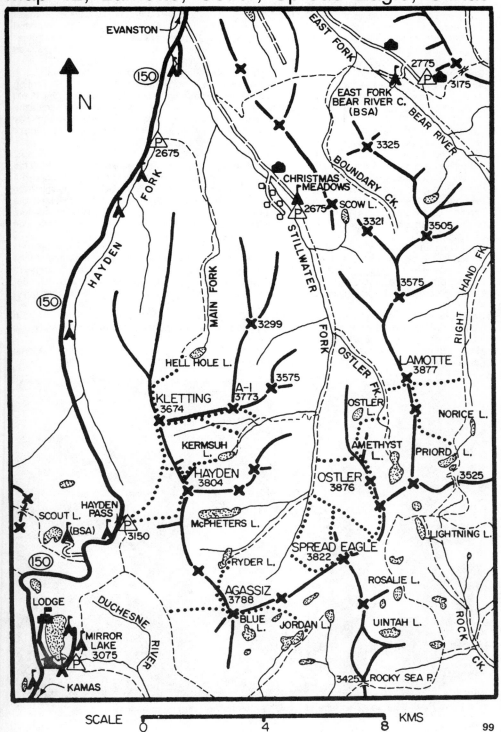

EVANSTON

150

N

EAST FORK

2775

3175

EAST FORK
BEAR RIVER C.
(BSA)

BOUNDARY CK.

BEAR RIVER

3325

P
2675

HAYDEN FORK

150

MAIN FORK

CHRISTMAS MEADOWS

2675 SCOW L.

3321

3505

STILLWATER

3575

RIGHT HAND FK.

3299

HELL HOLE L.

A-I
3773

3575

OSTLER FK.

FORK

LAMOTTE
3877

KLETTING
3674

OSTLER
L.

NORICE L.

KERMSUH
L.

AMETHYST
L.

PRIORD L.

HAYDEN
3804

OSTLER
3876

3525

SCOUT L.
(BSA)

HAYDEN
PASS
P
3150

McPHETERS L.

LIGHTNING L.

150

SPREAD EAGLE
3822

RYDER L.

ROSALIE L.

LODGE

DUCHESNE RIVER

AGASSIZ
3788

BLUE
L.

JORDAN L.

UINTAH L.

ROCK CK.

MIRROR
LAKE
3075

P

KAMAS

3425 ROCKY SEA P.

SCALE

0   4   8   KMS

Cathedral, Beulah and Yard Peaks, Uinta Mountains

Location   The peaks featured here are found in the north and northwest part of the Uinta Mountains, along the East Fork of the Bear River and the West Fork of Blacks Fork River. These peaks are some of the most rugged in the Uintas, and in some cases are definitely not "walk-ups." They are The Cathedral at 3726 meters; Yard Peak, 3873; and Beulah Peak, at 3827 meters. There are also several other rugged summits along the ridge north and south of Beulah, which rise to more than 3800 meters. The scenery around Allsop Lake is second to none.

Geology   The peaks here are composed of Precambrian quartzite of the Uinta Mtn. Group.

Access   Probably the best access trailhead is the one on the East Fork of the Bear River. By parking there, you can walk up into the Left Hand Fork drainage basin and climb all peaks discussed. One could also walk up the Right Hand Fork and down the West Fk. of Blacks Fork and back to one's car via the Bear R.--Smiths Fk. Trail, as did the author on one trip. Reach the East Fk. of Bear River from Highway 150, north of Mirror Lake. About two kms after turning off Highway 150, turn south to reach East Fork, or continue east toward Lyman Lake and the road up West Fk. of Blacks Fk.

Trail Information   All trails shown on the map are well used and well maintained, but one must route-find up to the summits, some of which are not easy. Beulah's easiest route seems to be from the west and the Left Hand Fork. The Cathedral can best be climbed from either the north or south ridge, but face routes are also possible. Yard peak is easily climbed from the south ridge, but also possible from the north and the cirque basin. The peaks between Beulah and Peak 3825 west of Dead Horse Lake can best be ascended from Allsop L. Climb carefully here as much of the rock is loose and brecciated, and can be dangerous. The northeast face of Yard and the east face of Beulah are for more experienced climbers.

Best Time and Time Needed   August and early September is the ideal time to climb. July weather is usually fine, but early July means wet campsites and snow and mosquitos, and late September means cold temps, especially at night. Once you're in the upper basins, strong climbers can climb a couple of peaks a day in some cases, and it's only about half a day from the trailhead on East Fork to the upper basins. Strong climbers can climb all of the peaks featured here in about three, maybe four days, round-trip.

Campgrounds   One can camp at the trailheads, or at many sites along the road leading to the trailheads. The road to East Fork Trailhead is very good, but the road up the West Fork of Blacks Fork is much rougher, thus the East Fork of Bear River is recommended.

Maps   Utah Travel Council Map 3—Northeastern Central Utah, Wasatch and Ashley National Forests, U.S.G.S. map Kings Peak (1:100,000) or High Uintas Primitive Area (1:75,000).

Red Knob Peak left, and east face of Beulah in the background (50mm lens).

Map 43, Cathedral, Beulah, Yard Peaks, Uintas

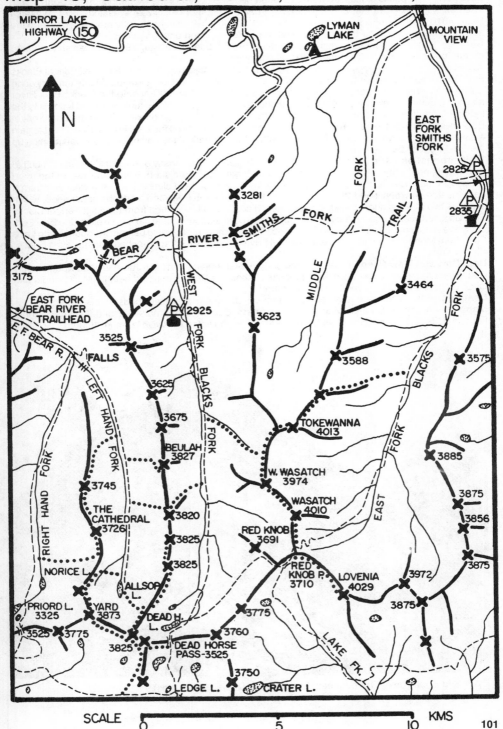

MIRROR LAKE HIGHWAY 150

LYMAN LAKE

MOUNTAIN VIEW

EAST FORK SMITHS FORK

N

2825 P

2835 P

3281

BEAR

RIVER

SMITHS

FORK

WEST

FORK

MIDDLE

FORK

TRAIL

3464

3175

EAST FORK BEAR RIVER TRAILHEAD

E.F. BEAR R.

FALLS

P 2925

3525

3623

3588

BLACKS

FORK

3575

LEFT HAND FORK

3625

3675

BEULAH 3827

TOKEWANNA 4013

EAST FORK

BLACKS FORK

3885

3745

W. WASATCH 3974

3875

3856

RIGHT HAND FORK

THE CATHEDRAL 3726

3820

WASATCH 4010

RED KNOB 3691

3875

NORICE L.

3825

3825

ALLSOP L.

RED KNOB P. 3710

LOVENIA 4029

3972

3875

PRIORD L. 3325

YARD 3873

DEAD H. L.

3775

3525 3775

3825

DEAD HORSE PASS-3525

3760

LAKE FK.

3875

3750

LEDGE L.

CRATER L.

SCALE

0   5   10   KMS

101

Tokewanna, Wasatch and Lovenia Peaks, Uinta Mountains

Location   The peaks discussed here are found near the center of the range, but on the north slope. The peaks are Tokewanna, at 4013 meters; a peak the author calls West Wasatch, 3974; Wasatch Peak, 4010; and the most southerly of the four, Mt. Lovenia, which rises to 4029 meters. They form the second loftiest part of the High Uintas, and are all found along one long ridge.

Geology   These summits are made up mostly of Precambrian quartzite, plus some red shales found on the top of Red Knob Pass and Peak, all belonging to the Uinta Mtn. Group.

Access   Possibly the single best access route is via the rather rough road up the West Fork of Blacks Fork. With your map, either a Utah state highway or the Utah Travel Council Map 3, locate the very good gravel road which runs from Utah State Highway 150 north of Mirror Lake, to the Blacks Fork River south of Mountain View, Wyoming. From a point just west of Lyman Lake, turn south and follow it to the trailhead. Another alternative would be to park at the end of the good gravel road on the East Fork of Bear River, then use the Bear River—Smiths Fork Trail, or the trail up the East Fork of Bear River to gain access. Another good alternative for people with a car is to park at the end of the good road running up the East Fork of Blacks Fork.

Trail Information   The trail up the West Fork of Blacks Fork is mostly good, but it's a little difficult to follow at its northern end , though it's impossible to get lost. There's a trail on both sides of the river, which you may have to ford on occasion. Tokewanna can be best climbed from the west and from a pass located between it and West Wasatch, or from Red Knob Pass and along the south ridge, which includes two of the highest peaks in the Uintas. It could also be climbed from the East Fork of Blacks Fork via a northeast ridge. Mt. Lovenia's summit can be scaled with equal ease from either the East Fork or the West Fork of Blacks Fork, and Red Knob Pass. A longer route would be from the south along Lake Fork, from Moon Lake. The high peaks east of Lovenia can best be approached from the East Fork of Blacks Fork.

Best Time and Time Needed   August and early September are ideal, but July has good weather. July also brings mosquitos, wet trails and campsites. After mid-September cold sets in. Most people can climb all peaks here in three to four days round-trip.

Campgrounds   There are hundreds of campsites along the approach roads in this area.

Maps   Utah Travel Council Map 3—Northeastern Central Utah, Wasatch and Ashley National Forests, U.S.G.S. map Kings Peak (1:100,000), or High Uintas Primitive Area (1:75,000).

From Red Knob Pass. The northeast face of Mt. Lovenia (50mm lens).

Map 44, Tokewanna, Wasatch, Lovenia, Uintas

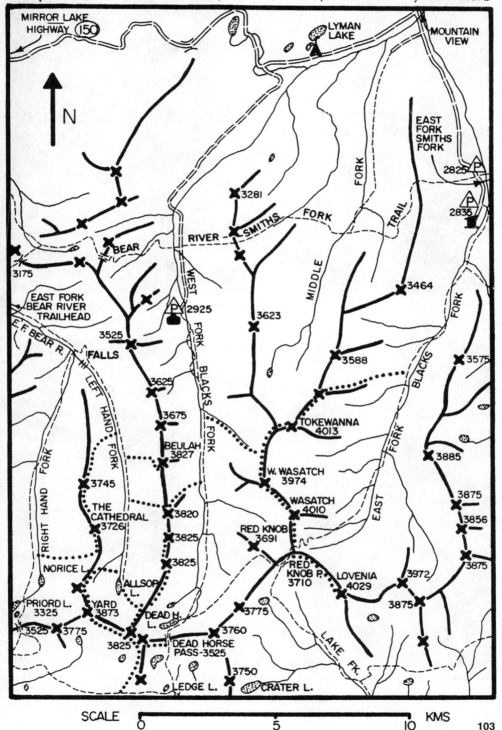

MIRROR LAKE HIGHWAY 150

LYMAN LAKE

MOUNTAIN VIEW

EAST FORK SMITHS FORK

2825

2835

3281

SMITHS FORK

RIVER

MIDDLE FORK

TRAIL

3464

3623

3588

3575

BLACKS FORK

BEAR

EAST FORK BEAR RIVER TRAILHEAD

E. F. BEAR R.

3175

WEST FORK

P 2925

3525

FALLS

3625

LEFT HAND FORK

BLACKS FORK

3675

TOKEWANNA 4013

BEULAH 3827

3885

W. WASATCH 3974

3875

3856

3745

THE CATHEDRAL 3726

3820

WASATCH 4010

RIGHT HAND FORK

RED KNOB 3691

EAST FORK

3825

3875

NORICE L.

3825

RED KNOB P. 3710

LOVENIA 4029

3972

ALLSOP L.

PRIORD L. 3325

YARD 3873

DEAD H. L.

3775

3875

3525

3775

3825

DEAD HORSE PASS-3525

3760

LAKE FK.

3750

LEDGE L.

CRATER L.

SCALE   0   5   10   KMS

Yard Peak viewed from the ridge running east (north face is to the right) (50mm lens).

From top of Beulah: Yard Peak, left; The Cathedral, center; North Cathedral, right (28mm lens).

Looking north from the top of Wasatch, at the south face of Tokewanna (28mm lens).

From the summit of Explorer: Cleveland at left, and Squaw in center (28mm lens).

105

Explorer, Squaw and Cleveland Peaks, Uinta Mountains

Location   Located in the very heart of the Uintas is a cluster of three high peaks sandwiched between the upper Rock Creek and Lake Fork Creek drainages. They are on a north-south ridge, just south of the main east-west summit ridge crossing the Uinta Mountains. They are Explorer Peak, 3873 meters; Squaw Peak, 3918; and Cleveland Peak at 3836 meters.

Geology   As with all or most of the Uinta Mtn. high summits, these peaks are made of the Precambrian quartzite rocks of the Uinta Mtn. Group. In the Uintas, the oldest rocks are found in the center of the range, while the younger rocks are found around the perimeter.

Access   The shortest route to these three summits is via Moon Lake, which is due north of Mountain Home. From this small community, just follow the signs north. Another way in from the south is via Rock Creek and the Upper Stillwater Campground and Trailhead. Get there from Mountain Home as well, but head off in a northwesterly direction. From the north are two routes: one is up the East Fork of Blacks Fork and the other up the West Fork. These northern routes are longer. Both maps and roads will change upon completion of the Upper Stillwater Reservoir on Rock Creek.

Trail Information   From Moon Lake, take the trail heading up Lake Fork, then further along, walk up Ottoson Creek to the pass southeast of Cleveland. All three summits can be climbed via this route. From Upper Stillwater, take the trail north and into either Squaw or Fall Ck. Basins, and from either place climb to the east. If using the West Fork of Blacks Fork, you'll have to cross Dead Horse Pass enroute, but there's no difficulty. If using the East Fork of Blacks Fork, you'll have to cross Red Knob Pass. Here again there are no problems along the trails, but the distance from the north is longer. The northern routes however, give one the chance to climb other even higher peaks along the way.

Best Time and Time Needed   The ideal time to hike here is in August and early September. July is fine except for wet campsites, some snow in places, and mosquitos. Take repellent at that time. After mid-September, very cold nights can arrive, but some years have fine weather into October. Plan one full day to reach the peaks, then strong hikers can climb all three in one day. And one day back out.

Campgrounds   There are campgrounds or campsites at each trailhead or along the way to the trailheads.

Maps   Utah Travel Council Map 3—Northeastern Central Utah, Wasatch and Ashley National Forests, U.S.G.S. map Kings Peak (1:100,000), or High Uintas Primitive Area (1:75,000).

The west face of Explorer Peak as seen from Ledge Lake (50mm lens).

Map 45, Explorer, Squaw and Cleveland, Uintas

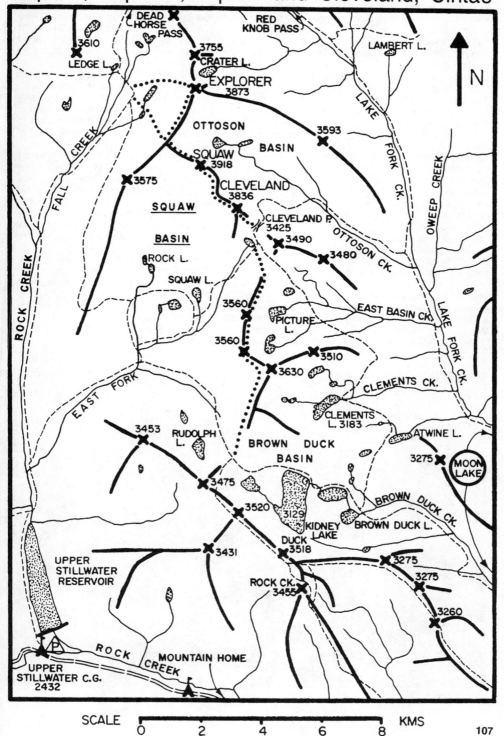

DEAD HORSE PASS

RED KNOB PASS

LAMBERT L.

3610

LEDGE L.

3755
CRATER L.

EXPLORER 3873

3593

OTTOSON BASIN

LAKE FORK CK.

OWEEP CREEK

SQUAW 3918

CREEK

3575

CLEVELAND 3836

SQUAW

BASIN

Cleveland P. 3425

3490

OTTOSON CK.

FALL

ROCK L.

3480

SQUAW L.

3560

PICTURE L.

EAST BASIN CK.

LAKE FORK CK.

ROCK CREEK

3560

3510

3630

CLEMENTS CK.

EAST FORK

3453

RUDOLPH L.

BROWN DUCK BASIN

CLEMENTS L. 3183

ATWINE L.

3275

MOON LAKE

3475

3520

3129

KIDNEY LAKE

BROWN DUCK CK.

BROWN DUCK L.

UPPER STILLWATER RESERVOIR

3431

DUCK 3518

3275

3275

ROCK CK. 3455

3260

UPPER STILLWATER C.G. 2432

ROCK

MOUNTAIN HOME

CREEK

N

SCALE 0 2 4 6 8 KMS

Squaw, Wilson, Red Castle, Powell Peaks, Uinta Mountains

Location   In the middle of the Uintas, and along the east-west summit ridge and watershed divide, lie four of the higher summits in the range. They are Squaw Peak at 3959 meters; Wilson Peak, 3979; Red Castle Peak, 3909; and Mount Powell at 4011 meters. These peaks are fairly typical of many other dome-shaped mountains in the Uintas, except for the north face of Red Castle. This one is very rugged and is perhaps the most fotogenic peak in the range, at least when viewed from the north or from Red Castle Lake.

Geology   Most of the rock here is the Precambrian quartzite. The name Red Castle comes from red rock making up most of this peak. It too is a crystaline rock originating from sandstone and shales.

Access   One can arrive at these peaks from several directions, including Yellowstone Creek and Lake Fork on the south, but the two main options are the East Fork of Blacks Fork and its Little East Fork, and the East Fork of Smiths Fork. Head due south out of Mountian View, Wyoming, and follow the signs to either the East Fork of Blacks Fork or Bridger Lake and China Meadows. Roads are good to each of these trailheads.

Trail Information   The trail which is both shorter and has the best views is the one coming in from East Fork of Blacks Fork. First begin on the Bear R.—Smiths Fork Trail, and head for Bald Mtn. From this trail and from around Bald Mtn. one has some fine views of Red Castle. This is a high altitude trail and very scenic. The other route begins at China Meadows and follows the East Fork of Smiths Fork. You'll likely see moose along this route. Still another possible access route is via the Little East Fork, and the trail over Squaw Pass. This gives one the chance to climb these summits from the south faces, which are easier. Follow the route symbols, as indicated. Mt. Powell can also be ascended from Henrys Fork Basin and Lake Blanchard. All these summits are easy to climb, except for some north faces, and the northern ramparts of Red Castle.

Best Time and Time Needed   August and early September are the best times to climb, but July has good weather. July also has mosquitos and sometimes wet campsites. After late September expect cold temps, especially at night. Early October often has fine weather, and can be fine for the prepared hiker. Most people can climb all peaks here in about four days, round-trip.

Campgrounds   There's a campground at China Meadows, but lots of quieter campsites on the access road. There are also good campsites at the trailheads on the East Fork of Blacks Fork.

Maps   Utah Travel Council Map 3—Northeastern Central Utah, Wasatch and Ashley National Forests, U.S.G.S. map Kings Peak (1:100,000), or High Uintas Primitive Area (1:75,000).

From Mt. Powell, one sees the north face of Red Castle Peak (50mm lens).

Map 46, Squaw, Wilson, R. Castle, Powell, Uintas

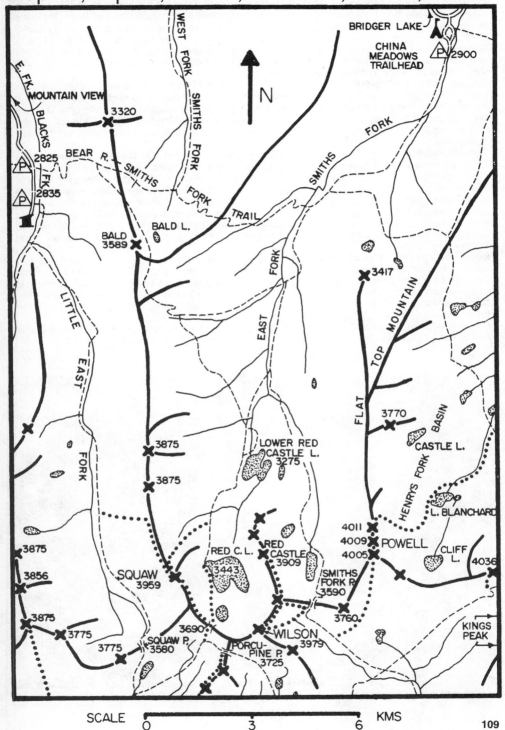

SCALE

0   3   6   KMS

Mt. Emmons and Emmons—Kings Peak Ridge, Uinta Mountains

Location The main peak featured here is Utah's third highest summit, Mt. Emmons, at 4097 meters. Also included are the other very high summits running northwest of Emmons to Kings Peak. There are five peaks on this ridge between Kings and Emmons, all but one are over 4000 meters. This is the roof of Utah. All are located in the heart of the range, due north of Mountain Home and Altamont, Utah.

Geology The heart of the Uintas, and including all higher peaks, is made up of Precambrian quartzite of the Uinta Mountain Group or Formation. These are folded and uplifted mountains, and it is the only major mountain range in America to run east-west.

Access With your Travel Council Map 3, locate Duchesne. Then drive due north out of the center of town to Mountain Home. From there again continue due north towards Moon Lake, but turn east at the turnoff and continue towards the Yellowstone Power Plant and finally to the campground where Swift Ck. enters Yellowstone Creek. One can also get there by driving north out of Altamont, or west from the mouth of the Uinta R. Canyon. All the higher roads near the mountain are gravel, but regularly maintained.

Trail Information One can approach Mt. Emmons from the Uinta River Trail and the Chain Lakes Basin, but by heading up Swift Creek you can have a chance to climb a number of other high summits, including the highest in the state, Kings Peak. Cross Swift Ck. and follow the signs up the Swift Ck. Trail into the Timothy Lakes Basin. This trail is well used and sign posted. From one of many locations in the upper basin, route-find up the slopes to the northeast or east to the summit of Emmons. Once on the ridge, walking is relatively easy. From Emmons, you can walk along this very high ridge all the way to Kings Peak. The author has done it several times, including a winter trip. A nice long hike would be to first climb Emmons via Swift Ck., then walk the ridge to Kings, and return via the good trail along Yellowstone Creek.

Best Time and Time Needed August and early September is the best time. July has good weather, but also wet campsites and mosquitos. Later in the season it's getting cold. Strong hikers could climb Emmons from Swift Creek in one long day, but for most it's a two day hike round-trip. To do the circle route suggested: Swift Creek, Emmons, Kings, then return via Yellowstone, is a long three-day hike.

Campgrounds Swift Creek Campground at the trailhead, or many campsites enroute to the trailhead.

Maps Utah Travel Council Map 3—Northeastern Central Utah, Ashley and Wasatch National Forests, U.S.G.S. map Kings Peak (1:100,000), or High Uintas Primitive Area (1:75,000).

Looking northeast across upper Swift Creek drainage at Mt. Emmons (50mm lens).

Map 47, Emmons, Emmons-Kings Pk. Ridge, Uintas

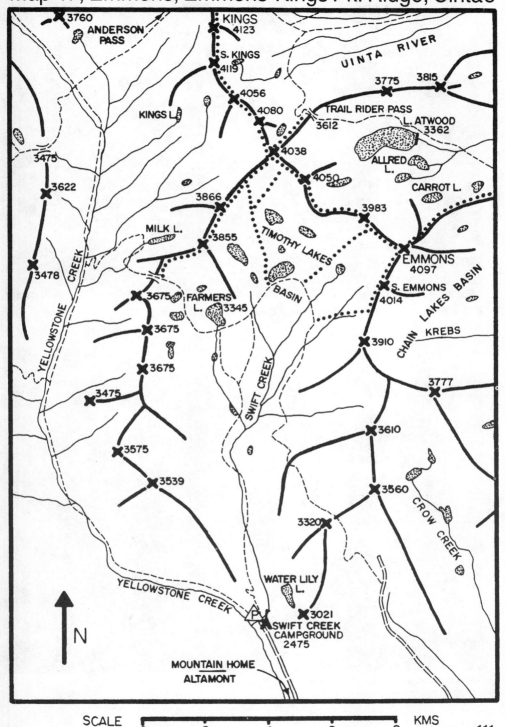

3760
ANDERSON PASS

KINGS 4123

S. KINGS 4119

4056

4080

KINGS L.

3475

3622

3478

YELLOWSTONE CREEK

3866

MILK L.

3855

3675 FARMERS L. 3345

3675

3675

3475

3575

3539

UINTA RIVER

3775   3815

TRAIL RIDER PASS
3612

L. ATWOOD 3362

4038

ALLRED L.

4050

CARROT L.

TIMOTHY LAKES

3983

EMMONS 4097

BASIN

S. EMMONS 4014

CHAIN LAKES BASIN

KREBS

3910

3777

SWIFT CREEK

3610

3560

3320

CROW CREEK

WATER LILY L.

P
3021
SWIFT CREEK CAMPGROUND 2475

YELLOWSTONE CREEK

N

MOUNTAIN HOME
ALTAMONT

SCALE   0   2   4   6   8   KMS

111

Wilson Peak, as seen from the top of Red Castle Peak (28mm lens).

The west face of Red Castle Peak and Red Castle Lake (50mm lens).

This is a winter scene showing north face of Henry's Fork Peak and Henry's Fork Basin (50mm lens).

A sheep camp at Mt. Leidy, near the trailhead above Hacking Lake (50mm lens).

Henrys Fork, Gilbert, and Kings Peak, Uinta Mountains

Location The peaks featured here include the highest in the state of Utah, but the normal access route is from Wyoming. They lie due south of Mountain View, Wyoming, and all are situated in the heart of the range. The highest is Kings Peak, 4123 meters; Gilbert, 4097, Henrys Fork Peak (author's name) at 4036 meters; and mentioned on another map, Mt. Powell at 4011 meters. The peaks to the south of Kings Peak are also very high.(Gilbert is half a meter higher than Emmons, but both are listed as 4097 meters.)

Geology All the higher peaks are made of the Uinta Mountain Group of rocks, which is almost all Precambrian quartzite. Around the perimeter of the range are younger sedimentary rocks.

Access Kings Peak can be approached from the southern slopes, from either Yellowstone or Swift Creeks, or the Uinta River, but these are longer routes. If you want to climb more than one peak, then the route from Mountain View, Wyoming and the Henrys Fork Campground is the best way. Simply follow the signs south out of Mountain View (the route to China Meadows is also from the north). The roads to each trailhead are good and maintained.

Trail Information If coming in on the Uinta R. route, follow trail signs to Lake Atwood, thence to Trail Rider Pass and on to Anderson Pass. If coming in from Yellowstone Ck., head in the direction of Anderson Pass. From the north, head into Henrys Fork Basin, which is a favorite among fishermen, and from there either take the trail over Gunsight Pass to Kings or Henrys Fk. Peaks, or route-find to Gilbert or Powell, or any of the other high summits in the area. All peaks and routes are easy, except for some of the north face routes on Henrys Fork Peak. Gilbert can be climbed from the north or south ridge, or the west face. Kings can be climbed from the north or south ridge, or from the east face. Henrys Fork Pk. can best be ascended from the south face, but its north face is perhaps the best challenge in the Uintas. Climb Mt. Powell from the north ridge or south face. The trail from China Meadows is another possible route to Henrys Fork Basin.

Best Time and Time Needed As in all areas of the Uintas, the months of August and early September are the ideal times to visit this region. July usually has good weather, but campsites are often still wet from winter snows, and there are plenty of mosquitos. Later in the season, say from mid-September, it's often too cold, but sometimes good weather can be had up until mid-October. A strong hiker can climb all four peaks in three or four days, round-trip.

Campgrounds There's a campground at each trailhead, and many campsites on the way in.

Maps Utah Travel Council Map 3—Northeastern Central Utah, Wasatch and Ashley National Forests, U.S.G.S. map Kings Peak (1:100,000), or High Uintas Primitive Area (1:75,000).

From the upper Yellowstone River. The west face of Kings Peak (50mm lens).

Map 48, Henrys Fk., Gilbert, Kings Peak, Uintas

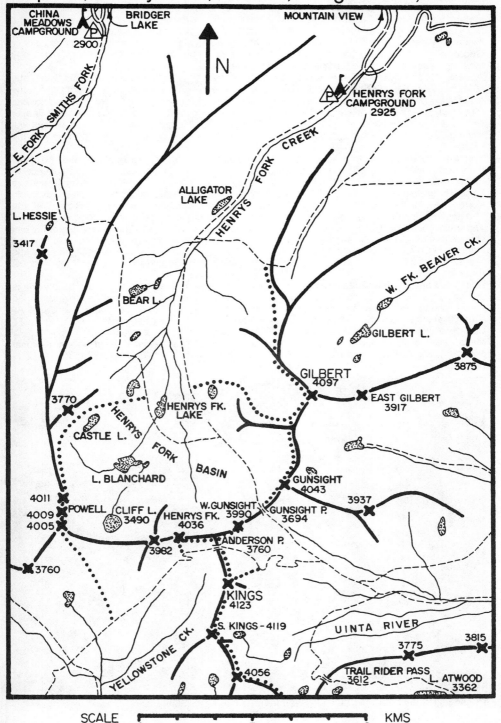

CHINA MEADOWS CAMPGROUND 2900

BRIDGER LAKE

MOUNTAIN VIEW

N

E FORK SMITHS FORK

HENRYS FORK CAMPGROUND 2925

HENRYS FORK CREEK

ALLIGATOR LAKE

L. HESSIE 3417

W. FK. BEAVER CK.

BEAR L.

GILBERT L.

GILBERT 4097

3875

3770

HENRYS FK. LAKE

EAST GILBERT 3917

CASTLE L.

HENRYS FORK BASIN

L. BLANCHARD

GUNSIGHT 4043

3937

4011
4009
4005

POWELL

CLIFF L. 3490

W. GUNSIGHT

HENRYS FK. 4036

3990

GUNSIGHT P. 3694

3982

ANDERSON P. 3760

3760

KINGS 4123

S. KINGS - 4119

YELLOWSTONE CK.

UINTA RIVER

3775

3815

4056

TRAIL RIDER PASS 3612

L. ATWOOD 3362

SCALE   0   3   6   KMS

Anne, Coffin, and the Burros, Uinta Mountains

Location The higher peaks or summits featured on this map include: North Burro, rising to 3867 meters; South Burro, 3876; Coffin Peak or Mountain, 3863; and the bench mark known as Anne, about 3875 meters. All these mountains are due south of Lonetree, Wyoming, and east of Gibert Peak, the second highest summit in Utah. They are also south and east of the popular fishery, Hoop Lake.

Geology These summits are all Precambrian quartzite, but the lower summits to the north (listed at 3095 and 2991 meters) are the overlying sedimentary rocks.

Access For all these peaks, first drive to Lonetree, Wyoming, located between Manila, Utah, and Mountain View, Wyoming. Just east of Lonetree and between mile posts 123 and 124, turn south at the sign stating Hoop Lake and the Beaver Creeks. Follow the signs to Hoop L., on a well-maintained road (but which is too slick in wet weather) to the lake. Or you can follow the signs to Middle Fork of Beaver Creek, and use the trail running to Beaver L. This latter road is good, but can also be slick in wet weather. The last 300 meters is steep and rocky, but all vehicles should be able to make it to the trailhead.

Trail Information From Hoop Lake campground, walk or drive across the dam, and take one of two trails—one running to Kabell and Island Lake, the other going up Burnt Ridge and towards Beaver Lake. These trails are well sign-posted and well used. To reach the summit of North Burro, one could walk up Kabell Ridge, or continue on past Island Lake to the pass of 3440 meters, and climb west towards South Burro. The ridge between the two is flat. The Burros can also be scaled from the Burnt Ridge Trail and Thompson Summit. The trailhead on Middle Fork of Beaver Ck. is on the edge of a logged-over area. This trail is good, and it runs 11 kms to Beaver Lake, again well sign-posted. From Beaver Lake, you can choose one of several routes to the high ridge to the south, then make your way to the west and the summits of Coffin or Anne, or to the east and to the Burros. One could also stay on the North Highline Trail as it runs west of Middle Fork, and from the first ridge top, walk south to the top of Coffin, thence, Anne.

Best Time and Time Needed August and early September are the best times to climb. July brings good weather, but also mosquitos and wet campsites. Strong hikers can climb both Burros from Hoop Lake in a long day, as well as Coffin and Anne in one long day from Middle Fork of Beaver Creek. All summits could be climbed in three or four days, round-trip, while camping at Beaver L.

Campgrounds Hoop Lake has a campground but campsites are everywhere.

Maps Utah Travel Council Map 3—Northeastern Central Utah, Wasatch and Ashley National Forests, U.S.G.S. map Kings Peak (1:100,000), or High Uintas Primitive Area (1:75,000).

The ridge just east of Coffin Summit. Seen from Beaver Lake (50mm lens).

Map 49, Anne, Coffin, the Burros, Uinta Mtns.

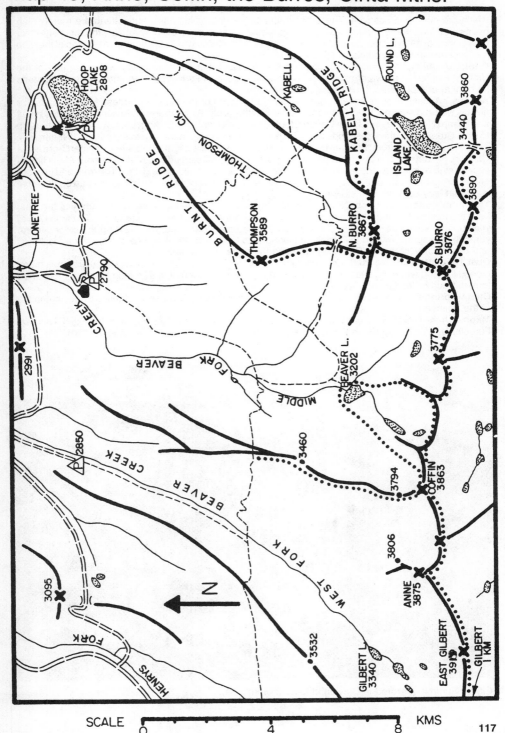

HOOP LAKE 2808

KABELL L.

ROUND L.

3860

3440

KABELL RIDGE

ISLAND LAKE

THOMPSON CK.

3890

BURNT RIDGE

THOMPSON 3589

N. BURRO 3867

S. BURRO 3876

LONETREE

2790

3775

BEAVER L. 3202

MIDDLE FORK BEAVER

CREEK

2991

3460

2850

BEAVER CREEK

3794

COFFIN 3863

3095

N

3806

WEST FORK

ANNE 3875

3532

GILBERT L. 3340

EAST GILBERT 391

GILBERT 1 KM

HENRYS FORK

Cleve and Clover Summits, Uinta Mountains

Location   These mountains are located due north of the Ute town of Whiterocks, and Neola, both of which are north of Roosevelt. These two summits are not really peaks, but instead are merely high points on a long and extended ridge. The two main high points are Cleve (probably meant to stand for Cleveland), at 3814 meters, and to the south Clover Summit rising to 3760 meters. (At the top of the map are several other high points which are south of Hoop Lake.)

Geology   All higher summits are composed of Precambrian quartzite rocks, which are part of the Uinta Mountain Group or Formation. Quartzite is sandstone which has been compressed or put under a lot of heat and pressure, thus changed to quartzite.

Access   Access is on relatively good roads, but because of the higher altitudes of these roads, it's always well into summer before anyone makes it to this area. To get there, drive north out of Roosevelt and toward Neola. Well into Uinta Canyon, look for and drive onto the Elkhorn Loop Road, which runs up to Pole Creek Lake, then descends to the Elkhorn Guard Station, thence on to the south to Whiterocks. That part of the road from the guard station to Pole Creek Lake is slightly better than the part from Uinta Canyon, but any car can be driven on either. From near the lake, head due north for about 7 kms till you see the sign pointing out the trailhead along the West Fork (of Whiterocks River). The trailhead is about one km from the main road. This last section of road is rough and rocky, but most cars can be driven at least part way up, if you go slow and easy.

Trail Information   To climb Clover Summit, it is probably best to just walk cross-country to the west from the trailhead, rather than along the trail. Just pick the easiest route up the face. To climb Cleve, walk up the well-used trail 9 or 10 kms to Cleveland Lake, then route-find west up the slopes to the summit. The author walked to Cleveland Lake and to the top of Cleve, then along the ridge to Clover, and back to the trailhead. This last part along the ridge is easy walking.

Best Time and Time Needed   You can get into this region only after about July 1, but July has many mosquitos and wet campsites. August and early September are better. The loop hike just mentioned took the author less than 7 hours, round-trip.

Campgrounds   There's a forest service campground at Pole Creek Lake, but there's a good campsite at the trailhead.

Maps   Utah Travel Council Map 3—Northeastern Central Utah, Ashley and Wasatch National Forests, U.S.G.S. map Kings Peak (1:100,000), or High Uintas Primitive Area (1:75,000).

Clover Summit, mirrored in Cleveland Lake (50mm lens).

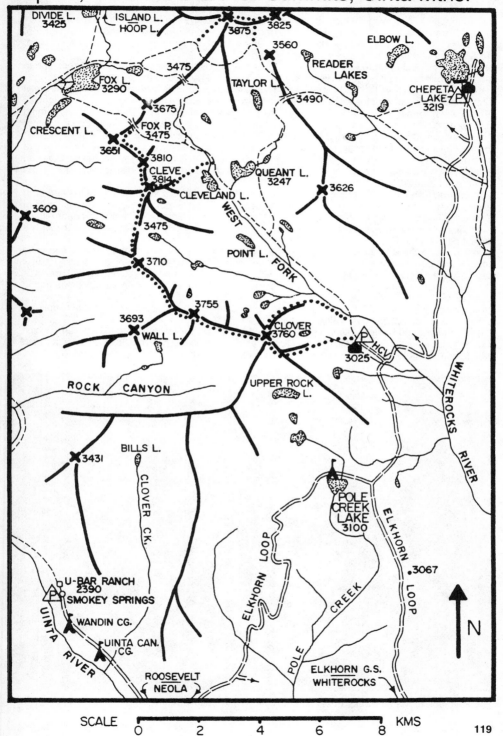

DIVIDE L.
3425

ISLAND L.
HOOP L.

3875

3825

ELBOW L.

3560

READER
LAKES

3475

TAYLOR L.

CHEPETA
LAKE P
3219

FOX L.
3290

3675

3490

CRESCENT L.

FOX P.
3475

3651

3810

CLEVE
3814

CLEVELAND L.

QUEANT L.
3247

3626

3609

3475

WEST

POINT L. FORK

3710

3755

CLOVER
3760

P
HCV

3693

WALL L.

3025

ROCK   CANYON

UPPER ROCK
L.

3431

BILLS L.

CLOVER CK.

WHITEROCKS RIVER

POLE
CREEK
LAKE
3100

.3067

ELKHORN LOOP

U-BAR RANCH
2390
P
SMOKEY SPRINGS

WANDIN CG.

UINTA CAN.
CG.

UINTA RIVER

ROOSEVELT
NEOLA

POLE   CREEK

ELKHORN LOOP

ELKHORN G.S.
WHITEROCKS

N

SCALE   0   2   4   6   8   KMS

119

Leidy and Marsh Peaks, Uinta Mountains

Location   These two peaks are the most easterly of all the peaks in the Uinta Mountains which rise above timberline. They are Mt. Leidy, at 3666 meters, and just to the south, Marsh Peak, reaching 3731 meters. Marsh Peak has a Diesel-powered radio facility at the summit, but no road and no trail to the top; it is serviced by helicopter. Both peaks are just to the west of the upper part of the Red Cloud Loop, which begins and ends in Maeser, just west of Vernal.

Geology   The geology here is the same as for the rest of the Uintas, the peaks consist of Precambrian quartzite. Younger sedimentary rocks lie at lower elevations and around the perimeter of the range.

Access   Access is from the Red Cloud Loop. This road can be found just west of Vernal, in the small suburb of Maeser. Look for the signs pointing out the loop road running north. If you're driving Highway 191, between Vernal and Flaming Gorge Reservoir, then you can reach the Red Cloud L. by turning west from the highway and onto the paved road running to East Park Reservoir. Further on is another road connecting this one with the upper part of the Red Cloud Loop. Once on the loop, look for the sign pointing out the way to Hacking Lake, which is near the trail leading to Leidy Peak. When you're immediately east of Marsh, look for the good road running northwest from a long straightaway. Cars can go about 3 kms, then must stop; for the way beyond and through an old logging area is very rocky and rough, even for 4WD's.

Trail Information   From near Hacking Lake, use a good trail running southwest past the corner of Leidy, which will be just in front of you at the car-park. The beginning of the trail which runs south of Marsh, is difficult to locate in an area of many old logging roads. Perhaps it's best to get near Ashley Twin Lakes, then simply walk west cross-country to the peak. Both peaks are easy climbs, with hardly a difficult pitch on them.

Best Time and Time Needed   August and early September are the best times, but July has good weather,and also mosquitos. Leidy is only 2–3 hours round-trip from that car-park, and Marsh Peak is about a long half day, round-trip, if you park at 3025 meters—a bit shorter if you have a HCV or 4WD. This author climbed both peaks the same day in about 5½ hours total walk time (walk times added together).

Campgrounds   This is a high and wild area, with abundant locations to camp. Hacking Lake makes a fine spot, as does Ashley Twin Lakes, if you can drive to it.

Maps   Be sure and have the Utah Travel Council Map 3—Northeastern Central Utah along, which shows the full length of the Red Cloud Loop. Also Wasatch and Ashley National Forests, U.S.G.S. map Dutch John (1:100,000), or High Uintas Primitive Area (1:75,000).

The east face of Marsh Peak, as seen from Ashley Twin Lakes (50mm lens).

Map 51, Leidy and Marsh Peaks, Uinta Mtns.

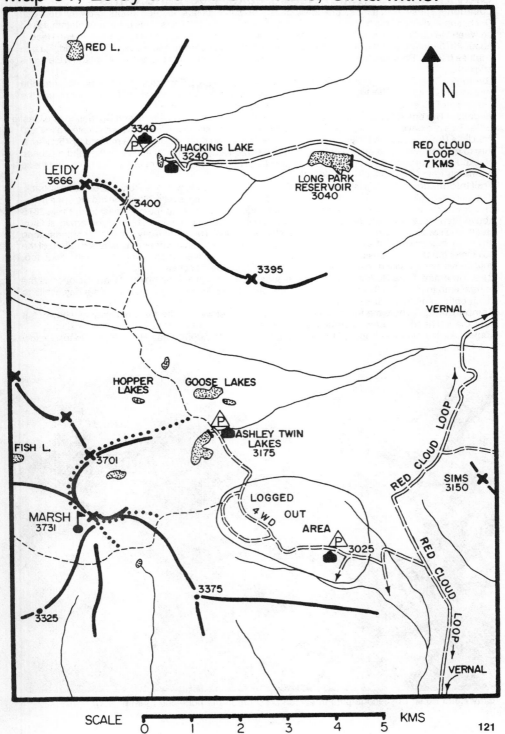

RED L.

3340

P

HACKING LAKE
3240

RED CLOUD
LOOP
7 KMS

LEIDY
3666

3400

LONG PARK
RESERVOIR
3040

N

3395

VERNAL

HOPPER
LAKES

GOOSE LAKES

P

ASHLEY TWIN
LAKES
3175

FISH L.

3701

RED CLOUD LOOP

SIMS
3150

LOGGED

4 WD

OUT

AREA

MARSH
3731

P

3025

RED CLOUD LOOP

3375

3325

VERNAL

Gray Head and Indian Head Peaks, Bad Land Cliffs

Location   These two almost unknown peaks or summits are located about halfway between Duchesne and Price, in a highland region known as the Bad Land Cliffs. This is the mountainous area between the Uinta Basin and the Castle Valley. Gray Head is 2894 meters altitude, while Indian Head is about 2910 meters (On the Ashley National Forest map this peak is also called "Grey Head," just to confuse things). Both summits lie in the area where the headwaters of Indian and Avintaquin Canyons originate.

Geology   The formations exposed here are the Green River Formation (on the peaks) and the Wasatch Formation (in the lower valleys). The color of the rock is gray, indicating both limestone and the presence of oil shale (Parachute Creek Member of the Green River F.).

Access   The one access road is Utah State Highway 191, which runs between Duchesne and Castle Gate. This is a paved highway, open year-round, and is the only paved link between Castle Valley and the Uinta Basin. About half a km north of the highest point on the road, the pass marked 2775 meters, turn to the northwest and drive along a dirt road between 2 and 3 kms. At that point the road has been blocked off. There are also roads up Avintaquin, Lake and the Right Fork of Indian Canyons, but these are rough roads and suitable only for 4WD's.

Trail Information   There's a trail heading north from the car-park, which is likely a deer hunters' track. It heads down into Sterling Hollow. Even without this trail the going is easy along the mostly open ridge. This trail runs to the top of Gray Head. To reach Indian Head, veer to the northeast from Peak 2875 above Sterling Hollow, and ridge-walk to the summit. A couple of summits before you arrive at Gray Head, you'll walk through a small stand of bristlecone pines. There are likely to be other stands along any of the high ridges in the area. The high, relatively dry and harsh environment, plus the nature of the soil (limestone), is responsible for the existence of these long-lived trees. If you stay on the ridge top, you'll have easy walking, plus have a chance to see the bristlecones.

Best Time and Time Needed   From about June 1 on through the deer hunt, or late October, is the normal time to hike. The hike to, and back from Gray Head will take most people half a day, while to climb both summits will take all day.

Campgrounds   There's a forest service campground just west of the main highway as shown, but near the trailhead there are several fine campsites.

Maps   Ashley National Forest, U.S.G.S. maps Price (1:100,000), Gray Head Peak, Jones Hollow (1:24,000).

Gray Head Peak. Bristlecone pine trees can be seen on the ridge-line (50mm lens).

Map 52, Gray Head, Indian Head, Bad Land Cliffs

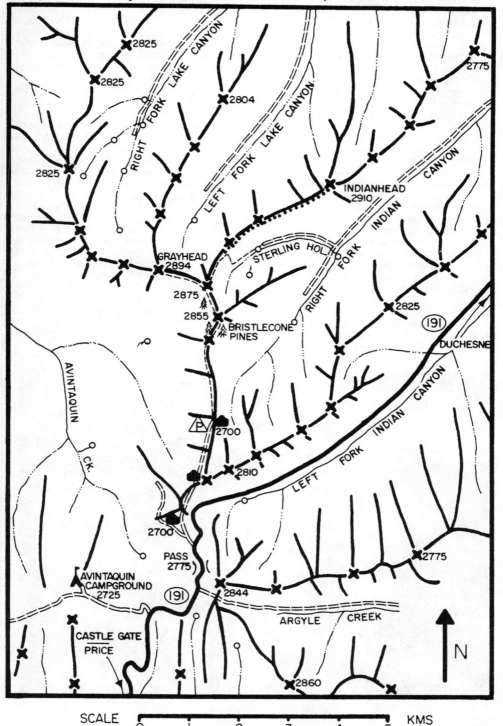

RIGHT FORK LAKE CANYON

LEFT FORK LAKE CANYON

INDIAN CANYON

×2825

×2825

2825

×2804

×2775

×2910 INDIANHEAD

GRAYHEAD
2894

2875

2855

BRISTLECONE
PINES

STERLING HOLLOW

RIGHT FORK INDIAN

×2825

191

DUCHESNE

AVINTAQUIN

CK.

P 2700

2700

×2810

LEFT FORK INDIAN CANYON

×2775

PASS
2775

AVINTAQUIN
CAMPGROUND
2725

191

×2844

ARGYLE CREEK

CASTLE GATE
PRICE

×2860

N

SCALE

0   1   2   3   4   5   KMS

Patmos Head, Book Cliffs

Location Few people in Utah know of the mountains and plateaus in eastern Utah near Price. The highest area is east and north of Dragerton, East Carbon City and Sunnyside. These are three small coal mining communities at the foot of the Book, Roan or Brown Cliffs. Various maps use different names. The highest summit is Bruin Point at 3135 meters. On top of this flat summit are radio towers. Next highest is Mt. Bartles at 3063 meters. But the peak of most interest to climbers is Patmos Head, rising to 3003 meters. Patmos Head has steep escarpments on all sides except for the ridge running north. On top are the remains of an old Heliograph Station dating from the 1880's.

Geology At the very summit of Patmos Head is the Green River Formation. Next is the Wasatch and North Horn Formations, followed by the Mesa Verde Group. It's in the Mesa Verde that the coal is being mined at the Geneva and Sunnyside Mines.

Access Drive southeast out of Price on US Highway 191-6, then directly east on State Road 123 running to East Carbon City. There are paved roads to the Geneva and Sunnyside mines. On the map, most trails shown are actually 4WD roads.

Trail Information This is not one of the popular weekend hiking areas in Utah; therefore, no trail system exists. But there are plenty of 4WD tracks. There's a road to the top of both Bruin Point and Mt. Bartles, but not to Patmos Head. So it's Patmos that'll be discussed here. If you have a nice car and don't like driving on rough, dusty roads, stop at the Geneva Mine and walk from there. Or drive about 2 kms further up the canyon and stop at a side road just above the water tanks. Walk along the canyon bottom north, sometimes on a 4WD road. Turn right in a canyon west of the summit and either go up that canyon, or up the prominent west ridge. There are easy grass and pine forest covered slopes, as well as a few cliffs to be skirted, but no major problems. Take all your own water, there's none in the canyons. Regular hiking boots are best here. Patmos Head can also be climbed from Range Creek (but you'll need a 4WD to get there), and from Number Two Canyon, but only after permission to pass the mine company works. Walking past or through this land shouldn't be a problem though.

Best Time and Time Needed Best time for hiking here would be June, September and October. July and August are fine too, but a little warm. Because of the steepness of the climb and the fact no trail exists, it will take an entire day for this climb for the average hiker. For a strong hiker, about half a day. Excellent views from the top of much of Utah's canyon and cliff country.

Maps Utah Travel Council Map 2 — Southeastern Central Utah, U.S.G.S. maps Price, Huntington (1:100,000), Woodside (1:62,500), Patmos Head, Bruin Point, Mt. Bartles, Sunnyside (1:24,000)

The southwestern slopes of Patmos Head viewed from just above the Geneva Mine (50mm lens).

Map 53, Patmos Head, Book Cliffs

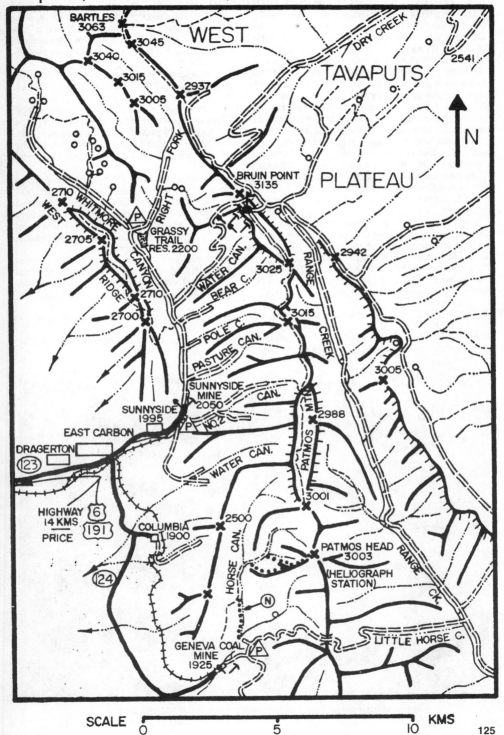

SCALE

0   5   10   KMS

Mt. Waas, Northern La Sal Mountains

Location   This map includes the northern half of the La Sal Mountains of southeastern Utah. This range is found just east of Moab,, and forms a beacon for travelers in the area.. The peaks here are from Geyser Pass north. The highest summit is Mt. Waas, at 3758 meters. Other well-known peaks are Manns, 3741 meters; Tomasaki, 3729; and Haystack, 3548 meters. In addition there are several other high summits along the main north-south ridge.

Geology   All higher peaks are composed of a granitic type rock called diorite porphyry. The mostly red rocks seen all around the mountain base are the familiar sandstones of the Colorado Plateau. The La Sals are one of eight laccolith mountains on the Plateau.

Access   Access is easy. Drive south out of Moab to the edge of town, and look for the prominent sign pointing out the way to the La Sal Mountains Loop Road. This well-used highway is paved almost all the way to Castleton, which is located just a few kms northeast of Moab. High on the mountain, you can turn to the east where the signs read: to Geyser Pass, Oowah Lake, Warner Lake or Miners Basin. (The author has been in Miners Basin, but not on the road leading there.) Warner Lake is probably the most centrally located of all the car-parks or trailheads.

Trail Information   Many of the trails shown are actually very old and eroded former mine exploration tracks, but the forest service has blocked off several to make them into regular hiking trails. All you'll need to do is to follow one of the trails from any of the five trailheads up to the mountains above timberline, then route-find to whichever summit you want. Once on the high ridges, the walking is very easy, and more than one peak can be climbed on one trip. The trail and car-park location just west of Geyser Pass are very difficult to find unless you know the place, but all others are rather visible. Each year more people are recreating here, so the trails are being used more all the time.

Best Time and Time Needed   Climb here from about mid-June through late October. Fall is the most colorful time to hike, but nights can be chilly. The author camped near Geyser Pass and climbed Tomasaki, then walked the ridge to Waas and to the Peak 3660; then he returned to camp via Miners Basin and Warner Lake, all in one long and tiring day. To do half this hike in one day is about all most people can do.

Campgrounds   At Warner and Oowah Lakes, but good campsites exist everywhere, many of which have a good water supply.

Maps   Utah Travel Council Map 2—Southeastern Central Utah, U.S.G.S. maps Moab, La Sal (1:100,000), Castle Valley, Polar Mesa, La Sal, La Sal Junction (1:62,500).

From the summit of Manns Peak, looking north toward Mt. Waas (28mm lens).

Map 54, Mt. Waas, Northern La Sal Mtns.

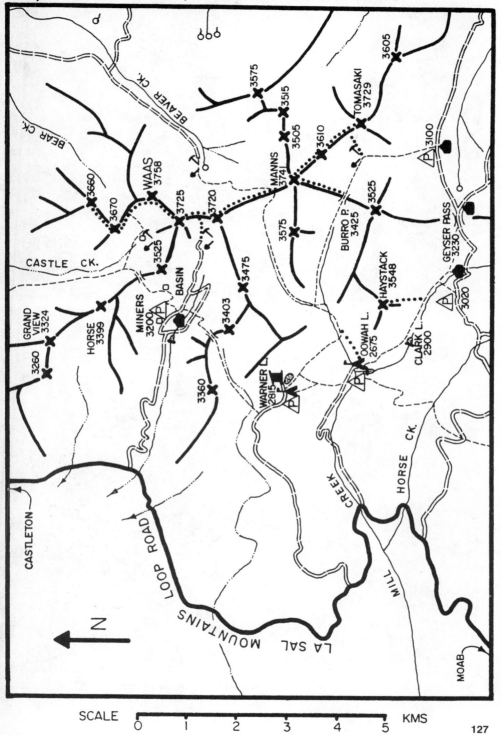

BEAVER CK.

BEAR CK.

3605

3575

3515

TOMASAKI
3729

3505

3610

P 3100

MANNS
3741

3660

WAAS
3758

3670

3725

3720

3525

BURRO P.
3425

GEYSER PASS
3230

3575

3525

3020

CASTLE CK.

3525

3475

HAYSTACK
3548

BASIN

GRAND
VIEW
3324

HORSE
3399

MINERS
3200

3403

OOWAH L.
2675

CLARK L.
2900

3260

3360

WARNER L.
2815

HORSE CK.

CASTLETON

LA SAL MOUNTAINS LOOP ROAD

MILL CREEK

MOAB

N

SCALE

0   1   2   3   4   5   KMS

127

It's either wading or swimming the better part of one 200 meter section of the Black Hole (35mm lens).

Tukuhnikivatz, far background, seen from the top of Mellenthin (50mm lens).

From Manns Peak, looking south at southern La Sal Mtns. (28mm lens).

Warner Lake with Haystack Mtn. left, Mellenthin right, in the La Sal Mtns. (50mm lens).

Mt. Peale, Southern La Sal Mountains

Location This map covers the southern half of the La Sal Mountains of southeastern Utah. This range is directly east of Moab, and forms an impressive skyline for that community. Included here is the highest summit in the La Sals, Mt. Peale, at 3877 meters. Also, Mellenthin, 3855 meters and Tukuhnikivatz, 3805. There are several other high summits on the ridge connecting these three peaks. Just to the south of this main cluster of summits is South Peak, at 3596 meters.

Geology The La Sals are one of eight laccolith mountains on the Colorado Plateau. The core of the range is a more resistant granitic type rock, sometimes called diorite porphyry. Surrounding the main summits are the sandstones common to the Plateau.

Access The main access road here is the La Sal Mountains Loop Road. It leaves the main highway several kms south of Moab, and runs up to the western slopes, then north and down to Castleton. It's paved all the way now except for one short section. High on the mountain, look for the sign pointing the way to Geyser Pass. This road is good for most of the way to the pass. One can also drive south out of Moab to La Sal Junction and turn east toward La Sal. About 8 or so kms beyond La Sal, look for a road sign pointing to the forest lands and La Sal Pass. This rough road gives access to Peale and to South Peak.

Trail Information From Geyser Pass, simply route-find up the slopes of Mellenthin. From this summit, one can ridge-walk on south to Tukuhnikivatz and Peale. Or one can drive to the old drill site at 3050 meters, just north of Tukuh., and route-find to anywhere on the mountain. The road to this trailhead may be given back to nature shortly though. From the area around La Sal Pass, one can again route-find north or south. This route is probably the easiest and shortest route to Mt. Peale, but the access road is rough and dusty. Once on the high ridges, the walking is very easy between summits, as is walking through the forest.

Best Time and Time Needed Climbing season here is from about mid-June on through late October, depending on the year. Early October is very colorful, but beware of early winter snow storms. To climb Mellenthin from Geyser Pass is about half a day. The same for Mt. Peale from the south, about half a day.

Campgrounds No campgrounds on this map, but there are plenty of very good campsites along small streams, especially near Geyser Pass.

Maps Utah Travel Council Map 2—Southeastern Central Utah, U.S.G.S. maps La Sal (1:100,000), La Sal Junction , La Sal (1:62,500).

From the summit of Mellenthin looking south at the north face of Mt. Peale (28mm lens).

Map 55, Mt. Peale, Southern La Sal Mtns.

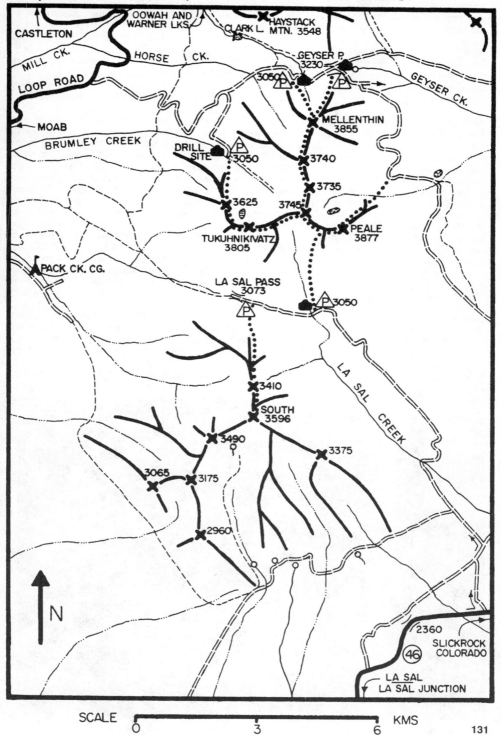

OOWAH AND WARNER LKS.

HAYSTACK MTN. 3548

CLARK L.

CASTLETON

MILL CK.

HORSE CK.

GEYSER P. 3230

LOOP ROAD

3050

P

GEYSER CK.

MOAB

BRUMLEY CREEK

MELLENTHIN 3855

P

DRILL SITE

P 3050

3740

3735

3625

3745

PEALE 3877

TUKUHNIKIVATZ 3805

PACK CK. CG.

LA SAL PASS 3073

P 3050

P

LA SAL CREEK

3410

SOUTH 3596

3490

3375

3065

3175

2960

2360

46

SLICKROCK COLORADO

LA SAL

LA SAL JUNCTION

N

SCALE

0   3   6   KMS

131

Mt. Ellen, Henry Mountains

Location   The Henry Mountains are located in southeastern Utah, almost due south of Hanksville, and west and northwest of Hite on the upper part of Lake Powell. This map covers the northern third of the range which includes the highest peak. This is Mt. Ellen, with a north and south ridge. The highest summits are on the north ridge and include the peak with the remains of an old Heliograph Station dating from the 1880's. (The actual platforms at the Heliograph Station date from much later times and surveys.) The altitudes are 3507 and 3512 meters. The south ridge includes the summits around Bomide Basin, the highest being 3481 meters. It has a small solar-powered radio transmitter on top.

Geology   The Henry Mountains are one of eight laccolith ranges on the Colorado Plateau. The core is an intrusive granitic type rock called diorite porophyry, with sedimentary sandstone rocks surrounding the core.

Access   The simplest access route is to turn south from the post office (100 E.) in Hanksville, and follow that road and signs to the Lonesome Beaver Campground in Sawmill Basin. The campground is just east of the highest peaks. This road is well used, but rough in spots, and any car can make it there with care. All peaks can be climbed from this one central location. Hanksville to the campground is about 35 kms. Access to Bromide Basin and the southern peaks can also be made from Highway 95 and mile post 26, near Bullfrog Junction. Head for Crescent Creek, the old site of Eagle City, and Bromide Basin. Any car can make it to the road junction just northeast of Bartons Peak, where water and a campsite can be found. Parts of this road are also rough, but well used mostly by pickups. Most roads on the map are rough, but generally passable to all vehicles, when care is taken.

Trail Information   There are no trails here to speak of. There are some game trails, including elk, deer and buffalo (and livestock), but there are a number of old mining roads or tracks which are not on this map or even the U.S.G.S. maps. These can be used in some cases. For Mt. Ellen, you can walk or drive up to Bull Creek Pass (3200 meters), and then walk the ridge north. Walk south to peaks on the south ridge. Or you can walk down the road to the Dandelion Picnic Site and locate the trail (actually an old logging road) which runs to the East Saddle. Higher up on this old road, look for an easy route up Ellen. For the peaks around Bromide Basin, park at the four-way junction east of the basin, and walk up the road to and past some old cabins and mines, then to the summits.

Best Time and Time Needed   Walking from the campground, strong hikers could climb the highest peak on both north and south ridges in one day, but most would prefer one day for the north ridge peaks, another for the south ridge peaks. Climbing season is from about June 1 through October.

Campgrounds   Lonesome Beaver CG. and Dandelion Picnic Site, and many other locations on Bull or Crescent Creeks.

Maps   Utah Travel Council Map 1—Southeastern Utah, U.S.G.S. maps Hanksville (1:100,000), Mt. Ellen, Bull Mtn. (1:62,500).

132   Looking south from the Heliograph Station on Ellen Peak (50mm lens).

Map 56, Mt. Ellen, Henry Mtns.

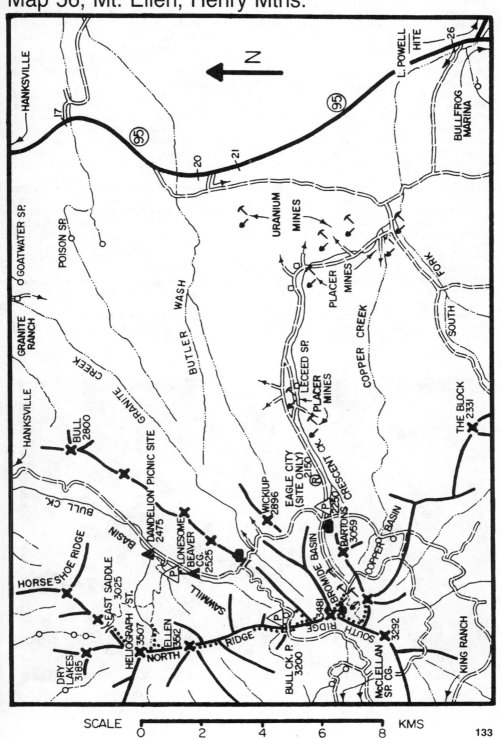

SCALE

0   2   4   6   8   KMS

Pennell and Hillers, Henry Mountains

Location   The two summits featured here are Mt. Pennell, at 3466 meters, and Mt. Hillers, 3225 meters. They are both part of the Henry Mountains of southeastern Utah, and are located due south of Hanksville and west of Hite, on Lake Powell. Just to the north is the highest peak in the range, Mt. Ellen, and to the southeast are the Little Rockies peaks of Mt. Ellsworth and Holmes.

Geology   The Henry Mountains are laccolith mountains, with their main summits or peaks composed of an intrusive granitic type rock known as diorite porphyry. The low lands around the peaks are sedimentary sandstones which make up the rest of the Colorado Plateau.

Access   One could reach these mountains from the west and north on rough dirt roads, but the logical way is via State Highway 276. This road runs south from Highway 95, the main link between Hanksville and Blanding, and ends on Lake Powell at Bullfrog. To reach Mt. Pennell the easiest way is to drive west from between mile posts 4 and 5, and head for the Trachyte Ranch, Farmers Knob, Coyote Benches and the upper part of Straight Creek. There's a very steep and rough track into the canyon, so it's best to camp and park where the road crosses Straight Creek. For Hillers, you can drive to Star Spring Campground. This section of road is very good and well maintained. The other roads on the map are passable to the higher clearance cars.

Trail Information   For Pennell, you can walk the road on the north side of the creek all the way to the southwest summit, where is located a solar-powered radio transmitter, then ridge-walk to the summit. Or you can walk along an old trail along the creek bed to the old Wolverton Mill site, then exit the bottom land for the road just mentioned, thence the summit. For Hillers, you can climb from Star Spring along the southeast ridge, which is rough and long, but it has bristlecone pines enroute. The easiest route to the summit of Hillers, but one which requires a longer and rougher drive, is the Cass Ck. route. Use a trail to the old Star Mine, thence to the summit. One can also climb Hillers from the Woodruff stone cabin, and mine, and along the south ridge. This route also has bristlecone pines.

Best Time and Time Needed   Best time to climb would be between about June 1 and late October. You'll need a full day for the climb of Hillers from Star Sp., but half a day via the Cass Ck. route. Pennell is an easy half-day hike from the campsite at 2400 meters.

Campgrounds   At Star Springs (BLM), but with campsites at any spring in the area.

Maps   Utah Travel Council Map 1—Southeastern Utah, U.S.G.S. maps Hite Crossing (1:100,000), Mt. Pennell, Mt. Hillers (1:62,500).

From just west of Star Spring, viewing the south face of Mt. Hillers (50mm lens).

Map 57, Pennell and Hillers, Henry Mtns.

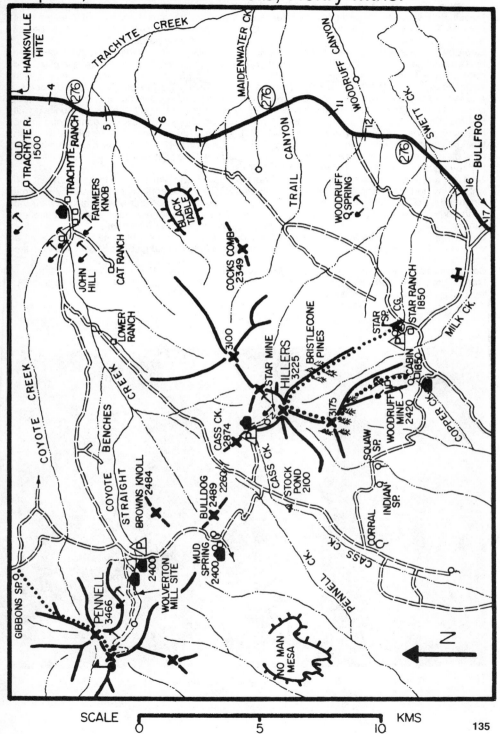

HANKSVILLE HITE

TRACHYTE CREEK

MAIDENWATER CK.

WOODRUFF CANYON

SWETT CK.

BULLFROG

276

OLD TRACHYTE R. 1500

TRACHYTE RANCH

FARMERS KNOB

JOHN HILL

CAT RANCH

BLACK TABLE

TRAIL CANYON

WOODRUFF Q SPRING

276

COCKS COMB 2349

STAR SP.

STAR RANCH 1850

C.G.

MILK CK.

LOWER RANCH

3100

STAR MINE

BRISTLECONE PINES

CABIN 1850

COYOTE CREEK

BENCHES CREEK

HILLERS 3225

3175

WOODRUFF MINE 2420

COPPER CK.

STRAIGHT COYOTE

CASS CK. 2874

CASS CK.

SQUAW SP.

BROWNS KNOLL 2484

BULLDOG 2489 2260

CASS CK.

STOCK POND 2100

INDIAN SP.

CORRAL

PENNELL CK.

CASS CK.

GIBBONS SP.

2400

MUD SPRING 2400

WOLVERTON MILL SITE

PENNELL 3466

NO MAN MESA

N

SCALE

0   5   10   KMS

135

Holmes and Ellsworth, Little Rockies (Henry Mountains)

Location   The peaks here are located due south of Hanksville, and west of Hite Marina on Lake Powell. Both summits are part of the Greater Henry Mountains, but are often referred to as the Little Rockies. The peaks are Mt. Holmes, 2417 meters, and Mt. Ellsworth, at 2510 meters. Mt. Ellsworth has a small solar-powered radio transmitter on the summit (serviced by helicopter).

Geology   These peaks, as with the rest of the Henry Mountains, are laccoliths; that is, they have been uplifted with the molten magma below not quite reaching the surface. The magma froze in place and cooled slowly, thus we have a granitic type rock called diorite porphyry at the core of the mountains, with sedimentary rocks surrounding the central mass. Later erosion exposed the granite rocks of the center.

Access   One could walk up from Lake Powell in Ticaboo or Four Mile Canyon, but the obvious way of access is Highway 276. Drive south from Hanksville, or west from Hite, till you see the signs pointing out Bullfrog. For Holmes, turn south from the highway near mile post 16. This is a sandy road in the beginning, so watch it. Further up you'll need a HCV, but you can drive nearly 3 kms up this old road with the right vehicle. For Ellsworth, look for m.p. 20, and turn east on another road, which can be driven by most pickups, or anything with higher than average clearance. The right vehicle can go about 3 kms up this road and be parked just before the granite dikes.

Trail Information   No trails, just route-find. From the car-park on Holmes, angle to the southeast and walk up the north face and ridge. The west face is very rugged. The north face route is easy, on what otherwise is a difficult looking mountain. Mt. Ellsworth can be climbed from one of several routes, but the north ridge is perhaps best. Route-find up the ridge to the first peak, then ridge-walk to the highest summit. This too is an easy climb. Look for desert big horn sheep on both peaks.

Best Time and Time Needed   Spring or fall are ideal ; winters can be a fun time too, depending on snow cover (which is usually very little). Summers are hot as hell. The author climbed both peaks on the same day in 35 degree C. heat.

Campgrounds   Best campsite is at Star Springs and campground, 7 kms from Highway 276.

Maps   Utah Travel Council Map 1—Southeastern Utah, U.S.G.S. maps Hite Crossing (1:100,000), Mt. Hillers, Mt. Ellsworth (1:62,500).

The west face of Mt. Holmes, seen from Highway 276 (100mm lens).

Map 58, Holmes and Ellsworth, Little Rockies

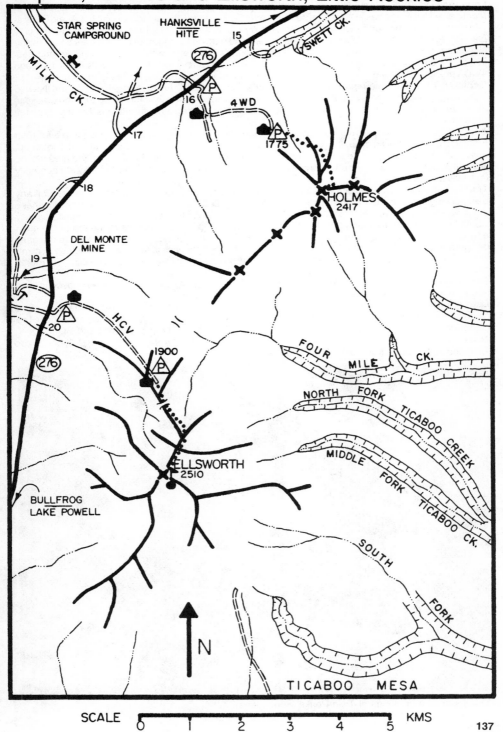

STAR SPRING
CAMPGROUND

HANKSVILLE
HITE

15

SWETT CK.

MILK CK.

276

16

4 WD

1775

P

17

HOLMES
2417

18

DEL MONTE
MINE

19

20

276

HCV

1900

P

FOUR MILE CK.

NORTH FORK TICABOO CREEK

MIDDLE FORK TICABOO CK.

ELLSWORTH
2510

BULLFROG
LAKE POWELL

SOUTH FORK

N

TICABOO MESA

SCALE

0 1 2 3 4 5   KMS

137

Abajo Peak, Abajo Mountains

Location The Abajo Mountains are located in the extreme southeastern corner of Utah just west of Monticello. This range has a number of summits over 3000 meters, the highest of which is Abajo Peak at 3463 meters. On the northeastern slopes of Abajo Peak is the Blue Mountain Ski Resort. It's the only place to ski in southeastern Utah. Abajo Peak is forested right up to the summit. The higher south-facing slopes are grass covered, while the north-facing slopes are covered with spruce, fir and aspen trees. Logging is a minor local industry. On top of Abajo Peak is a radio tower. During summer months good 4WD vehicles can make it to the summit, but there are many good hiking routes to the top as well.

Geology The Abajo Mountains have been made the same as the La Sals, Henrys, and Navajo Mountains. They are known as laccolith mountains. Moulton magma was forced up through cracks in the earth, but failed to reach the surface. But it did deform or push up other formations. Later erosion left the intrusive body exposed.

Access By far the best all around route to reach the higher summits of the Abajo is the paved road running west out of Monticello. It's paved for about 10 kms, to the Buckboard Campground. Higher up, this road is steep, but good up to the Indian Creek Guard Station. One can also reach the area via the Natural Bridges N.M. on the south side of the range and from various other roads, but they are generally less well maintained.

Trail Information Because of the nature of the topography and vegetation, there are very few if any backpacking trails in the Abajos. Instead it's mostly 4WD tracks one encounters. Even with these setbacks, hiking and climbing can still be enjoyed. To climb Abajo Peak, the least complicated way would be to drive to the Blue Mountain Ski Resort, then simply follow the lifts to the top of the main north-south summit ridge, thence south to the summit. A second choice would be to drive to the pass between Abajo and Horsehead Peaks and climb from there. This pass is the best route to use to climb Horsehead as well. From near this same pass, The Twins and North Peaks can also be climbed. Plenty of small streams and water in the canyons.

Best Time and Time Needed All peaks in the Abajos are one day climbs. The hiking season is from about June 1 through October, and in some years into November.

Campgrounds Both Buckboard and Dalton Spring Campgrounds are fee-use areas, but good campsites can be found in the area east of the peaks. The forest service has forbidden camping in the higher portions of the range, because it's a culinary watershed for both Monticello and Blanding.

Maps Utah Travel Council Map 1 — Southeastern Utah, Manti-La Sal National Forest, U.S.G.S. maps Blanding (1:100,000), Monticello, Mt. Linnaeua (1:62,500)

The south face or slopes of Twin Peaks (50mm lens).

Map 59, Abajo Peak, Abajo Mtns.

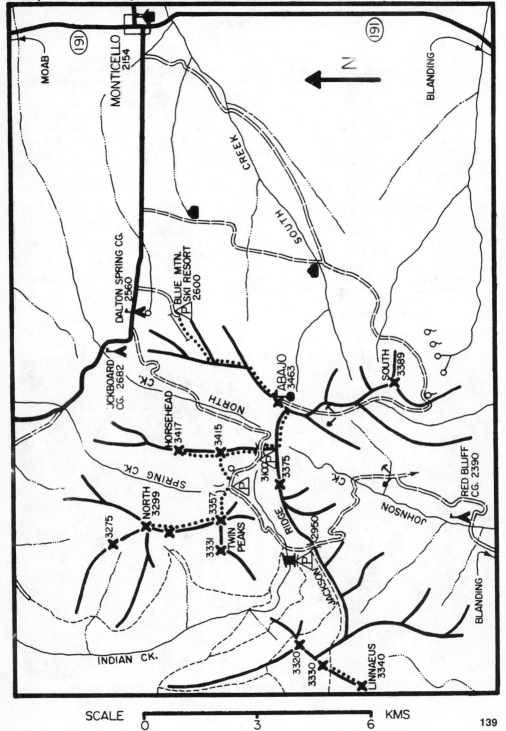

SCALE

0   3   6   KMS

139

Navajo Mountain, Navajo Nation

Location   Navajo Mountain is located in extreme southern Utah immediately next to the Arizona state line, to the east of Rainbow Bridge and Lake Powell, and south of the San Juan River Arm of Lake Powell. The entire mountain sits on Navajo Tribal Lands.

Geology   Navajo Mountain is one of eight ranges on the Colorado Plateau which are known as laccolith mountains. The flat-lying rocks of the Colorado Plateau were pushed up by molten magma from below. As the magma neared the surface, it cooled and froze in place. Later erosion **will** expose this central core, but as yet it is beneath the sandstone strata making up the Plateau.

Access   This is the only mountain in Utah that you'll have to leave the state in order to make the climb. The thing you must do is go to Page, Arizona, and drive east and southeast on Highway 98. At a point due south of the mountian, and where the sign points out the way to Navajo Mountain and Inscription House, turn north. Or you can drive down through Monticello, Blanding and Mexican Hat, Utah, then enter the Navajo Nation and go on to Kayenta. From Kayenta drive west to the junction of Highway 98, then use this highway to reach the Inscription House turnoff. At that point drive north on a well-used gravel and sandy road (to be paved in the next few years) to Navajo Mountain Trading Post. There you can get fuel and food, and other last minute supplies and information about the trip. To reach the base of the mountain, drive back south of the trading post about one km, and turn west. Follow this rough road 6 or 7 kms and park at the bottom of a steep section of road. Four wheel drives can make it to the summit to service a radio facility, but you should plan to walk.

Trail Information   The easiest way up is to follow this very steep and rough road to the summit, but you can walk cross-country to save several kms on the southeast face. Another route possibility would be to park near the Rainbow Lodge ruins, and climb it from the south.

Best Time and Time Needed   This is an easy one-day hike from about any route, but carry water in your car and pack. Climb from about May through the first of November.

Campgrounds   No campgrounds anywhere near, but there is lots of open space. But beware, there are Navajos living everywhere in scattered sites around the mountain. You might ask someone from a local home if it's OK to camp in that area. It is in a way private land!

Maps   U.S.G.S. maps Navajo Mtn., Kayenta (1:100,000), Navajo Mtn. (1:62,500) in Utah, and Chaiyahi Flat, Chaiyahi Rim NE (1:24,000), both in Arizona.

Navajo Mtn. from the south, and from near the Navajo Mtn. Alliance Church (50mm lens).

Map 60, Navajo Mtn., Navajo Nation

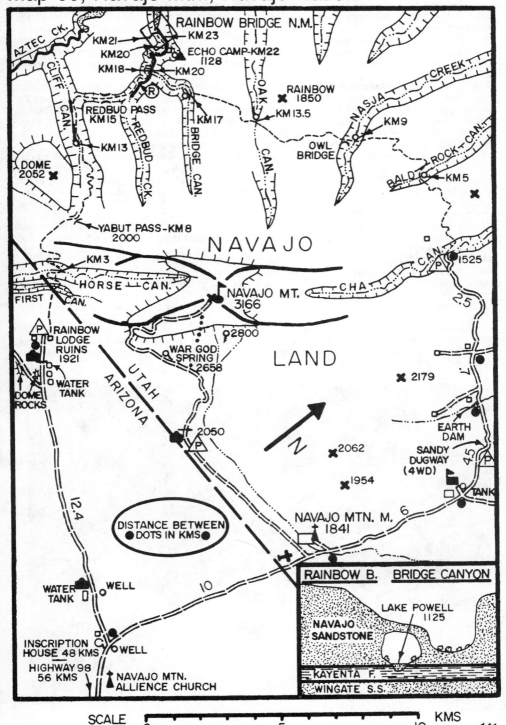

RAINBOW BRIDGE N.M.

AZTEC CK.

KM21
KM23
KM20
ECHO CAMP-KM22
1128
KM18
KM20
KM17
REDBUD PASS
KM15
KM13
DOME
2052
CLIFF CAN.
REDBUD CK.
BRIDGE CAN.
OAK CAN.
RAINBOW
1850
KM13.5
NASJA CREEK
KM9
OWL
BRIDGE
BALDIO
KM5
ROCK CAN.

YABUT PASS-KM8
2000

NAVAJO

KM3
HORSE CAN.
FIRST CAN.
NAVAJO MT.
3166
CHA CAN.
2.5
1525

P
RAINBOW
LODGE
RUINS
1921
WATER
TANK
DOME
ROCKS
UTAH
ARIZONA
WAR GOD
SPRING
2658
2800
LAND
2179

2050
P
N
2062
1954
EARTH
DAM
SANDY
DUGWAY
(4WD)
4.5
P
TANK

12.4
DISTANCE BETWEEN
DOTS IN KMS
NAVAJO MTN. M.
1841
6

10
WATER
TANK
WELL
RAINBOW B. BRIDGE CANYON
LAKE POWELL
1125
NAVAJO
SANDSTONE
INSCRIPTION
HOUSE 48 KMS
WELL
HIGHWAY 98
56 KMS
NAVAJO MTN.
ALLIENCE CHURCH
KAYENTA F.
WINGATE S.S.

SCALE
0
5
10
KMS

141

Zion Narrows

Location and Access   The Zion Narrows is one of the most famous canyon hikes in the world. The reasons are, it has some of the best narrows around, and is located in Zion National Park. This hike is found in the upper portions of Zion Canyon, the main and most-visited part of the park. You can drive to the bottom part of the narrows via the paved canyon highway. If you're interested in doing the full length of Zion Canyon and all it's narrows, you must drive 3 kms beyond the east entrance of the park on the main highway running to Mt. Carmel Junction. At that point is a reasonably good dirt road running north 29 kms to the Chamberlain Ranch.

Trail or Route Conditions   From the car-park at Chamberlain Ranch, you first walk on an old ranch road, then along the creek bed. Plan to be in the water wading about ¼ of the time. In the stream it's slippery, so take a *light weight walking stick* (it's also useful when probing the deeper holes). There is a short paved trail up from the bottom car-park about 1½ kms to where the canyon really narrows. *Have a good weather forecast* before doing this trip; flash floods have killed in the past.

Elevations   Chamberlain Ranch is about 1735 meters, bottom car-park is 1344.

Hike Length and Time Needed   From the ranch to the bottom car-park is about 20 kms. This can be done in one day, but it's a tiring hike, so most people do it in 2 days. A car shuttle is a necessity, so look for other hikers in the visitor   center, or hire help in Springdale to shuttle your car. If time is limited and/or the shuttle too difficult, you can do as most people do: walk up canyon from the bottom end. In half a day, you can walk up stream to about Orderville Canyon, and see the lower end of the narrows. Consider seeing Goose, Kolob and Deep Creeks if you have time. They also have narrows.

Water   Water from side canyons is generally safe to drink, but main stream water should be purified before using. Camping is legal in the canyon, but not below Big Spring (park ranger now tell hikers to boil even spring water?).

Map   USGS or BLM map Kanab (1:100,000), or Zion National Park (1:31,680).

Main Attraction   This canyon is at or near the top of the authors best hikes list.

Ideal Time to Hike   Because you'll be in the water and wet so much of the time, do this hike in warm weather, from about mid June through late September. Earlier in the season the water is cold and high. Late in the season it's just too cold. Because of some deep holes, small children should not attempt this hike.

Hiking Boots   Wading boots or shoes.

Author's Experience   The author has gone up from the bottom three times trying to get better fotos. Use fast film and keep cameras in plastic sacks or in day packs. Drowned cameras are common in this canyon, because of the slippery rocks.

Wading in the North Fork of the Virgin River deep inside Zion Narrows (50mm lens).

Map 61, Zion Narrows

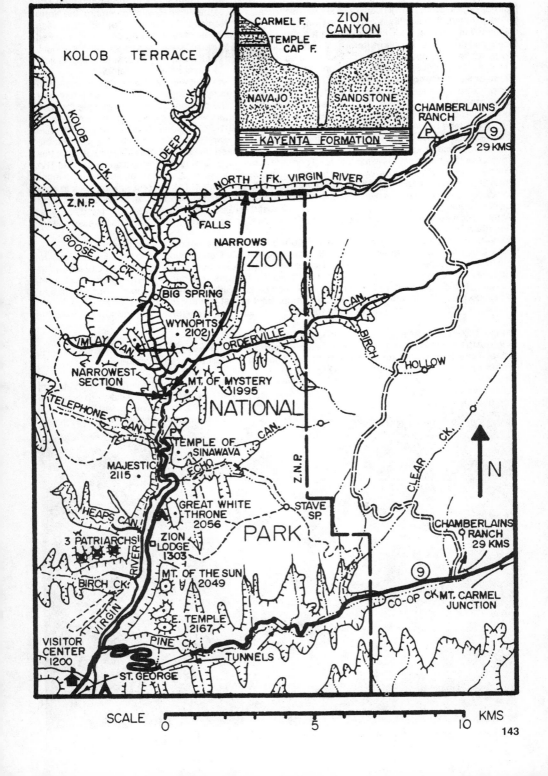

KOLOB TERRACE

ZION CANYON

CARMEL F.

TEMPLE CAP F.

NAVAJO SANDSTONE

KAYENTA FORMATION

KOLOB CK.

DEEP CK.

CHAMBERLAINS RANCH

9 29 KMS

NORTH FK. VIRGIN RIVER

Z.N.P.

FALLS

NARROWS

ZION

GOOSE CK.

BIG SPRING

WYNOPITS 2102

IMLAY CAN.

ORDERVILLE

BIRCH CAN.

HOLLOW

NARROWEST SECTION

MT. OF MYSTERY 1995

TELEPHONE CAN.

NATIONAL

CAN.

Z.N.P.

CLEAR CK.

N

TEMPLE OF SINAWAVA

MAJESTIC 2115

ECHO

GREAT WHITE THRONE 2056

STAVE SP.

PARK

CHAMBERLAINS RANCH 29 KMS

HEAPS CAN.

3 PATRIARCHS

ZION LODGE 1303

MT. OF THE SUN 2049

9

BIRCH CK.

VIRGIN RIVER

E. TEMPLE 2167

PINE CK.

CO-OP CK. MT. CARMEL JUNCTION

VISITOR CENTER 1200

TUNNELS

ST. GEORGE

SCALE 0   5   10   KMS

Parunuweap Canyon

Location and Access   Parunuweap Canyon lies between Mt. Carmel Junction and Springdale. The stream flowing through this canyon is known as the East Fork of the Virgin River. Remember, the North Fork of the Virgin River flows out of Zion Canyon and the Zion Narrows. The lower half of this canyon lies within Zion National Park. Most people drive about 3 or 4 kms south of Mt. Carmel Junction to a locked gate and park. One can also enter where Mineral Gulch and Meadow Creek cross Highway 9; or about 5 kms east of the park entrance, you can drive south to an overlook area, and enter via Mineral Gulch. This last 8 km drive is a dusty and sometimes rough road, and usable in dry weather only.

Trail or Route Conditions   If you begin near Mt. Carmel J., you can walk across private property with no problem, while following a ranch road about 5 kms into the canyon. Beyond the road you merely walk down and through the creek. But there's a minor problem at the canyon bottom. Just outside the park boundary lies Shunesburg and some private lands. Park rangers ask hikers to seek prior permission to cross this land before hiking. Call the Jim Trees Ranch at 801-772-3230 and get permission which is easy and free; or do a second route up Stevens Wash and down Gifford Canyon, which ends near the tunnel entrance on Highway 9. There is some kind of old sheep trail there, but before you attempt this route, talk to rangers at the visitors center. There are some deep holes in the narrows section called The Barracks, and occasional *quick sand* (this isn't as bad as some have reported). You never sink in more than 30 or maybe 40 cms. But it can be scary the first time you try it. Take a long walking stick to help locate more solid walking, which is usually in the middle of the stream. An *air mattress* would be a good piece of equipment here in case you have to ferry packs across pools. Also have a *rope* handy as well. At the falls, walk to the left. Some consider this hike more difficult than the Zion Narrows Hike, so do that first, then Parunuweap.

Elevations   Top of the canyon is about 1600 meters, while the bottom is less than 1200.

Hike Length and Time Needed   From the trailhead near Mt. Carmel Junction to the falls is 25 kms; to the mouth of Stevens Wash 34 kms; and to the highway below Shunesburg about 42 kms (trailhead to Highway 9). Plan to do this in two days, but camp outside the park boundary, or have a permit to camp in the park. From Parunuweap Canyon, through Stevens and Gifford Canyon is about 8 kms with lots of elevation gain. This is not recommended though. Best to just call the ranch for permission.

Water   There are many springs along the way, but treat river water (park rangers now tell hikers to boil even spring water?).

Map   USGS or BLM map Kanab (1:100,000).

Main Attraction   Challenging hike for experienced hikers, narrows and Powell M. Plaque.

Ideal Time to Hike   Summer. With all the wading you'll do, hike in warm weather.

Hiking Boots   Wading boots or shoes.

Author's Experience   The author parked between mile posts 48 and 49, and entered through Mineral Gulch. At the park boundary, he lowered pack over one falls and ferried pack across a deep pool. The trip took two days, 14 hours total walk-time, and he hitch-hiked back to his car (in early June).

The narrows of Mineral Gulch, a tributary of Parunuweap Canyon (28mm lens).

Map 62, Parunuweap Canyon

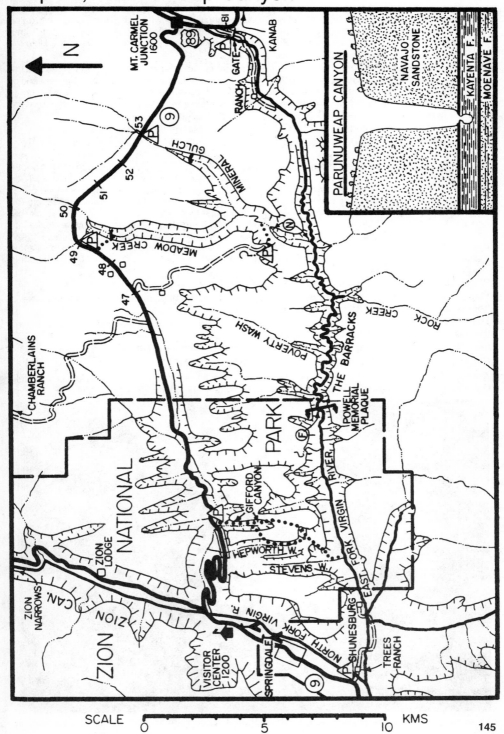

SCALE 0   5   10   KMS

145

Lower Escalante River

Location and Access The lower end of the Escalante River lies between Bryce Canyon on the West, Lake Powell on the south, and Capitol Reef N. P. on the east. Drive east from the Bryce Canyon area on Highway 12, or south from Torrey and Fruita on this same paved highway. At a point about 7 kms southeast of Escalante town, turn south on the Hole-in-the-Rock Road. This road ends at the Hole-in-the-Rock, just above Lake Powell, a distance of 92 kms.

Trail or Route Conditions In this whole mapped area, there are only a couple of real trails. One is at the end of the road, where a trail goes down into the Hole-in-the-Rock, and another rises out of the very end of Coyote Gulch to the bench lands above. Otherwise you walk down the creek bed, which is sometimes wet, sometimes dry. All the major canyons on the west side have flowing water, while the canyons on the east are generally dry.

Elevations Trailheads are between 1400 and 1700 meters, while the lake is 1125.

Hike Length and Time Needed The most popular outing is this: Drive 8 kms down 40 Mile Ridge to a dry water tank. Then walk north to Hamblin Arch in the Coyote Gulch, and descend. Walk down to very near the Escalante R., then just before the trail goes off a ledge with a log ladder, turn uphill to the south, and follow a trail to a crack in the rock where hikers can squeeze through to the top of the Navajo. Then walk on a trail back to your car, a total distance of about 22 kms, and a one day hike. Most however prefer to camp one night or more. One can also park at the head of Hurricane Wash, and walk down into the Coyote. You can spend a day, or more here. Another popular hike is to drive to the Egypt car-park (but check the bottom of 25 Mile Wash before proceeding through - as it is sometimes sandy) and hike into either Harris, the Escalante, or 25 Mile Wash, and make a loop hike. This hike takes one or more days. A nice day-hike is to park at the 40 Mile Gulch Trailhead and walk down this gulch, then up Willow Creek, passing Broken Bow Arch on the way. For a verbal description of other canyon hikes, consult the book, *Hiking the Escalante* (no maps included).

Water Most canyons have year-round water and very few cattle. Carry water in your car.

Map USGS or BLM map Escalante and Smokey Mountain (1:100,000), or Hiking the Escalante River, from BLM offices in all of Utah or Escalante (1:62,000).

Main Attraction Natural arches, deep undercuts and canyons, hanging gardens. Coyote Gulch is on the authors best hikes list (and there are more good ones).

Ideal Time to Hike Spring or fall, but because of wading, summer is OK too.

Hiking Boots Wading boots or shoes for all canyons.

Author's Experience He has gone down Coyote G. twice, as well as Willow Ck. and Hole in the Rock. Before entering this region, stop at the BLM and National Park Service office in Escalante.

From the bench land above, we see Coyote Wash and Jacob Hamblin Arch in the Navajo Sandstone.
(28mm lens.)

Map 63, Lower Escalante River

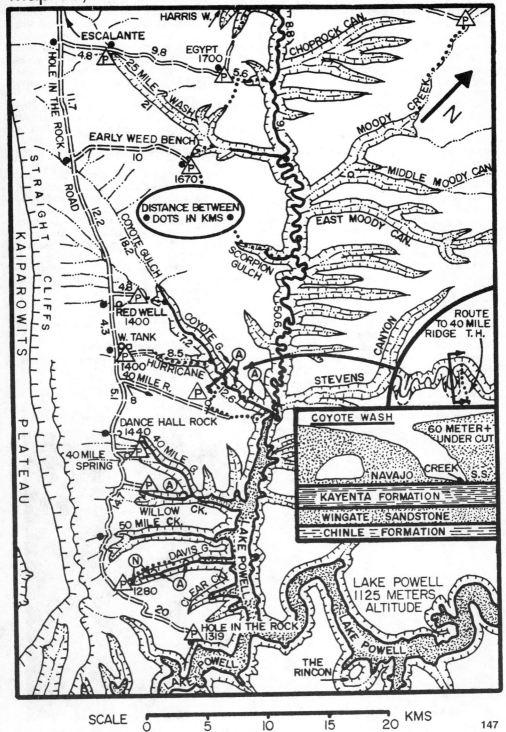

HARRIS W.

ESCALANTE

EGYPT 1700

CHOPROCK CAN.

4.8

9.8

5.6

25 MILE WASH

21

MOODY CREEK

N

EARLY WEED BENCH

10

1670

MIDDLE MOODY CAN.

HOLE IN THE ROCK

11.7

ROAD

DISTANCE BETWEEN DOTS IN KMS

EAST MOODY CAN.

12.2

COYOTE GULCH

18.2

SCORPION GULCH

50.6

4.8

RED WELL 1400

4.3

W. TANK

1400

COYOTE G.

7.2

ROUTE TO 40 MILE RIDGE T.H.

HURRICANE

8.5

40 MILE R.

8

5.1

12.6

STEVENS CANYON

DANCE HALL ROCK 1440

COYOTE WASH

60 METER+ UNDER CUT

40 MILE SPRING

40 MILE G.

NAVAJO CREEK S.S.

KAYENTA FORMATION

WINGATE SANDSTONE

CHINLE FORMATION

WILLOW CK.

50 MILE CK.

LAKE POWELL

LAKE POWELL 1125 METERS ALTITUDE

N

DAVIS G.

1280

CLEAR CK.

20

HOLE IN THE ROCK 1319

LAKE POWELL

LAKE POWELL

THE RINCON

STRAIGHT CLIFFS

KAIPAROWITS PLATEAU

SCALE

0   5   10   15   20   KMS

Paria River and Buckskin Gulch

Location and Access   One of the best known canyon hikes on The Plateau is the Paria River and its main tributary, the Buckskin Gulch. This hike begins in Utah and ends at Lee's Ferry in Arizona. To reach the trailhead, drive along Highway 89 (the main road linking Kanab Utah and Page Arizona), to a point about 58 kms east of Kanab, and 48 kms west of Page, where the Paria River crosses the highway (between mile posts 20-21). You'll see the Paria River Ranger Station on the south side of the road. From that point you can drive 3 kms south to the Whitehouse Ruins, and the beginning of the hike to Lee's Ferry. To reach the head of the Buckskin, drive west on Highway 89 about 8 kms from the ranger station (m.p. 26). Just west of the Cockscomb Ridge, the House Rock Valley Road heads south about 6 and/or 10 kms to the Buckskin Trailheads.

Trail or Route Conditions   There are no trails except for the path leading into the Paria from the trailhead. You merely walk down the creek bed. In the case of the Paria, you'll be walking in water much of the time. The amount of flow in the river depends on upstream irrigation and the time of year, but it's seldom more than ankle deep. The lower Buckskin has running water too, but for most of the year this canyon is dry except for an occassional pool. Walking is generally easy, but most exciting in the Buckskin.

Elevations   Head of Buckskin, 1470 meters; Paria Trailhead, 1341; and Lee's Ferry, 990.

Hike Length and Time Needed   From Whitehouse to Lee's Ferry is about 54 kms, or a 2 or 3 day hike, depending on side trips. Add 16 kms on to the 56, and you have 72 kms from the Buckskin Trailhead to Lee's Ferry. That for most people is 3 to 4 days. But if you walk to Lee's Ferry, you've got to have two cars, or hitch hike back. There are people at Marble Canyon who run shuttle services. One solution to the car problem is to park at Buckskin Trailhead, then walk down the Buckskin, and up the Paria. This is 37.5 kms, plus the road walk of 14 kms. That's two long days, maybe three. Might ask other hikers to help in eliminating the 14 km road walk. The Buckskin is the best part of the hike, as it averages 4 to 5 meters in width for around 20 kms. There are many campsites enroute (along the Paria), but *always camp on high ground, use a stove, take a 10 meter long nylon rope (to get down the rockfall at KM 24.2 in the Buckskin)*(Steps have now been cut in the rockfall boulders, but take a rope anyway.) *and have a good weather forecast.* August has bad storms and flooding—beware.

Water   Plan to camp at springs, or purify Paria River water.

Map   USGS or BLM maps Smokey Mountain and Glen Canyon City (1:100,000), or Paria Plateau and Lee's Ferry (1:62,500), or BLM's Paria Canyon Primitive Area.

Main Attraction   Perhaps the best and longest narrows anywhere (Buckskin Gulch).

Ideal Time to Hike   Because of shade and wading, late spring through early fall, but many people do this hike in winter now (but only after a long dry spell).

Hiking Boots   Wading boots or shoes.

Author's Experience   The author hiked down the Paria and into the Buckskin, and back in 7 hours round-trip. On a second trip he hiked down the Paria and up the Buckskin, camping one night enroute. The deep, dark narrows of the Buckskin are endless, so take fast film and a camera stand for best fotos.

Buckskin Gulch of the Paria River. The best narrows hike on the Colorado Plateau (35mm lens).

Map 64, Paria River-Buckskin Gulch

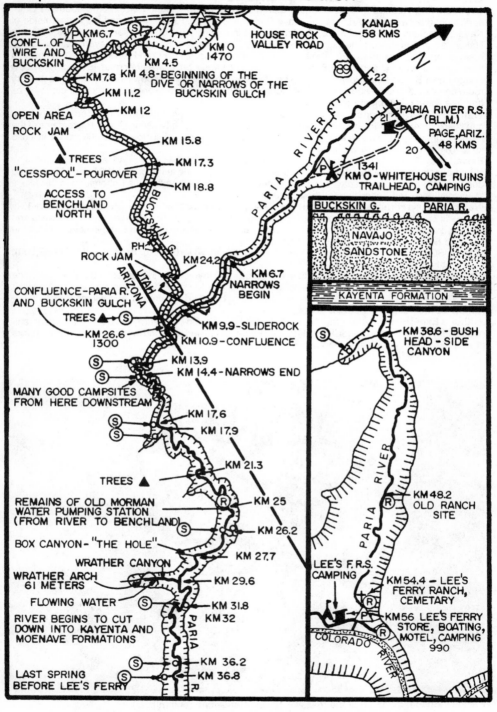

CONFL. OF WIRE AND BUCKSKIN

KM 6.7

KM 0 1470

KM 4.5

KM 4.8 - BEGINNING OF THE DIVE OR NARROWS OF THE BUCKSKIN GULCH

HOUSE ROCK VALLEY ROAD

KANAB 58 KMS

N

22

PARIA RIVER R.S. (B.L.M.)

PAGE, ARIZ. 48 KMS

21

20

KM 7.8

KM 11.2

KM 12

OPEN AREA

ROCK JAM

TREES

"CESSPOOL"-POUROVER

KM 15.8

KM 17.3

KM 18.8

ACCESS TO BENCHLAND NORTH

P.H.

ROCK JAM

KM 24.2

CONFLUENCE-PARIA R. AND BUCKSKIN GULCH

TREES

KM 26.6 1300

ARIZONA UTAH

BUCKSKIN G.

KM 6.7 NARROWS BEGIN

KM 9.9 - SLIDEROCK

KM 10.9 - CONFLUENCE

KM 13.9

KM 14.4 - NARROWS END

MANY GOOD CAMPSITES FROM HERE DOWNSTREAM

KM 17.6

KM 17.9

KM 21.3

TREES

REMAINS OF OLD MORMAN WATER PUMPING STATION (FROM RIVER TO BENCHLAND)

R

KM 25

KM 26.2

BOX CANYON - "THE HOLE"

WRATHER CANYON

KM 27.7

WRATHER ARCH 61 METERS

FLOWING WATER

KM 29.6

KM 31.8

KM 32

RIVER BEGINS TO CUT DOWN INTO KAYENTA AND MOENAVE FORMATIONS

PARIA

KM 36.2

KM 36.8

LAST SPRING BEFORE LEE'S FERRY

PARIA R.

T341

KM 0 - WHITEHOUSE RUINS TRAILHEAD, CAMPING

BUCKSKIN G.   PARIA R.

NAVAJO SANDSTONE

KAYENTA FORMATION

KM 38.6 - BUSH HEAD - SIDE CANYON

PARIA RIVER

KM 48.2 OLD RANCH SITE

LEE'S F.R.S. CAMPING

KM 54.4 - LEE'S FERRY RANCH, CEMETARY

R

KM 56 LEE'S FERRY STORE, BOATING, MOTEL, CAMPING 990

COLORADO RIVER

SCALE   0   5   10   KMS

149

Cliff Canyon and Rainbow Bridge

Location and Access The canyons featured on this map are found in extreme southern Utah, sandwiched between the Arizona line, Lake Powell and the San Juan River, and the western side of Navajo Mountain. But to get there, one must drive in from the Arizona side and through the Navajo Nation. Locate and drive the highway connecting Page and the Shonto and Kayenta areas of the reservation. This is Highway 98. About 83 kms from Page, or 22 kms from Highway 160, turn north on the Navajo Mtn. Road, and drive 68 kms on a gravel and sandy, but all weather road, to the old Rainbow Lodge ruins. Before Lake Powell came to be, this was the route to Rainbow Bridge N.M. (a secondary route comes in from the north side of the mountain). Nowadays, many boaters come to the bridge, as the lake waters lie beneath the monument.

Trail or Route Conditions This old trail isn't used much any more, but it's still good enough that you can't get lost. At the spring in Cliff Canyon, you'll find an old toilet; and at Echo Camp, the remains of the former tourist campsite under a huge overhang. From Yabut Pass, you'll drop about 700 meters in 4 or 5 kms. This is the hard part when coming back out.

Elevations From about 2000 meters, down to about 1125 at the bridge and lake.

Hike Length and Time Needed From the Rainbow Lodge ruins to the bridge is 21 kms. This can be done round-trip in one long day, but you'd better take 2 or 3. Remember, the bottom end of this hike is at low altitude, and hotter than at the trailhead.

Water About a km before the lodge ruins is a water tank and tap (this is where the good road ends), as well as in several locations along the road leading to the trailhead. The Navajos use these wells and taps for domestic use. Always carry water in your car. There's year-round live water in several places in Cliff and Bridge Canyons, as well as at Echo Camp.

Map USGS or BLM maps Navajo Mountain and Kayenta (1:100,000), or Navajo Mtn (1:62,500), Chaiyahi Flat and Chaiyahi Rim (1:24,000).

Main Attraction Deep and narrow Navajo Sandstone Canyons and the largest natural bridge in the world. The lake provides great swimming, but the place is too crowded sometimes.

Ideal Time to Hike Spring or fall are best but it can be hiked in summer and winter.

Hiking Boots Any dry weather boots or shoes.

Author's Experience The author camped, with the permission of a nearby resident, at the water tank near the lodge ruins, then began early. He hiked to the bridge and returned, all in one day, with 11 hours of walk time. Don't try this, it's too much for one day.

Rainbow Bridge, made up of the massive Navajo Sandstone (50mm lens).

Map 65, Cliff Canyon-Rainbow Bridge

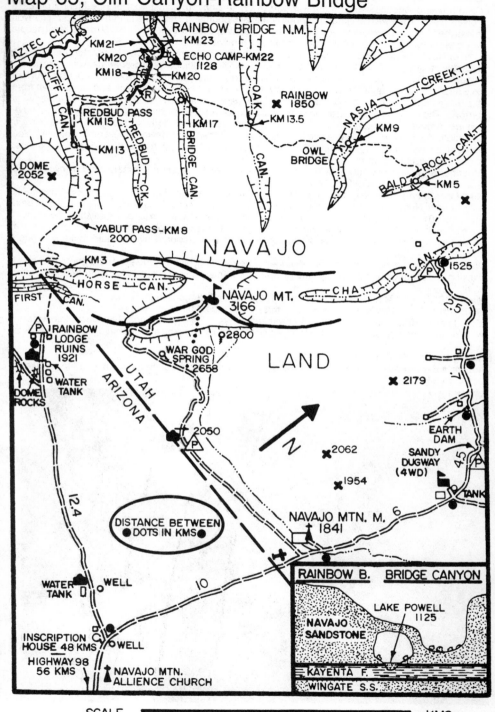

AZTEC CK.

CLIFF CAN.

RAINBOW BRIDGE N.M.
KM 21
KM 23
KM 20
ECHO CAMP-KM 22
1128
KM 18
KM 20

REDBUD PASS
KM 15
KM 13
KM 17

RAINBOW
1850
KM 13.5

DOME
2052

OAK CAN.

REDBUD CK.

BRIDGE CAN.

OWL
BRIDGE

NASJA CREEK

KM 9

BALD

ROCK CAN.

KM 5

YABUT PASS-KM 8
2000

N A V A J O

CAN.

P 1525

KM 3

HORSE CAN.

FIRST CAN.

NAVAJO MT.
3166

CHA

2.5

2800

LAND

RAINBOW
LODGE
RUINS
1921

WAR GOD
SPRING
2658

UTAH
ARIZONA

WATER
TANK

DOME
ROCKS

2179

2050
P

N

EARTH
DAM

2062

SANDY
DUGWAY
(4WD)

1954

TANK

DISTANCE BETWEEN
DOTS IN KMS

NAVAJO MTN. M.
1841

6

4.5

P

12.4

WATER
TANK

WELL

10

RAINBOW B.   BRIDGE CANYON

INSCRIPTION
HOUSE 48 KMS
WELL

HIGHWAY 98
56 KMS

NAVAJO MTN.
ALLIANCE CHURCH

NAVAJO
SANDSTONE

LAKE POWELL
1125

KAYENTA F.

WINGATE S.S.

SCALE   0   5   10   KMS

151

Lower White Canyon

Location and Access This, the lower part of White Canyon, is just east of Hite Marina on Lake Powell. It's also due west of Natural Bridges National Monument. The entire length of this lower canyon is less than 2 kms from Highway 95. This makes for easy access, with no dirt or 4WD roads. Most people would want to stop at mile post 57, enter the canyon and come out at m.p. 55.

Trail or Route Conditions There is no trail anywhere in this canyon, and it's completely unknown as a hikable canyon. It's likely that some have tried to hike up its length, but only prepared hikers can make it through the "Black Hole". The author hiked up from Lake Powell to the bottom of the Black Hole, but had no way to get cameras and maps through dry. He then took his overnight pack and came down from m.p. 61, camping enroute, but couldn't get his large pack and air mattress through the half meter wide narrows. The third try he made it through. It's a dry canyon (except for the Black Hole) but you must have a *small diameter inner tube*, or some *float device* to take camera, clothes, maps, etc., through in a dry condition. You must *swim* most of one 200 meter section, then swim or wade most other potholes. You might also have a *short rope*, to get non-rock-climbers out of the canyon near m.p. 55. This is the most exciting narrows hike on the Colorado Plateau.

Elevations Mile post 57 is about 1400 meters, the Black Hole is about 100 meters deep, mile post 55 is at about 1300, and Lake Powell, 1125 meters.

Hike Length and Time Needed In at m.p. 57, down canyon, out at m.p. 55, and back to ones car is only 12 kms. Normally that's half a day, but with the excitement of the Black Hole, plan to take all day. From m.p. 61, down canyon to the lake is about 26 kms. This is too much for a one day hike, so it would have to be done in two days. But be warned; getting a large pack through a half meter wide place, with a 90 degree turn while swimming is difficult. A group of well prepared hikers could make it through however.

Water It's a dry canyon except for a number of permanently filled potholes. There should be good drinking water in potholes here any time of year (but with a influx of hikers, you better treat the water first).

Map USGS or BLM map Hite Crossing (1:100,000), or Browns Rim (1:62,500).

Main Attraction The Black Hole. One of three or four best hikes in this book.

Ideal Time to Hike Hot summer weather with temps 35°C or higher, if possible. Black Hole water is frigid, and hypothermia is a big danger. Keep clothes dry by stripping and swimming in shorts or swim suit.

Hiking Boots Wading boots or shoes

Author's Experience On the third try, the author was prepared, and made the m.p. 57 to 55 hike in less than 5 hours.

You'll have to swim through most of the Black Hole of Lower White Canyon (28mm lens).

Map 66, Lower White Canyon

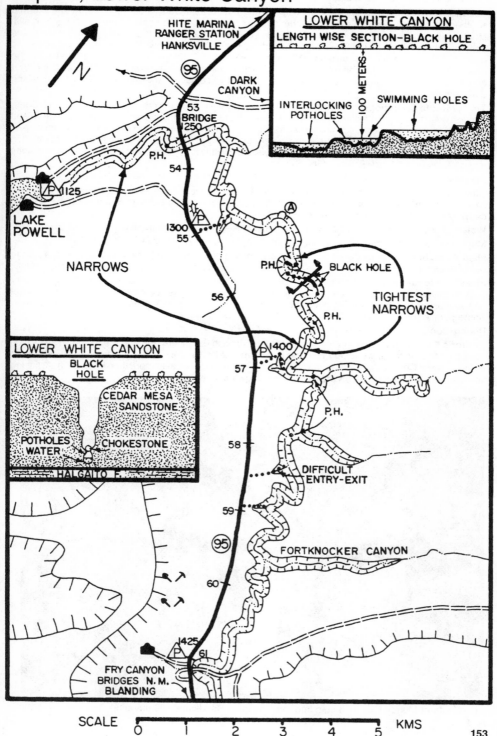

LOWER WHITE CANYON
LENGTH WISE SECTION—BLACK HOLE

100 METERS

INTERLOCKING POTHOLES

SWIMMING HOLES

HITE MARINA
RANGER STATION
HANKSVILLE

95

DARK CANYON

53 BRIDGE 1250

P.H.

54

LAKE POWELL

1125

NARROWS

1300
55

56

A

P.H.

BLACK HOLE

TIGHTEST NARROWS

P.H.

LOWER WHITE CANYON

BLACK HOLE

CEDAR MESA SANDSTONE

POTHOLES WATER

CHOKESTONE

HALGAITO F.

1400

57

P.H.

58

DIFFICULT ENTRY-EXIT

59

95

FORTKNOCKER CANYON

60

1425

61

FRY CANYON
BRIDGES N. M.
BLANDING

SCALE   0   1   2   3   4   5   KMS

153

The Chute, of Muddy Creek, San Rafael Swell

Location and Access   This hike, a walk down The Chute of the Muddy Creek, is located in the extreme southern end of the Swell. It's found on the inside of the Reef, and in between the big Wingate Walls. Muddy Creek in this section cuts down through the Coconino Sandstone, thus making a very narrow and deep trench, the same as the San Rafael River does in the north as it flows through the Black Boxes. To get to this canyon, exit I-70 at mile post 129 and drive south to Tomsich Butte; or leave Highway 24 (the road connecting Hanksville and I-70) at Temple Junction, and drive west and south to Tomsich Butte. You could also drive to the Delta Mine (Hidden Splendor), but you'd have to walk upstream from there. Going down canyon is easier.

Trail or Route Conditions   There is no trail--you simply walk down the creek bed. From Tomsich Butte, turn left or east and drive as far as you can. That will be just before the stream crossing. Park there and walk along a very old and faded mining road as shown, for about 2 kms, then it's "in the water." In the part labeled Coconino Narrows, you'll be in the water about 50% of the time, but while in the area of the log jam, you'll be in water 90% of the time. The water is usually only ankle deep, and there are no obstructions as one finds in the Black Boxes of the San Rafael River.

Elevations   River bed near Tomsich Butte 1554 meters; at the bottom end 1450 meters.

Hike Length and Time Needed   From Tomsich Butte to the Delta Mine is about 25 kms, one way. This can be done in one day, but you'd need two cars. It's perhaps best to begin and end the hike at one car-park, making it a long day-hike, in and out.

Water   Forget the water you'll be walking in for drinking, it has to be treated. Take your own.

Map   USGS or BLM map San Rafael Desert (1:100,000), or Wild Horse (1:62,500).

Main Attraction   A deep, dark and narrow canyon, and one that is "unknown" to this date. Maybe the best narrows hike in the Swell.

Ideal Time to Hike   Spring through fall, but if it's too early in the season or too late, the waters will be very cold. Summer might be best, as you're in the water so often. Winter is out of the question. There is about half as much water in Muddy Creek as in the San Rafael River, so the big, deep holes just aren't there. Some people run it in kayaks during the last week or two of May.

Hiking Boots   Wading boots or shoes.

Author's Experience   The author camped at the Tomsich Butte car-park, and walked down stream on April 19, 1986. His feet were very cold the first couple of hours, then things warmed up. He walked to within 4 kms of Chimney C., and returned (8 hours). The water was never more than knee deep. At the log jam you walk under logs which are lodged in narrows above you.

The Chute of Muddy Ck., as it cuts into the Coconino Sandstone (50mm lens).

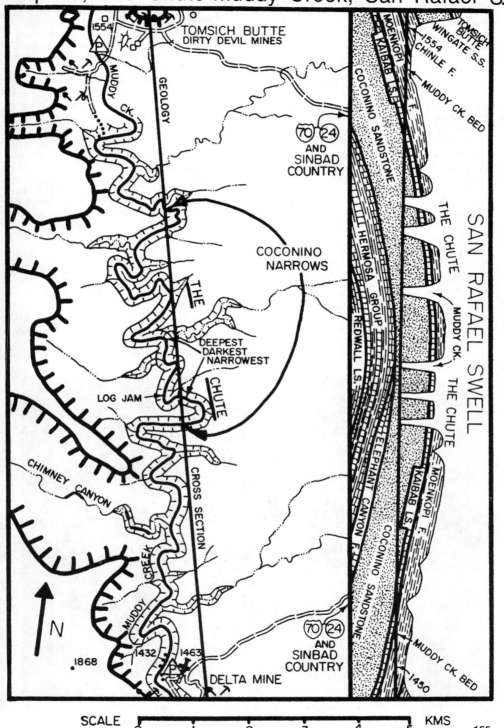

1554
TOMSICH BUTTE
DIRTY DEVIL MINES

MUDDY CK.

GEOLOGY

70 24
AND
SINBAD
COUNTRY

COCONINO
NARROWS

THE

DEEPEST
DARKEST
NARROWEST

LOG JAM

CHUTE

CHIMNEY CANYON

CROSS SECTION

MUDDY CREEK

N

.1868   1432   1463

DELTA MINE

70 24
AND
SINBAD
COUNTRY

SAN RAFAEL SWELL

TOMSICH
BUTTE
1554
WINGATE S.S.
CHINLE F.
MOENKOPI F.
KAIBAB LS.
MUDDY CK. BED

COCONINO SANDSTONE

HERMOSA GROUP

REDWALL LS.

THE CHUTE
MUDDY CK.
THE CHUTE

ELEPHANT CANYON F.

KAIBAB LS.
MOENKOPI F.

COCONINO SANDSTONE

MUDDY CK. BED

1450

SCALE   0   1   2   3   4   5   KMS

155

Little Wild Horse Canyon, San Rafael Swell

Location and Access   These two canyons are found very near Goblin Valley State Park, which is on the southeast side of the San Rafael Swell. Goblin Valley is about halfway between Interstate Highway 70 and Hanksville, just off Highway 24. At Temple Junction near mile post 137, turn west on a paved road for about 8 kms. Then turn left or south onto a good all-weather sand and gravel road. Follow this road for 12 kms to Goblin Valley, or turn to the west as shown on the map and proceed to the campsite where Little Wild Horse Canyon comes out of the Reef.

Trail or Route Conditions   Going up Bell, you walk in the dry creek bed. As the canyon widens and opens up, you'll find an old mining road which can be used to reach the upper part of Little Wild Horse Canyon. Then once again, you make your way down the dry creek bed. The author was here after a two or three week dry spell and had no problem, but if you're there soon after rains, you may have some wading to do in the many small potholes that line Little Wild Horse Canyon. Even if the potholes have water in them, they are not serious obstacles.

Elevations   Little Wild Horse Canyon car-park is about 1550 meters; inside the Swell is 1720.

Hike Length and Time Needed   From the car-park, up Bell, across the Swell to Little Wild Horse, then back to the car-park is about 13 kms. This can be done in as little as 4 hours, but you'll want to spend time in the narrows of Little Wild Horse Canyon. This is one of the best narrows of any canyon on the Colorado Plateau. The walls aren't so high, but as flood waters cut through the Navajo Sandstone, they have left all kinds of shapes and erosion features. The narrows are perhaps 3 kms long, but for about 1 km the width is from .75 to 2 meters wide. At a place or two, it would be difficult to take a frame pack through. One of the best day hikes around.

Water   Carry water in your car and in your pack.

Map   USGS or BLM map San Rafael Desert (1:100,000), or Wild Horse (1:62,500).

Main Attraction   The narrows of Little Wild Horse.

Ideal Time to Hike   Spring, fall or winter warm spells or the early mornings of summer.

Hiking Boots   Dry weather boots or shoes; but after rains, wading shoes.

Author's Experience   The author camped at the mouth of Little Wild Horse, then walked up Bell, crossed over, and came down Little Wild Horse. That took just over 4 hours. Don't forget your camera. The author has put this on his best hikes list, and because there's no river to wade, and because there are no major obstacles, it's a fun and safe hike for the whole family. But remember, don't do this one if storm clouds are gathering.

You'll find about 3 kms of narrows like this in Little Wild Horse Canyon (28mm lens).

Map 68, Little Wild Horse Canyon, San Rafael S.

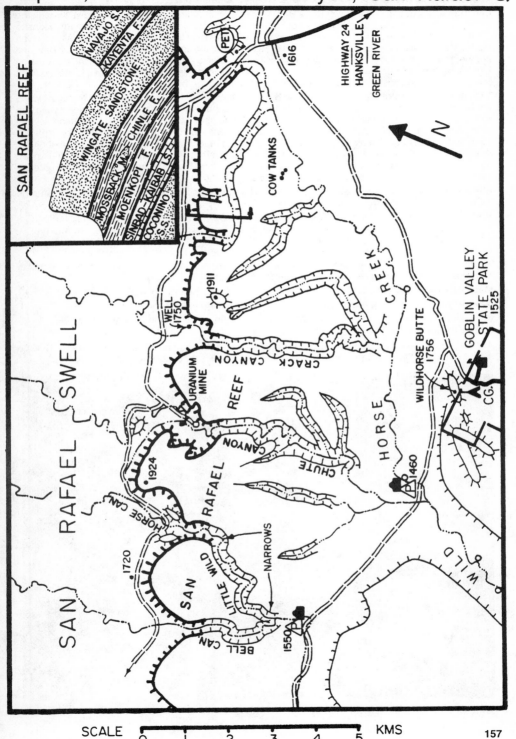

SAN RAFAEL REEF

NAVAJO S.
KAYENTA F.
WINGATE SANDSTONE
MOSSBACK M. CHINLE F.
MOENKOPI F.
SINBAD KAIBAB LS.
COCONINO S.S.

PET.

1616

HIGHWAY 24
HANKSVILLE
GREEN RIVER

N

COW TANKS

1911

WELL 1750

URANIUM MINE

REEF CANYON

CRACK CANYON

HORSE CREEK

WILDHORSE BUTTE 1756

GOBLIN VALLEY STATE PARK 1525

CG.

SAN RAFAEL SWELL

1924

CHUTE CANYON

1460

SAN RAFAEL REEF

EAST HORSE CAN.

SAN

LITTLE WILD HORSE CAN.

NARROWS

1720

BELL CAN.

1550

WILD

SCALE   0   1   2   3   4   5   KMS

Lower Black Box (Swazys Leap), San Rafael Swell

Location and Access   The Lower Black Box is located on the San Rafael River as it flows through the northern part of the San Rafael Swell. To get there, exit I-70 at mile post 129, and drive north 9 kms to Sinkhole Flat. A sign there will put you on the road. Follow this road to the Jackass Benches as shown on the map. From this circle road, there is a 4WD or HCV track to the upper part of the Lower Black Box, and another to the lower end of the Box. For people with nicer vehicles, it's possible to park at the rest area on I-70 between mile posts 140-141. Or one can also exit I-70 near mile post 145, and drive to the mouth of Black Dragon Canyon, with it's lovely campsite beneath a huge overhang.

Trail or Route Conditions   Besides the 4WD or HCV tracks, there's a trail-of-sorts on the east side to the Box which connects the upper and lower ends. At the upper end is Swazys Leap, a 3 meter-wide gap with the river 17 meters below. It has an old livestock bridge across it, which the author used several times. If you park on I-70, you'll have to route-find cross-country to the lower end of the Box. If you park at the mouth of B. Dragon, walk up canyon on an old mining road, then cross-country to the Box bottom. Walking through the Lower Black Box is almost totally in the river in the upper end of the hike. You'll need an *inner tube* if you want to keep your pack and camera dry. You'll float or swim part of the time. There are several small rockfalls in the upper part, but no major obstacles.

Elevations   Swazys Leap is about 1350 meters; the bottom end of the Box is about 1300; and the Jackass Benches car-park, about 1700 meters.

Hike Length and Time Needed   The hike through the Box is about 8 kms. If you camp and park at car-park 1700, the round-trip will be about 28-30 kms. This is similar to the distances from I-70 or B. Dragon Canyon. This means a very long day, or an easier two-day trip. With a 4WD or HCV, you can drive to Swazys Leap, hike the river, then return on the east side trail, making it an easier day.

Water   Carry water in your car and on your back. There are springs with good water in the upper part of this hike, but lower springs are sulphur. Treat the river water.

Map   USGS or BLM map San Rafael Desert (1:100,000), or Tidwell Bottoms (1:62,500).

Main Attraction   A deep, dark canyon which is on the author's best hikes list.

Ideal Time to Hike   Warm or hot weather after spring run-off (late June through September).

Hiking Boots   Wading boots or shoes.

Author's Experience   The author was here several times, but when he hiked the Lower Black Box, he did it from Black Dragon Canyon, with a total walk time of 9-1/2 hours (one day).

Swazys **Leap** and bridge over the upper part of the Lower Black Box (28mm lens).

Map 69, Lower Black Box, San Rafael Swell

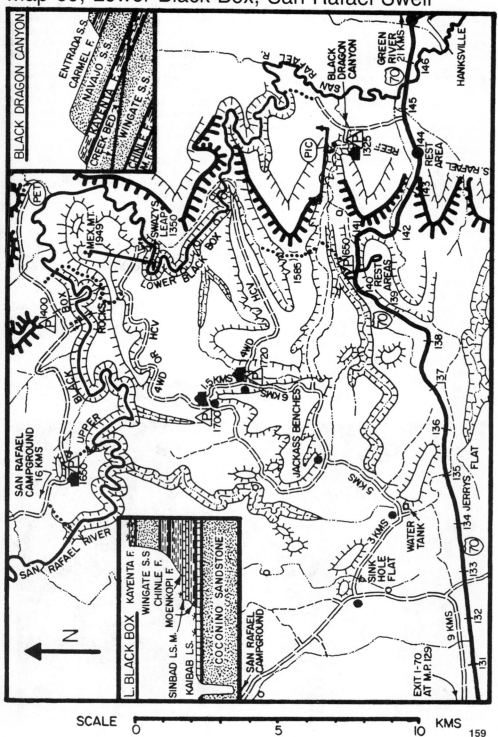

BLACK DRAGON CANYON

ENTRADA S.S.
CARMEL F.
NAVAJO S.S.
KAYENTA F.
CREEK BED
WINGATE S.S.
CHINLE F.
M.F.

PET

MEX. MT. 1949

SWAZYS LEAP 1350

LOWER BLACK BOX

SAN RAFAEL R.

BLACK DRAGON CANYON

GREEN RIVER 21 KMS

70

146

145

144 REST AREA

143

142

141

140 REST AREAS

139

138

137

136

135 JERRYS FLAT

134

133

70

132

131

HANKSVILLE

S. RAFAEL

PIC

1325

REEF

1650

1585

HCV

1400

BOX

ROCKS

BLACK

UPPER

4WD OF HCV

4WD

1720

1.5 KMS

6 KMS

1700

JACKASS BENCHES

5 KMS

WATER TANK

3 KMS

SINK HOLE FLAT

9 KMS

EXIT I-70 AT M.P. 129

SAN RAFAEL CAMPGROUND 16 KMS

1650

SAN RAFAEL RIVER

SAN RAFAEL CAMPGROUND

N

L. BLACK BOX
KAYENTA F.
WINGATE S.S.
CHINLE F.
MOENKOPI F.
SINBAD LS. M.
KAIBAB LS.
COCONINO SANDSTONE

SCALE 0   5   10 KMS

159

Upper Black Box, San Rafael Swell

Location and Access   The Upper Black Box is located on the San Rafael River as it flows through the northern part of the San Rafael Swell. It's about 30 kms due west of Green River town, and not far north of Interstate Highway 70. To get there, exit I-70 at mile post 129, and drive north to the San Rafael Campground. Or from the north, drive south from Price on Highway 10, and turn toward Cleveland and Buckhorn Wash between mile posts 56 and 57; or turn east from betwen mile posts 49 and 50, and drive toward Buckhorn Wash. Follow the Buckhorn Wash Road to the campground just mentioned on the San Rafael R. Across the river from the campground turn east, and follow the river about 16 kms. Park where there is a small stock pond on the right, and a butte on the left.

Trail or Route Conditions   When hiking the Upper Black Box one must walk in the river from 25% to 50% of the time. There is no trail. From the car-park at 1650 meters, walk in a SSE direction for about one km (a compass helps, or set your sights on two buttes on the distant horizon). At that point you should be able to view the San Rafael R. on the left and a shallow drainage coming in from the right. Look for stone cairns following an old stock trail down into the Box. About 3/4 the way through the Box, you'll come to a rockfall (rocks, on the map). At that point you'll need a short rope to get yourself, cameras, pack, etc., over the drop off in a dry condition. If you have nothing to damage in water, then just jump the two meters *but there may be rocks under the water!* If you have no rope, then you can exit to the left, or north, with some steep but relatively easy rock climbing. If you stay in the Box, you can walk out the bottom end very easily, then walk back to your car on the road.

Elevations   The car-park is 1650 meters; the river at the entry point is about 1475; and the river exit about 1400 meters.

Hike Length and Time Needed   From the entry car-park to the bottom of the Box is about 14 kms. Add another 14 or so kms for the walk back on the road. Round-trip distance is about 28 kms. You can shorten this distance by 5 kms, by exiting at the rockfall. To do this hike with one car, it's a very long day-hike; with two cars, a shorter day-hike.

Water   Carry water in your car and on your back. Or treat the river water.

Map   USGS or BLM maps Huntington and San Rafael Desert (1:100,000), Red Plateau and Beckwith Peaks (1:24,000), The Wickiup (1:62,500).

Main Attraction   A steep, deep and dark canyon, where you'll need an *inner tube and short rope* to get all the way through. Petroglyphs are NE of Mexican Mtn.

Ideal Time to Hike   Warm or hot weather after spring run-off (late June through September).

Hiking Boots   Wading boots or shoes.

Author's Experience   The author walked, waded and swam down to the rockfall, and had to exit. Then back to the car in 7 hours total walking time. But the lower part might be the best. The author puts this canyon on his best hikes list.

You'll need an inner tube to get through the Upper Black Box safely and dry (28mm lens).

Map 70, Upper Black Box, San Rafael Swell

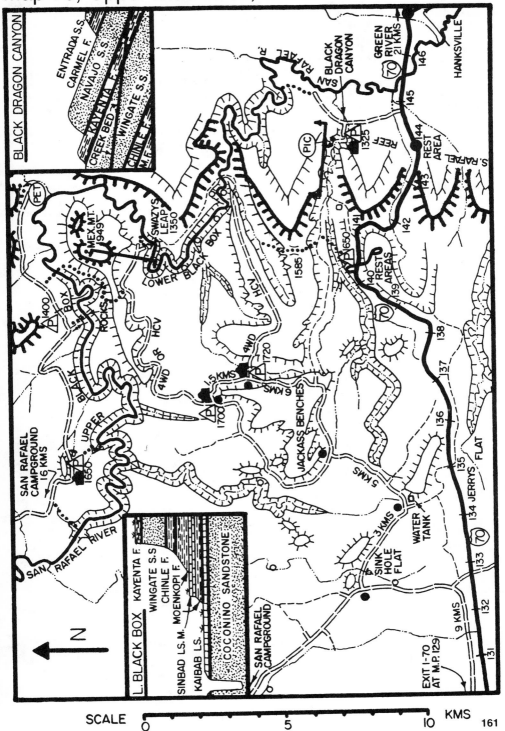

BLACK DRAGON CANYON

Entrada S.S.
Carmel F.
Navajo S.S.
KAYENTA
CREEK BED F.
WINGATE S.S.
CHINLE F.
M.F.

L. BLACK BOX
KAYENTA F.
WINGATE S.S
CHINLE F.
SINBAD LS. M. MOENKOPI F.
KAIBAB LS.
COCONINO SANDSTONE

SAN RAFAEL CAMPGROUND

HANKSVILLE

GREEN RIVER 21 KMS

BLACK DRAGON CANYON

SAN RAFAEL R.

146
145
144
143
142
141
142
138
137
136
135
134 JERRYS FLAT
133
132
131

REST AREA

S. RAFAEL

REST AREAS

PIC

1325

1350 SWAZYS LEAP

MEX. MT. 1949

PET

1400

BOX

BLACK ROCKS

LOWER BLACK BOX

1585

1650

1700

1720

1.5 KMS

6 KMS

4WD OR HCV

HCV

4WD

JACKASS BENCHES

5 KMS

3 KMS

WATER TANK

SINK HOLE FLAT

9 KMS

EXIT I-70 AT M.P. 129

SAN RAFAEL CAMPGROUND

SAN RAFAEL CAMPGROUND 16 KMS

1650

UPPER BLACK

SAN RAFAEL RIVER

N

SCALE 0   5   10 KMS

Road and Lime Canyons

Location and Access   Road and Lime Canyons are located due north of Mexican Hat and Valley of the Gods, and east of State Highway 261. They are also just south of Fish and Owl Creeks and east of Grand Gulch Primitive Area. Drive north from Mexican Hat, or south from near Bridges N. M. and Highway 95 to mile post 19. At that point locate a road, and sign stating, Cigarette Spring—9 miles (14 kms). From this Cigarette Spring Road (239), one can reach Road or Lime Canyon. There are many places to camp, including Cigarette Spring, the best site around.

Trail or Route Conditions   There are no trails in any of these canyons. You simply walk down the mostly dry creek beds, or cross a nearly flat mesa top. Don't forget a compass; it helps a lot when moving across the Cedar Mesa.

Elevations   The car-parks at the head of both Road and Lime Canyons are at about 1950 meters, whereas the bottom end of each drainage is about 1500 meters.

Hike Length and Time Needed   From the head of Road, down canyon and up Cigarette Spring Canyon to the spring, is about 24 kms. To walk down Lime, then up on the mesa to Cigarette Spring, is about the same length of hike as in Road Canyon. From the Spring back to one's car is from 8 to 10 kms. To do either of these canyons and loop from the canyon heads, would be one long day for anybody. But shorter hikes can be made into the canyons and return.

Water   The author found short stretches of running water in Road, as shown by heavy black lines. He hiked upper Lime C. in February and found lots of ice, indicating a reliable water source. Cigarette Spring is wonderful. Stockmen have put a metal tank beneath a small overhang which catches dripping water; and it's in the shade and cool. But always carry water in your car.

Map   USGS or BLM map Bluff (1:100,000), or Cedar Mesa (1:62,500).

Main Attraction   Scenery is just so so, but the real attractions here are the Anasazi Indian ruins. At one location in Road C., are several well preserved kivas (ceremonial sites). These are perhaps the best preserved kivas the author has seen.

Ideal Time to Hike   Spring, fall or winter warm spells, or an early morning start in summer.

Hiking Boots   Any dry weather boots or shoes.

Author's Experience   The author left his car-park camp, walked down Road, then took the short-cut to Cigarette Sp., and walked back Road 239 to the car in about 7½ hours. A good trip, and one of the best places on The Plateau to see ruins in a natural state. He also day-hiked Lime C. from the road beginning at mile post 16.

Road Canyon has some well preserved Anasazi ruins like this one (28mm lens).

Map 71, Road and Lime Canyons

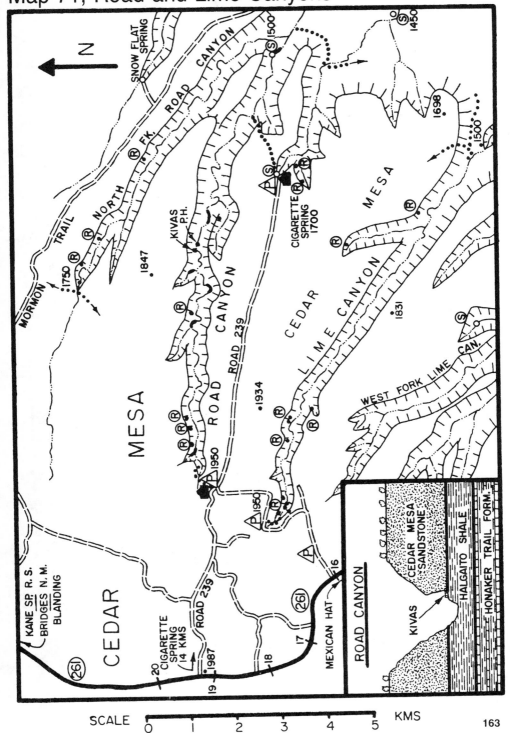

SCALE 0 1 2 3 4 5 KMS

Fish and Owl Creek Canyons

Location and Access   These two canyons, Fish and Owl, are located to the south of the Abajo Mountains and Highway 95, to the east of Grand Gulch and Highway 261, and due north of Mexican Hat. To get there from the junction of Highways 95 and 261, drive south about 8 kms and look to the east or left side of the highway for a side road numbered 253 (between mile posts 28 and 29). This side road junction is also about 1½ kms south of the Kane Gulch Ranger Station, the trailhead entry point to Grand Gulch. From the highway, drive southeast about 8 kms on Road 253 to an old drill hole site, which is the trailhead. You can camp here, but take your own water.

Trail or Route Conditions   The best way to do this circle route (so as not to back track) is to go in a clock-wise direction. The reason for this is that it's easier to find the route from the trailhead to Fish Creek, than from Fish Creek to the trailhead. So to begin, walk in a north northeasterly direction, using a compass until you reach a point where two of Fish Creeks tributaries meet. Then search for one of two (or three) routes down into the canyon. Once in the canyon you walk down the creek bed. There's water in places, but you can avoid wading. Later, you walk up Owl Creek until you reach a waterfall near the 1585 meter point. Locate a trail on the north side, and follow it back to the trailhead, and visit a cliff dwelling very near the top of the mesa enroute.

Elevations   Trailhead altitude is 1895 meters; confluence of the two creeks is 1460

Hike Length and Time Needed   From the trailhead to Fish Creek, then up Owl Creek and back to the trailhead is about 25 kms round-trip; or a rather long day for most hikers. Many people do the hike in two days. If you have but half a day, you could enter Owl Creek Canyon, visit some ruins and one of two big pourover pools, and return.

Water   There's running water in both creeks; Fish Creek even has small minnows in one stretch. The author saw no cattle, so the water should be unpolluted.

Map   USGS or BLM map Bluff (1:100,000) or Bluff and Cedar Mesa (1:62,500).

Main Attraction   This is one of the better places in Utah and the Colorado Plateau to visit Anasazi Indian ruins in a wilderness setting. There are also ruins in McCloyd Canyon and the North Fork of Road Canyon.

Ideal Time to Hike   Spring, fall or winter dry spells, or early mornings in summer.

Hiking Boots   Any dry weather boots or shoes.

Author's Experience   The author camped at the trailhead and did the round-trip in one day, or a total time of 8½ hours.

Just one of the ruins you'll find in the upper part of Owl Creek (28mm lens).

Map 72, Fish and Owl Creek Canyons

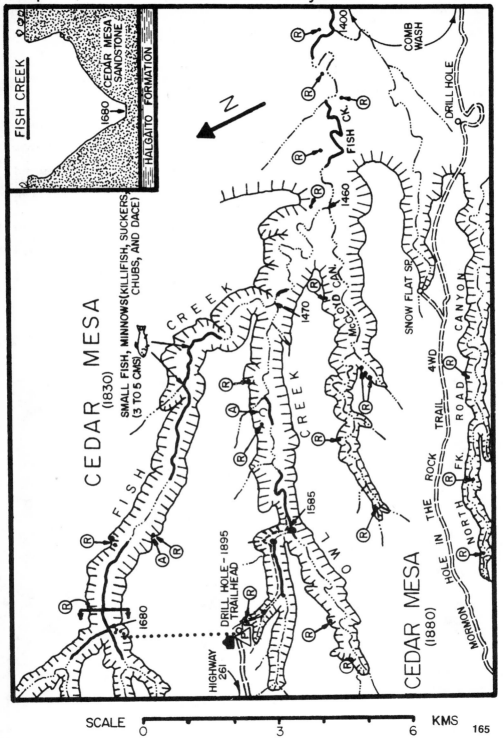

Grand Gulch

Location and Access   Grand Gulch is located just south of Natural Bridges National Monument, east of Highway 263, and west of Highway 261. The normal starting point is from the Kane Gulch Ranger Station, about 7 kms south of the junction of Highways 95 and 261 (near mile post 29). Another popular entry point is Bullet Canyon. To get there drive about 11 kms south of the Kane G. Ranger Station, then turn right or west (between m.p. 21 and 22). It's 3 kms to the trailhead. A third entry point is at Collins Spring. Drive about 10 kms southwest from the junction of Highways 95 and 263, then turn south on Road 218 and drive another 10 kms to the trailhead. From Highway 261, you can also reach the head of Slickhorn Canyon (mile posts 21 or 23).

Trail or Route Conditions   The entire length of Grand Gulch is part of an official primitive area. As time goes on there are hiker developed trails in the making particularly down canyon from Kane Gulch R.S., in Bullet Canyon, and below Collins Spring. Even if there are no trails, the walking is easy in the usually dry creek beds.

Elevations   Kane Gulch R.S. is at 1950 meters, as is the trailhead at Bullet Canyon, Collins Spring is 1560 meters altitude and the San Juan River about 1125 meters.

Hike Length and Time Needed   To walk all the way down to the San Juan R. and up Slickrock Canyon to the car-park indicated, is about 110 kms. A strong hiker could do that in as little as 5 days, but he would need two cars (or make a long road walk). But it would take most people a week for this marathon; maybe longer if you enjoy the ruins. A shorter trip would be down Grand and up Bullet, a distance of about 39 kms from trailhead to trailhead.

Water   The upper part of Grand G. has a number of springs and intermittent seeps, but check with the ranger and talk with other hikers as to the whereabouts of water in the canyon. The amount changes from season to season. Always have water in your car, and carry a couple of large jugs into the canyon for water storage.

Map   USGS or BLM maps Blanding, Bluff, and Navajo Mountain (1:100,000), or Bears Ears, Cedar Mesa and Grand Gulch (1:62,500).

Main Attraction   The best place to see Indian ruins on the Colorado Plateau.

Ideal Time to Hike   Spring, fall or early mornings in summer.

Hiking Boots   Any dry weather boots or shoes.

Author's Experience   The author started one afternoon, and walked all the next day (down Grand, and up Bullet). Total walk time, 13 hours. If it's your first time in such a setting you'll want more time in the ruins.

Grand Gulch is the best place to view Anasazi ruins (35mm lens).

Map 73, Grand Gulch

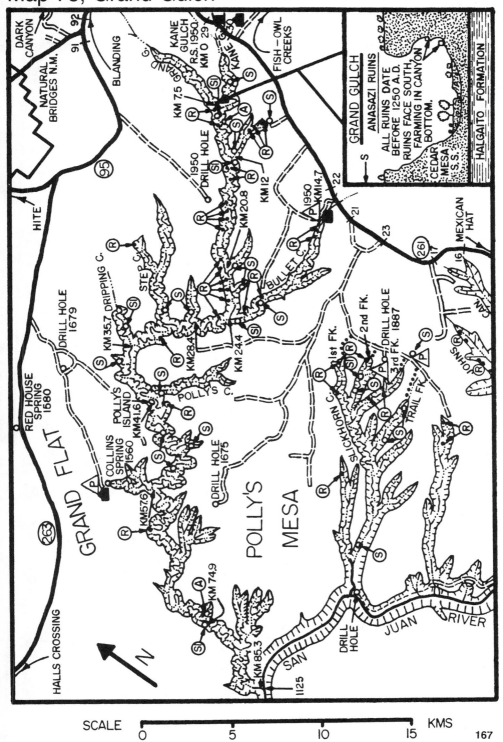

SCALE

KMS

0   5   10   15

Mule Canyon

Location and Access   Mule Canyon is located about half way between Blanding and Natural Bridges National Monument, and is just north of Highway 95. To get there, drive south, then west, out of Blanding about 45 kms. Or head east from Lake Powell till you reach the Mule Canyon Ruins. From those road-side ruins continue about one more km to the Texas Flat Road (between mile posts 102 and 103). From the beginning of this road, drive one km to gain access to the South Fork of Mule or about two kms to reach the North Fork. The best place to park is in between the two canyons under some juniper trees.

Trail or Route Conditions   There are no trails into either the North or South Fork of Mule Canyon, but it's easy to walk right up the mostly dry creek bed. What water there is can be avoided, and there's very little brush.

Elevations   The car-park is at about 1800 meters, while in the bottoms of the upper canyons it's about 2000 meters.

Hike Length and Time Needed   In either the North or South Forks, the distance from the car-park to the head of the canyon is about 10 kms. To hike up either canyon and return the same way is a rather short hike, but with all the ruins to see, it'll take you a long day in each fork. Another possibility is to go up South Fork and then route-find over the divide and enter the North Fork. The author found a route out of South Fork, but didn't take the time needed to find a route into or out of the North Fork.

Water   The map shows the running water at the time of the authors visit. In drier times there could be much less water, but the presence of many Anasazi ruins indicates a permanent water supply. There's an excellent spring and campsite at the head of Dog Tank Draw.

Map   USGS or BLM map Blanding (1:100,000), or Bear Ears and Brushy Basin Wash (1:62,500).

Main Attraction   This is one of the best canyons on The Plateau to visit Anasazi ruins in a natural state, and without having park rangers around telling you to be careful. The South Fork has more ruins than the North, but both canyons are worth a visit. One ruin in South Fork stands against a wall, and is unique.

Ideal Time to Hike   Spring and fall are best, but winter dry spells can be pleasant, and summers aren't too hot because of altitude.

Hiking Boots   Any dry weather boots or shoes.

Author's Experience   The author spent two days here, one in each canyon. Each hike lasted about 6 hours (the author has seen many ruins, so you'll surely want to spend more time there than he did). If this is the first time you've seen ruins, plan to spend a full day in each canyon.

One of many ruins seen in North Mule Canyon (50mm lens).

Map 74, Mule Canyon

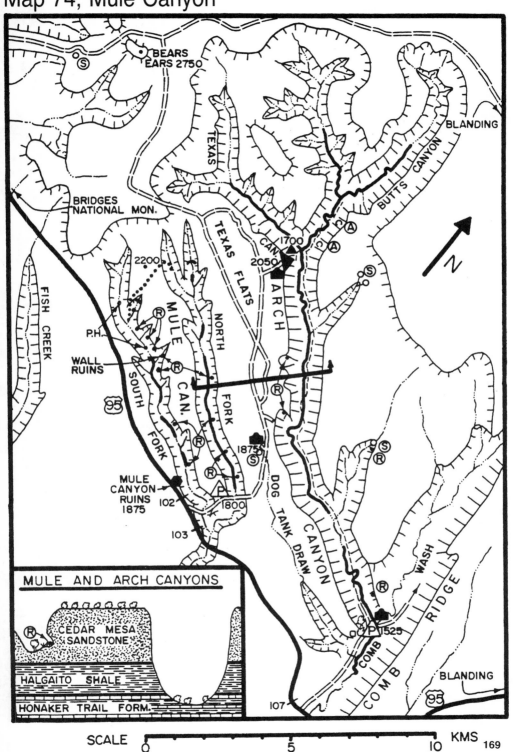

BEARS
EARS 2750

TEXAS

BLANDING

BRIDGES
NATIONAL MON.

TEXAS FLATS

BUTTS CANYON

TEXAS CAN.

ARCH

1700

2050

2200

A

A

S

FISH CREEK

MULE

R

P.H.

WALL
RUINS

R

NORTH FORK

CAN.

SOUTH FORK

95

R

R

R

S

S

R

1875

R

DOG TANK DRAW

CANYON

MULE
CANYON
RUINS
1875

R

102

1800

103

WASH

RIDGE

R

COMB

COMB

1525

BLANDING

107

95

N

MULE AND ARCH CANYONS

R
CEDAR MESA
SANDSTONE

HALGAITO SHALE

HONAKER TRAIL FORM.

SCALE 0   5   10 KMS 169

List of Utahs 4000 meter Peaks (all in the Uinta Mtns.)

In Utah, there are 21 peaks or mountains over 3962 meters (13,000 feet). Of these, 15 are over the 4000 meter mark. All of the 21 peaks listed below are in the Uinta Mountains. Some have no names, and some have been named by the author. The elevations have come from the old USGS maps at 1:24,000 scale, and have been converted to metric. Has anyone climbed all 15 or 21 peaks? The author thought he had them all, but later found East Lovenia to be on this magic list, so he still has some climbing to do.

1. Kings Peak 4123
2. Kings Peak South 4119
3. Gilbert Peak 4097
4. Mt. Emmons 4097
5. Unnamed Peak (Kings—Emmons Ridge) 4080
6. Unnamed Peak (Kings—Emmons Ridge) 4056
7. Unnamed Peak (Kings—Emmons Ridge) 4050
8. Gunsight Peak (author's name) 4043
9. Unnamed Peak (Kings—Emmons Ridge) 4038
10. Henrys Fork Peak (author's name) 4036
11. Mt. Lovenia 4032
12. South Emmons (author's name) 4014
13. Mt. Tokewanna 4013
14. Mt. Powell (3 summits) 4005, 4009, 4011
15. Wasatch Peak 4010

Other Peaks over 3962 meters (13,000 feet). All in the Uinta Mtns.

16. West Gunsight (author's name) 3994
17. Unnamed Peak (Kings—Emmons Ridge) 3983
18. West Henrys Fork Peak (author's name) 3982
19. Wilson Peak 3979
20. West Wasatch (author's name) 3974
21. East Lovenia (author's name) 3972

List of Peaks over 3600 meters outside the Uinta Mtns.

1. Mt. Peale—La Sal Mtns. 3878
2. Mt. Mellenthin—La Sal Mtns. 3855
3. Mt. Tukuhnikivatz—La Sal Mtns. 3806
4. Mt. Waas—La Sal Mtns. 3759
5. Manns Peak—La Sal Mtns. 3742
6. Mt. Tomasaki—La Sal Mtns. 3729
7. Delano Peak—Tushar Mtns. 3709
8. Mt. Belknap—Tushar Mtns. 3699
9. Mt. Baldy—Tushar Mtns. 3689
10. Ibapah Peak—Deep Creek Range 3684
11. Mt. Holly—Tushar Mtns. 3057
12. Haystack Mtn.—Deep Creek Range 3664
13. Mt. Nebo—Wasatch Mtns. 3637

(There are 10 minor peaks or summits along the high ridges in the La Sal Mountains which exceed the 3600 meter level, but may or may not be classified as separate peaks.)

(Mt. Timpanogos—Wasatch Mtns. .... 3582)

Red Mountain, seen from the pass between Red and Ibapah Peaks – Deep Creek Range (50mm lens).

Between High Creek and Naomi Peaks, sits High Creek Lake (55mm lens).

Heliograph Stations in Utah

Heliograph is the name of an instrument having a mirror set upon a tripod, which is used to send signals by using the rays of the sun. These contraptions were used in the early years of geodetic surveys in the western USA. Some of these first surveys in Utah were made from about 1882 on through the late 1880's.

The Heliographs were set upon high and prominent peaks, then triangulation measurements were taken to determine altitudes and locations. On some major summits, surveyers were camped for extended periods of time. On those summits stone sleeping huts and flat triangulation platforms were constructed. Some of these old structures are still standing and therein lies the reason for adding the subject to this book.

The map shows the Utah stations. This information comes from the U.S. Coast and Geodetic Survey of 1883 and uses names of peaks used at that time. Some names have changed: North Ogden is now likely to be Ben Lomond Peak; Vernon is probably Black Crook Peak in the Sheeprock Mountains; Gosiute is Ibapah Peak; Oak Creek is Fool Peak in the Canyon Range; Wasatch is Heliotrope Mtn. east of Gunnison; and La Sal must be Mt. Waas in the La Sal Mountains. Jeff Davis Peak just inside Nevada, is now called Wheeler Peak.

The author has been on top of all these summits except Pilot, Pioche and Cliff (in the eastern Book Cliffs somewhere), and has found some kind of ruins at or near the top of each. The very best ruins are found on the top of Belknap and Ibapah (Gosiute). At the very summit of each peak can be found several small stone huts. All that remain of course are the stone walls. They originally had either tents on top to form the roofs, or some kind of wooded roofs. There are scattered wood pieces at each site, some of which must have been used as platform or tripod material.

Other peaks which have some limited amounts of ruins are: Nebo, just south of the south summit, and Fool Peak (Oak Creek) just west of the summit and down a bit. Both of these are simple tent platforms, but some artifacts such as nails and broken bottles still can be found. On other peaks, camping places were simply not observed or were less noticeable. Mt. Ellen (Henry Mountains) also has some well preserved ruins or platforms just under its summit.

About the only reading material the author has found about these Heliograph Sations has been in the old US Coast and Geodetic Survey reports dating from the early 1880's. These documents are found in only a few of the larger libraries of the state.

(Recently the author spoke to 80 year old Charles B. Hunt (1986), who conducted geologic surveys in the Henry Mountains in the 1930's. He said the platforms seen today on top of Ellen Peak didn't exist in his day. It appears that at least some of the ruins seen in the Henry Mountains and perhaps other summits, were not all from the 1880's.)

One of the better preserved Heliograph Stations is on top of Ibapah Peak (50mm lens.)

Heliograph Stations of Utah

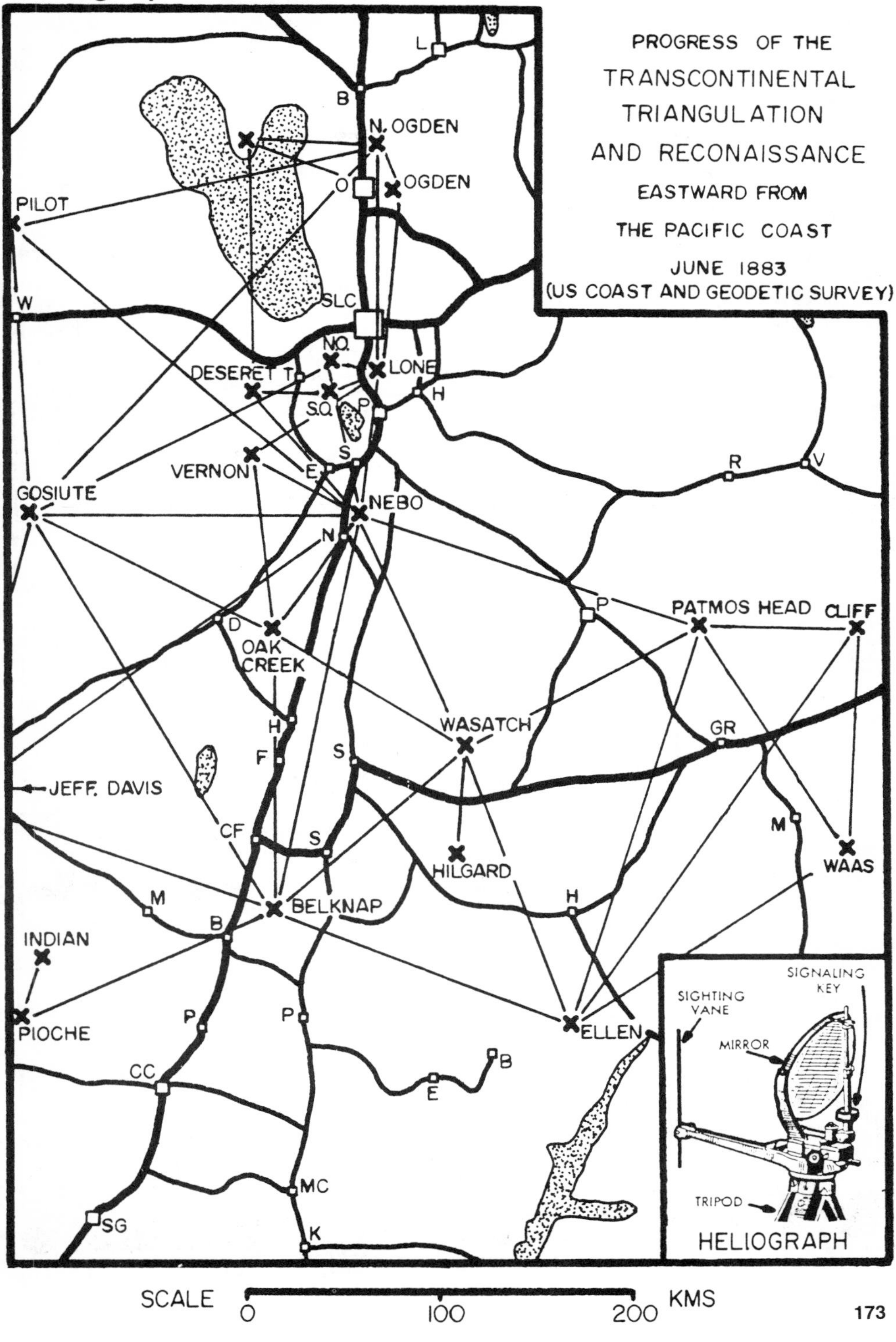

PROGRESS OF THE
TRANSCONTINENTAL
TRIANGULATION
AND RECONAISSANCE
EASTWARD FROM
THE PACIFIC COAST
JUNE 1883
(US COAST AND GEODETIC SURVEY)

L

B

N. OGDEN

OGDEN

O

PILOT

W

SLC

N.O.

DESERET T.

LONE

H

S.Q.

P

VERNON

E

S

GOSIUTE

NEBO

N

R

V

D

PATMOS HEAD

CLIFF

OAK
CREEK

P

H

WASATCH

GR

F

S

JEFF. DAVIS

M

CF

S

HILGARD

WAAS

M

B

BELKNAP

H

INDIAN

PIOCHE

P

P

ELLEN

CC

B

E

MC

SG

K

SIGNALING
KEY

SIGHTING
VANE

MIRROR

TRIPOD

HELIOGRAPH

SCALE   0   100   200   KMS

173

Climographs of Utah

There are great climatic changes from northern Utah to the south eastern corner. Elevation directly affects the temperature, as does a town's situation in a valley or basin. Rainfall amounts vary greatly from north to south. The northern and western parts of the state receive the greatest amount of precipitation in fall, winter and especially in spring. But the south eastern portion of Utah has its highest precip in late summer — early fall. Compare Logan with Monticello. The northern part of Utah gets most of its precip from storms coming into the state from the northwest, west, or from the southwest. Southeastern Utah has higher amounts of precip from summer time thunder storms. This moisture usually comes from the south, around Baja California or the Gulf of Mexico. The Wasatch Front in northern Utah is affected by the Great Salt Lake. Areas from Brigham City to Salt Lake City occasionally have "lake effect" or "lake enhanced" storms. Of all valley locations in Utah, the higher bench areas of Bountiful receive the highest amounts of precipitation.

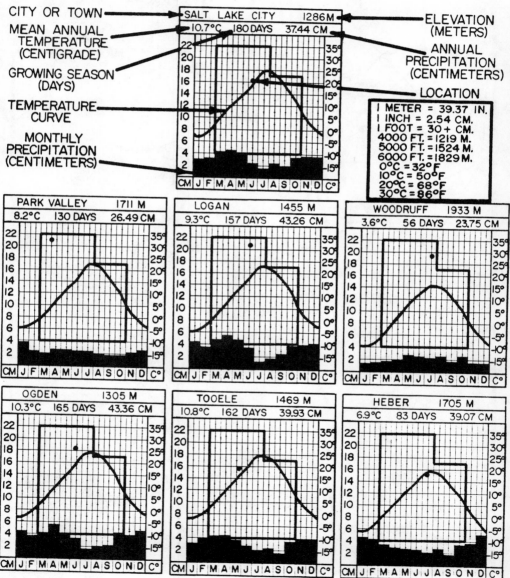

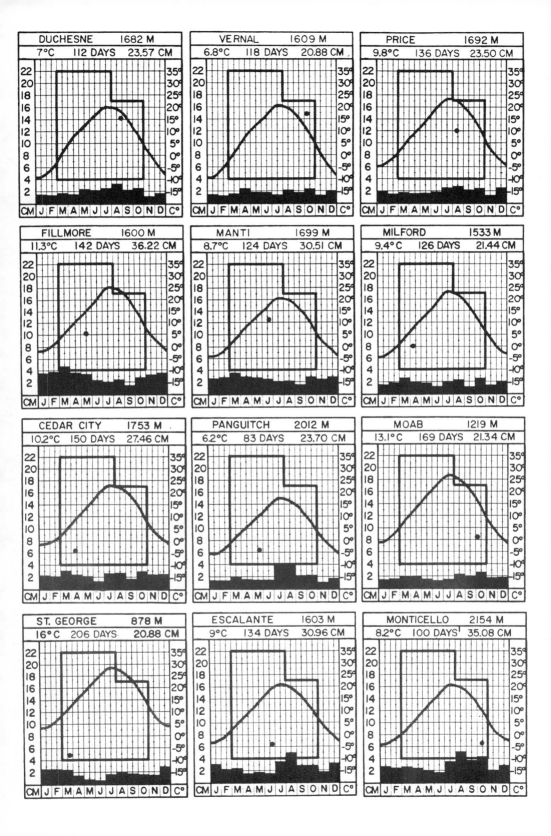

Bristlecone Pines of Utah and the Western USA

If you're hiking or climbing in southwestern or western Utah, you should be aware of some of the trees in that region. The trees in question are the bristlecone pines, found only in the Great Basin of Utah, Arizona, Nevada and California. Depending on the book you read the official name is either *Pinus aristate* or *Pinus longaeva*. The name doesn't matter; the thing to remember is that it is likely the oldest living thing in the world. To the authors' knowledge, the oldest tree found is on Wheeler Peak in eastern Nevada. It's 4900 years old! In the White Mountains of California, east of Bishop, one is 4300 years old. The map shows the distribution according to several sources and the authors own climbs. The author has been to almost all these mountain areas, and questions the locations of some stands. He doubts bristlecone pines live on the Sevier Plateau (and in Colorado according to only one source), because of the higher amounts of moisture received, and other factors.

Typically, the bristlecone pine lives above 3000 meters, on poor rocky soil, and especially on soils derived from limestone. They grow 5 to 10 meters in height, are up to one meter in diameter, have needles in sets of 5, and have chocolate-colored cones with short bristles on the tips. The branches have needles clustered on the last 25 to 30 cms, and have the appearance of a fox tail. Trees are usually twisted, gnarled and squat and often half dead. Some have only a narrow piece of bark running up one side of the trunk which supports life. The most interesting trees are those on wind-swept ridges and other exposed locations, which often times grow horizontal instead of up.

In Utah, here are the known sites where bristlecone pines are found. The Deep Creek Range, on Swasy, Notch, Frisco and Indian Peaks, in the higher portions of the Wah Wah Mountains, and the northern part of the Mountain Home Range (just north of Indian Peak). They are likely to be in the Pine Valley Mountains, and on several scattered locations in Cedar Breaks National Monument and nearby plateaus. The stand most easily reached is the one on Spectra Point in Cedar Breaks, N.M. It's only about 1 km from the visitor center.

Outside of Utah they are found on Mt. Humphreys, Arizona, and in the White Mountains of California. They're also on most of the higher peaks of central and southern Nevada.

If you have seen bristlecone pine trees anywhere not listed on this map, please inform the author of their locations so they can be plotted on the next edition or printing of this book.

From Spectra Point, Cedar Breaks N.M.; bristlecone pines, Cedar Breaks and Brian Head (35mm lens).

Bristlecone Pines of Utah, Western USA

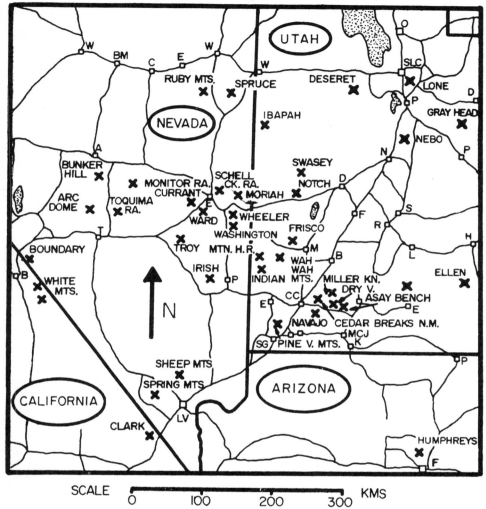

Since the first edition the author has found several other stands of bristlecone pine. A tip from Ann Cheves led the author to the south slopes of Gray Head Peak, between Price and Duchesne. They are likely to be on other high summits in that area as well. Darel and Karen Neilson reported a small stand of about 10 trees on the south face of Lone Peak, but this author has some doubts. The soil there is derived from granite, not limetone, and the climate is much wetter than in other locals. Someone (and the name has been lost) stated there were some bristlecones on Deseret Peak, but that hasn't been confirmed. Another person said they were growing at the head of Henderson Canyon, just east of Pine Lake, and northeast of Bryce Canyon N.P. Yet another person thought bristlecones were in the San Rafael Swell, but the author has doubts, due to lower altitudes and lack of proper soil. The author, however, found a stand on the south and southeast ridges of Mt. Hillers, above the Star Campground, and the Woodruff Mine.

Geology of Utah

The short introduction to Utah geology in this book is not intended to make geologists out of climbers and hikers but merely to give the reader a simple introduction to the processes which form the mountains and plateaus of Utah.

The following map shows the locations of the geologic cross sections shown on the next four pages. In addition to the cross sections shown here, there are small cross sections on a number of other maps, especially the canyons on the Colorado Plateau.

The first cross section shows the Wellsville and Bear River Mountains in northern Utah. It runs on a line from about Honeyville just north of Brigham City, into the Cache Valley, to the top of Mt. Logan, and on east. Most of the formations in this area are limestone and dolomite. The area has been faulted and various blocks have been uplifted in relation to others. Therefore we have fault block mountains. Along with the faulting, great pressure has tilted some formations to about 45 degrees. These two mountain ranges are similar to other smaller mountains in the Great Basin of western Utah.

The next area is the Uinta Mountains. These mountains are a large oblong dome-shaped structure running east-west. The earth's crust buckled and forced the Uintas up, then later erosion wore down the higher regions. The result is the oldest rocks are exposed at the center of the range, with progressively younger rocks being exposed at the outer edges. The heart of the Uintas is composed of various layers of quartzite rock.

The Wasatch Plateau is another uplifted region, with all the beds of rock still in a horizontal position. The top of the plateau, generally known as the "Skyline Drive", is very flat. Along either side, near Ephraim and Castle Dale, there are faults running north-south. The rocks here are sandstone, lime-stone and an occasional vein of shale.

The next geologic cross section is that of the Henry Mountains and nearby Waterpocket Fold. This is on the Colorado Plateau, famous for its very flat-lying sandstone beds. But the sandstone bedding has been disrupted by the intrusive body which forms the heart of the Henrys. This was moulten magma in the beginning, but later cooled before reaching the surface. Later erosion left the diorite porphyry exposed. It is seen in the highest summits of the Henry Mountains. Crustal pressure caused some folding of the upper crust, resulting in the Waterpocket Fold, to the west of the Henrys. The Henry Mountains are known as laccolith mountains or sometimes laccolithic intrusions. Within the confines of the Colorado Plateau are 8 such mountains or ranges falling into this category. Besides the Henrys they are: the La Sal, Abajo and Navajo Mountains in Utah; the Rico, Ute and La Plata Mountains in Colorado; and the Carrizo Mountains in Arizona.

The last cross section is that of the central Wasatch Mountains. This runs from about Grandview Peak in the north, to Lone Peak in the south. Lots of limestone here, as well as shales, conglomerates, quartzites and finally granite. These formations have been bent in several places running north-south, and this whole range has been uplifted on the east side of the Wasatch Fault. This fault forms the zone between mountain and valley all along the Wasatch Front. Around Lone Peak and in Little Cottonwood Canyon, an intrusive body has also caused uplifting. This rock is usually known as temple granite but geology maps call it quartz monzonite.

One of the best single sources of information is the Geological Highway Map of Utah, put out by B.Y.U. Geology Dept. It has the geologic map of Utah, cross sections, and some brief explanations.

Here are several of the better known formations in Utah and how they were formed.

Oquirrh Formation (mostly limestone) — It was layed down in warm shallow seas, and was later uplifted. Composed mostly of marine shells, and corals (seen in central Wasatch Mts.).

Little Cottonwood Quartz Monzonite (granite) — Molten magma pushed up from below, but never reached the surface. It cooled very slowly, forming the salt and pepper crystals.

Uinta Mt. Group (quartzite) — It's usually metamorphosed (combining of heat and pressure) sandstone. The grains are then recrystallized, forming a hard and tough rock.

Navajo Sandstone — Sand is made by erosion of other rocks, then usually wind blown, often near shallow seas and in a desert setting. Grains are then cemented by lime or iron oxide.

Locations of Geologic Cross Sections

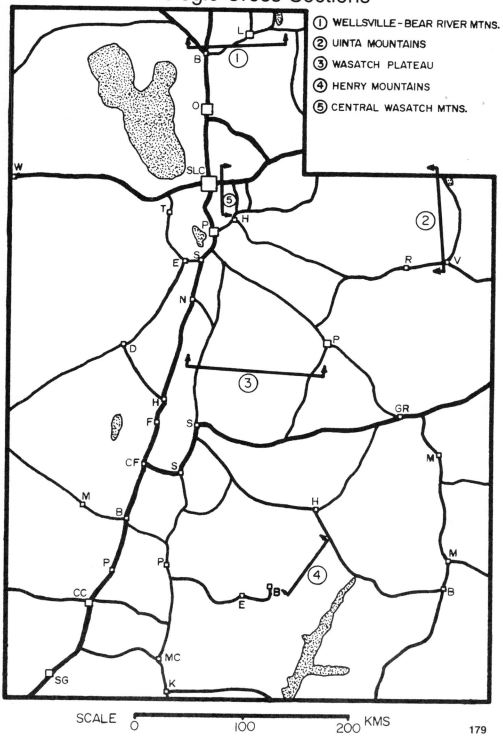

① WELLSVILLE – BEAR RIVER MTNS.
② UINTA MOUNTAINS
③ WASATCH PLATEAU
④ HENRY MOUNTAINS
⑤ CENTRAL WASATCH MTNS.

SCALE
0   100   200 KMS

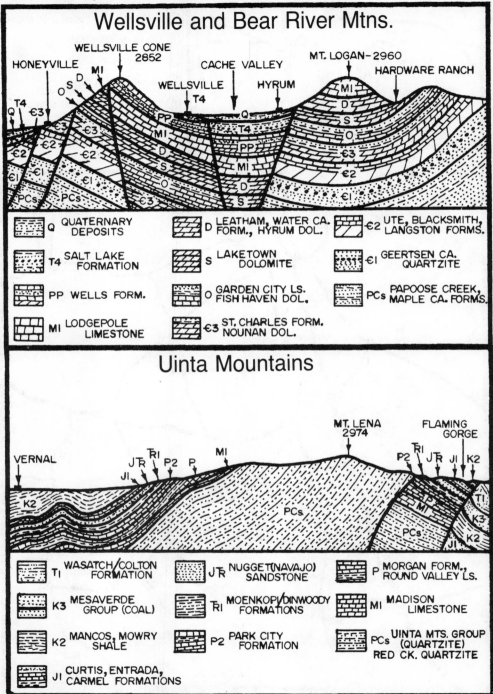

Wellsville and Bear River Mtns.

HONEYVILLE
WELLSVILLE CONE 2852
CACHE VALLEY
MT. LOGAN-2960
HARDWARE RANCH
WELLSVILLE
HYRUM

Q	QUATERNARY DEPOSITS
T4	SALT LAKE FORMATION
PP	WELLS FORM.
MI	LODGEPOLE LIMESTONE
D	LEATHAM, WATER CA. FORM., HYRUM DOL.
S	LAKETOWN DOLOMITE
O	GARDEN CITY LS. FISH HAVEN DOL.
€3	ST. CHARLES FORM. NOUNAN DOL.
€2	UTE, BLACKSMITH, LANGSTON FORMS.
€1	GEERTSEN CA. QUARTZITE
PCs	PAPOOSE CREEK, MAPLE CA. FORMS.

Uinta Mountains

VERNAL
MT. LENA 2974
FLAMING GORGE

TI	WASATCH/COLTON FORMATION
K3	MESAVERDE GROUP (COAL)
K2	MANCOS, MOWRY SHALE
JI	CURTIS, ENTRADA, CARMEL FORMATIONS
JR̄	NUGGET(NAVAJO) SANDSTONE
R̄I	MOENKOPI/DINWOODY FORMATIONS
P2	PARK CITY FORMATION
P	MORGAN FORM., ROUND VALLEY LS.
MI	MADISON LIMESTONE
PCs	UINTA MTS. GROUP (QUARTZITE) RED CK. QUARTZITE

Wasatch Plateau and Henry Mountains

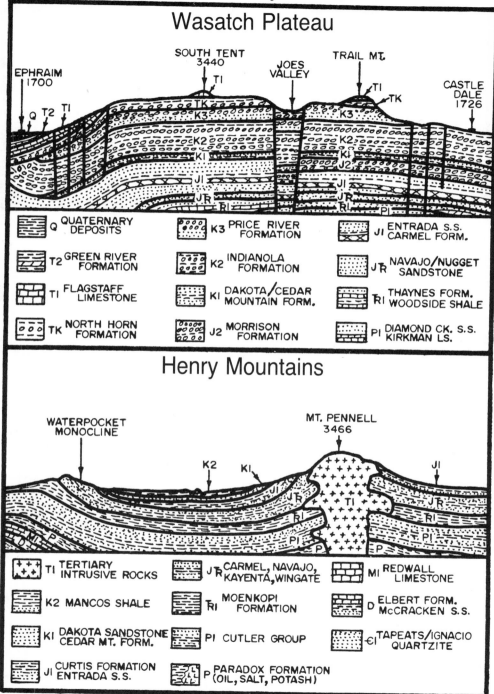

Wasatch Plateau

EPHRAIM 1700
SOUTH TENT 3440
JOES VALLEY
TRAIL MT.
CASTLE DALE 1726

Q QUATERNARY DEPOSITS	K3 PRICE RIVER FORMATION	JI ENTRADA S.S. CARMEL FORM.
T2 GREEN RIVER FORMATION	K2 INDIANOLA FORMATION	JR NAVAJO/NUGGET SANDSTONE
TI FLAGSTAFF LIMESTONE	KI DAKOTA/CEDAR MOUNTAIN FORM.	TRI THAYNES FORM. WOODSIDE SHALE
TK NORTH HORN FORMATION	J2 MORRISON FORMATION	PI DIAMOND CK. S.S. KIRKMAN LS.

Henry Mountains

WATERPOCKET MONOCLINE
MT. PENNELL 3466

TI TERTIARY INTRUSIVE ROCKS	JR CARMEL, NAVAJO, KAYENTA, WINGATE	MI REDWALL LIMESTONE
K2 MANCOS SHALE	TRI MOENKOPI FORMATION	D ELBERT FORM. McCRACKEN S.S.
KI DAKOTA SANDSTONE CEDAR MT. FORM.	PI CUTLER GROUP	€I TAPEATS/IGNACIO QUARTZITE
JI CURTIS FORMATION ENTRADA S.S.	P PARADOX FORMATION (OIL, SALT, POTASH)	

Central Wasatch Mtns.--North

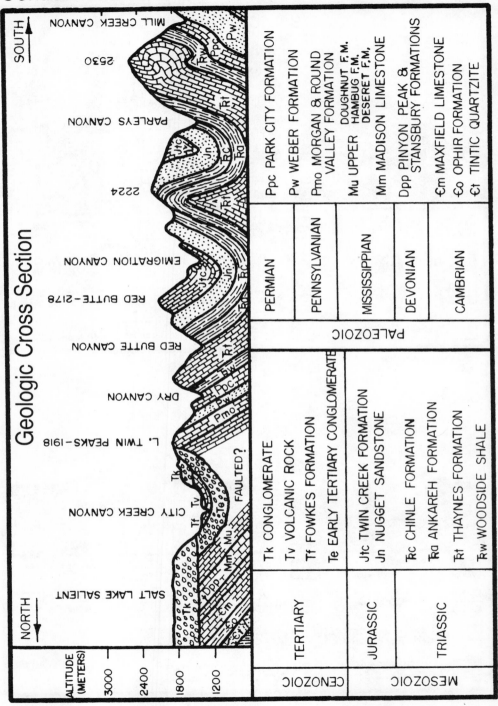

Geologic Cross Section

NORTH

SOUTH

ALTITUDE (METERS)	
3000	
2400	
1800	
1200	

SALT LAKE SALIENT

CITY CREEK CANYON

L. TWIN PEAKS-1918

RED BUTTE CANYON

RED BUTTE-2178

EMIGRATION CANYON

2224

PARLEYS CANYON

2530

MILL CREEK CANYON

FAULTED?

CENOZOIC	TERTIARY	Tk CONGLOMERATE
		Tv VOLCANIC ROCK
		Tf FOWKES FORMATION
		Te EARLY TERTIARY CONGLOMERATE
MESOZOIC	JURASSIC	Jtc TWIN CREEK FORMATION
		Jn NUGGET SANDSTONE
	TRIASSIC	Rc CHINLE FORMATION
		Ra ANKAREH FORMATION
		Rt THAYNES FORMATION
		Rw WOODSIDE SHALE

PALEOZOIC	PERMIAN	Ppc PARK CITY FORMATION
		Pw WEBER FORMATION
	PENNSYLVANIAN	Pmo MORGAN & ROUND VALLEY FORMATION
	MISSISSIPPIAN	Mu UPPER DOUGHNUT F.M. HAMBUG F.M. DESERET F.M.
		Mm MADISON LIMESTONE
	DEVONIAN	Dpp PINYON PEAK & STANSBURY FORMATIONS
	CAMBRIAN	€m MAXFIELD LIMESTONE
		€o OPHIR FORMATION
		€t TINTIC QUARTZITE

Central Wasatch Mtns.--South

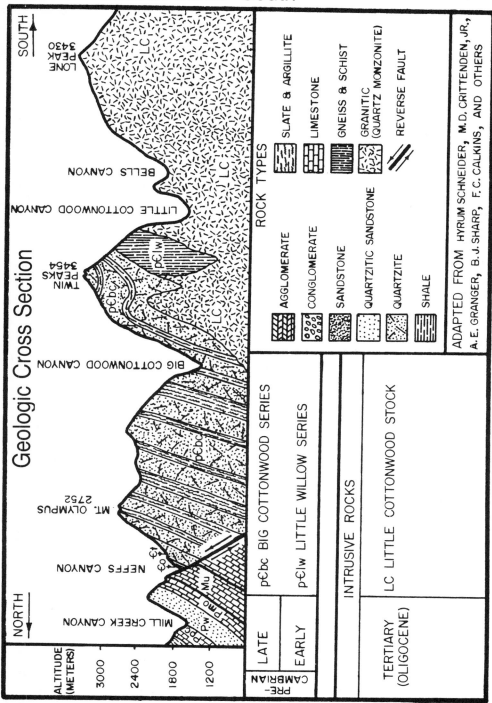

Geologic Cross Section

ROCK TYPES

SLATE & ARGILLITE
LIMESTONE
GNEISS & SCHIST
GRANITIC (QUARTZ MONZONITE)
REVERSE FAULT

AGGLOMERATE
CONGLOMERATE
SANDSTONE
QUARTZITIC SANDSTONE
QUARTZITE
SHALE

ADAPTED FROM HYRUM SCHNEIDER, M. D. CRITTENDEN, JR., A. E. GRANGER, B. J. SHARP, F. C. CALKINS, AND OTHERS

PRE-CAMBRIAN	LATE	pЄbc BIG COTTONWOOD SERIES
	EARLY	pЄlw LITTLE WILLOW SERIES
	INTRUSIVE ROCKS	
TERTIARY (OLIGOCENE)		LC LITTLE COTTONWOOD STOCK

ALTITUDE (METERS)
3000
2400
1800
1200

SOUTH
LONE PEAK 3430
BELLS CANYON
LITTLE COTTONWOOD CANYON
TWIN PEAKS 3454
BIG COTTONWOOD CANYON
MT. OLYMPUS 2752
NEFFS CANYON
MILL CREEK CANYON
NORTH

LC
pЄlw
pЄbc
Mu
Pwa
Pmo
€t

Utahs Anasazi and Fremont Indians

In southeastern Utah canyons, some of which are included in this book, are found many archaeological ruins, and petroglyphs and pictographs, left behind by what now is know as the Anasazi and Fremont Indians. The following is an excerpt adapted from the information in the BLM publication, "Grand Gulch Primitive Area" (map).

|The Basketmakers were the earliest known inhabitants of Grand Gulch. This culture is thought to have derived from an earlier nomadic people whose livelihood was based on hunting and gathering. As yet no artifacts have been discovered in the Gulch which pre-date the Basketmakers. When the nomadic people learned to plant and cultivate corn introduced from the south (as well as squash and beans and the domestication of turkeys), they became more sedentary and the Basketmaker culture evolved. It flourished here from 200 to 600 A.D. They built pit houses made of mud, caked over stick walls and roofs. Their name was derived from the finely woven baskets they made. They also used flint tools and wooden digging sticks. The most prevalent remains of the Basketmaker culture in the Gulch are their slab-lined storage cists. These may still be seen on the mesa tops or on high ledges protected from the weather (and rodents).

A series of droughts apparently drove the people into the surrounding mountains. When they returned around 1050 A.D., their culture had been influenced by the Mesa Verde people to the east and the Kayenta people from the south. As time passed the Mesa Verde influence predominated in the Grand Gulch area.

The Basketmaker culture had developed into the Pueblo culture. The Pueblo culture is characterized by the making of fine pottery with some highly decorated; the cultivation of cotton and weaving of cotton cloth, and the high degree of architectural and stone masonry skill seen in the cliff dwellings in the Gulch. They also developed irrigation of their crops by building checkdams and diversion canals. These have been found on the mesa tops near Dark Canyon and tributary canyons to the Colorado River. The kiva, a round ceremonial structure found in Grand Gulch, is still in use by the modern day descendants of the Anasazi, the Hopi and New Mexico Pueblo Indians.

Grand Gulch is also known for the diversity of rock art scattered throughout. The rock art consists of both petroglyphs (pecked into the rock) and pictographs (painted on with pigments). As the figures do not represent a written language, the meaning of the various panels is left to our imaginations.

Periods of drought in the 12th and 13th centuries, plus depletion of natural resources and pressure from nomadic Indians from the north, are thought to be some possible reasons for the abandonment of

A close-up of Newspaper Rock, located on the paved highway running to The Needles (55mm lens).

Utah's Anasazi and Fremont Indians

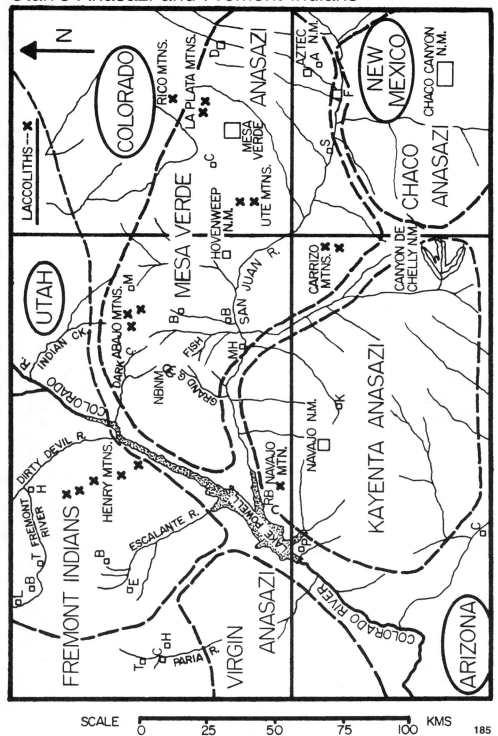

N

LACCOLITHS --- ✕

COLORADO

NEW MEXICO

RICO MTNS. ✕
LA PLATA MTNS. ✕ ✕

D □

AZTEC N.M. ▲
A ▲
□ F

CHACO CANYON N.M. □

MESA VERDE □
C ○

HOVENWEEP N.M. □
UTE MTNS. ✕ ✕

S ○

CHACO ANASAZI

ANASAZI

UTAH

MESA VERDE

M ○
INDIAN CK.
DARK ABAJO MTNS. ✕ ✕ ✕
C ○
NBNM □
GRAND G. ○ ○ FISH

B ○
B ○
SAN JUAN R.
MH ○

CARRIZO MTNS. ✕ ✕

CANYON DE CHELLY N.M.

COLORADO R.

K ○

KAYENTA ANASAZI

DIRTY DEVIL R.
T □ FREMONT RIVER H ✕
HENRY MTNS. ✕ ✕ ✕ ✕
B ○
E ○
ESCALANTE R.

NBNM □

NAVAJO MTN. ✕
RB □
C ○

NAVAJO N.M. □

FREMONT INDIANS

L ○
B ○
B ○

LAKE POWELL
P ✕
R ○

C ○

VIRGIN ANASAZI

PARIA R.
T ○ C ○ □ H

COLORADO RIVER

ARIZONA

this region. By the late 1300's, the Anasazi moved south into Arizona and southeast into the Rio Grande Valley of New Mexico.]

Places where Anasazi ruins can be found are in Grand Gulch, Fish and Owl Creeks, Mule, Dark, Roads and Lime Canyons, and in various other canyons not covered in this book. The map shows the general boundaries of the Mesa Verde Anasazi, to which Utahs Anasazi belonged. It also shows the land areas occupied by other groups of Anasazi during the same time period, namely the Virgin, Kayenta and the Chaco Anasazi. It also shows part of the land covered by the Fremont Indians. Evidence of the Fremonts is found in the Escalante River drainage, in Capital Reef National Park and the Fremont River system in that same area. View their rock art on panels at Newspaper Rock and in the Fremont River Gorge.

The Fremonts were people who lived in this area during the same time period as the Anasazi. The main populations of Fremonts apparently lived in Castle Valley (southwest of Price) and in Nine Mile Canyon. They ranged from Utahs high plateaus, to the Uinta Mountains, south to the Escalante River, and east into Colorado. They hunted and fished, and grew corn, squash and beans, using some primitive irrigation ditches. But they differed from the Anasazi in these ways: They built less durable homes in the river bottoms or on ridges, but not under cliffs. They used animal skins to make moccasins, instead of using sandals as worn by the Anasazi. They depended on hunting much more than their cousins to the southeast. They didn't grow or use cotton, or raise turkeys. And the ceremonial kiva was apparently never used or developed. It appears the Colorado River was a cultural and physical impediment.

Evidence shows the Fremont culture thrived from about 950 A.D. until 1250 or 1300 A.D. It's thought they too were driven out by drought. It's also thought that they remained in the same general area and their descendants are now the Utes and Southern Piutes.

Anasazi ruins in Natural Bridges National Monument (35mm lens).

Utah Maps and Dealers

The Utah Travel Council publishes a series of 8 maps covering the state of Utah. These maps are 1:250,000 scale, and have contour lines. These maps are especially good for areas not covered by the national forest maps, and for areas in the Great Basin and the southeastern part of the state. Because of the intermediate scale, they bridge the gap between state highway and forest service or U.S.G.S. maps. These can be purchased at all the national park visitor centers, many of the other outlets listed below, and at the Utah Travel Council Office, 300 North Main Street, Salt Lake City, Utah.

The U.S. Forest Service maps can normally be purchased at any of the forest service offices or ranger stations. The Intermountain Regional Forest Headquarters in Ogden has all forest service maps for the state and intermountain area. Forest service maps are especially good for the Uinta Mountains, because they show lakes. Sign posts on trails normally point the way to lakes, not mountains. Forest service maps are also good when it comes to showing access roads, and whether they are maintained or not.

Bureau of Land Management (BLM) maps can be purchased at any of their offices throughout the state, but these are often inferior to other maps.

At the time of publication of this book, most but not all, of the new metric — 1 : 100,000 scale maps have been completed. Both the U.S.G.S. and the BLM make their own series of this map, but the U.S.G.S. ones are normally better because they're one color and are much less confusing and easier to read. There are some problems with these maps, but none too serious. Some 4WD roads don't show up clearly, some 4WD roads have been eliminated, and they fail to show many man-made features. But they do cover larger areas than the 1 : 24,000 scale maps, thus one map can be bought instead of 3 or 4. A good feature about these maps is they are metric. At one time the USA began a movement to change over to the metric system. Even Congress had a schedule, but when Ronald Reagan got to the White House, the movement went backward instead of forward. This author has been to 129 countries since he began traveling in 1970, and can safely state that the USA is the one and only country in the world which doggedly clings to the old inferior English system of measurement. Even the English and Canadians have made the change, so why not us?

Dealers for Topographic Maps In Utah

(USGS maps 1 : 250,000, 1 : 100,000 (Metric), 1 : 62,500, and 1 : 24,000 scale, and national parks and monuments of various scales)

Arches National Park
Visitor Center

Brian Head
Brian Head Nordic Ski Center

Bryce Canyon National Park
Visitor Center

Canyonlands National Park
Needles Visitor Center

Capitol Reef National Park
Visitor Center

Cedar City
Mountain View Real Estate
110 North, Main

Cedar Breaks N.M.
Federal Building

Cedar Breaks National Monument
Visitor Center

Delta
Portraits Forever Studio
242 East, Main

Duchesne
Jerry D. Allred and Associates
121 North, Center

Green River
Ken Sleight Expeditions
16 North, Long St.

Kanab
Utah Properties, Inc.
30 West, Center

Wilderness Sports
240 South, 100 East

Logan
Trailhead Sports
35 West, 100 North

Moab
Arches National Park HQ.
Canyonlands National Park HQ.
Bridges National Monument HQ.
125 W. 200 S.

The Times Independent
35 East, Center

Tourist Information Center
North Highway

Ogden
Great Basin Engineering, Inc.
3505 Grant Ave.

Weber State College Bookstore
3750 Harrison Blvd.

Park City
Timberhaus Ski & Sports
628 Park Ave.

Index Map for 1:100,000 Scale Metric Maps

GROUSE CREEK	TREMONTON	LOGAN	TOPOGRAPHIC MAPS PRINTED AND	
NEW FOUNDLAND MOUNTAINS	PROMONTORY POINT	OGDEN	DISTRIBUTED BY THE U.S. GEOLOGICAL SURVEY (INTERMEDIATE SCALE)	
BONNEVILLE SALT FLATS	TOOELE	SALT LAKE CITY	KINGS PEAK	DUTCH JOHN
WILD CAT MOUNTAIN	RUSH VALLEY	PROVO	DUCHESNE	VERNAL
FISH SPRINGS	LYNNDYL	NEPHI	PRICE	SEEP RIDGE
TULE VALLEY	DELTA	MANTI	HUNTINGTON	WEST WATER
WAH WAH MTS. NORTH	RICHFIELD	SALINA	SAN RAFAEL DESERT	MOAB
WAH WAH MTS. SOUTH	BEAVER	LOA	HANKSVILLE	LA SAL
CEDAR CITY	PANGUITCH	ESCALANTE	HITE CROSSING	BLANDING
ST. GEORGE	KANAB	SMOKEY MTN.	NAVAJO MTN.	BLUFF

Provo
Utah Office Supply Co.
69 East Center Street
Salt Lake City
Federal Building (USGS)
125 South State

Holubar Mountaineering
3975 Wasatch Blvd.

Intermountain Aerial Surveys
2078 West 2300 South

Kirkham's Outdoor Products
3125 South State

Photo-Blue
370 South, West Temple

Sunset Sports Center
1110 East 7200 South

Timberline Sports, Inc.
3155 Highland Drive

Wasatch Mountain Touring
779 East, Third South
Snowbird
Timberhaus Ski & Sport
Snowbird Village
Springdale
Zion Natural History Assn.
St. George
Spoke and Pedal
90 South, 100 East
Timpanogos Cave National Mon.
Visitor Center
Torrey
Boulder Mountain Realty

Bushnell Real Estate, Inc.
Vernal
Bitter Creek Books
672 West, Main
Zion National Park
Visitor Center

US Geological Survey Sales Offices

All USGS Topographic maps may be purchased over the counter or by mail order from:

Branch of Distribution
U.S. Geological Survey
Federal Center
Denver, Colorado

A limited stock of the standard topographic quadrangle maps is maintained for over-the-counter sales only at:

1012 Federal Building
1961 Stout Street
Denver, Colorado

1036 General Service Building
19th & F Streets N.W.
Washington, D.C.

Public Inquiries Office
USGS National Center, Room 1C402
12201 Sunrise Valley Drive
Reston, Virginia

Map Reference Libraries In Utah

Cedar City
Library, Southern Utah State College
Logan
Library, Utah State University
Ogden
Library, Weber State College

Provo
Library, Brigham Young University
Salt Lake City
Library, University of Utah
Salt Lake City Public Library

U.S. Forest Service Offices and Ranger Stations

ASHLEY NATIONAL FOREST
Headquarters
437 East Main
Vernal, Utah

Duchesne Ranger District
85 West Main Street
Duchesne, Utah

Flaming Gorge Ranger District
Dutch John Unit
P.O. Box 157
Dutch John, Utah

Green River Unit
1540 Uinta Drive
Green River, Wyoming

Manila Unit
Manila, Utah

Roosevelt Ranger District
150 South 2nd East
Roosevelt, Utah

Vernal Ranger District
650 North Vernal Avenue
Vernal, Utah

DIXIE NATIONAL FOREST
Headquarters
82 North 100 East
Cedar City, Utah

Cedar City Ranger District
82 North 100 East
Cedar City, Utah

Enterprise Ranger Station
Enterprise, Utah

Escalante Ranger District
Escalante, Utah

Pine Valley Ranger District
196 East, Tabernacle Street
St. George, Utah

POWELL RANGER DISTRICT
225 East Center
Panguitch, Utah

Teasdale Ranger District
Teasdale, Utah

FISHLAKE NATIONAL FOREST
Headquarters
170 North Main Street
Richfield, Utah

Beaver Ranger District
190 North 100 East
Beaver, Utah

Castle Dale Ranger Station
Castle Dale, Utah

Ephraim Ranger Station
Ephraim, Utah

Ferron Ranger Station
Ferron, Utah

Fillmore Ranger District
390 South Main
Fillmore, Utah

Loa Ranger District
150 South Main
Loa, Utah

Manti Ranger Station
Manti, Utah

Monticello Ranger Station
Monticello, Utah

Mt. Pleasant Ranger Station
Mt. Pleasant, Utah

Richfield Ranger District
55 South 100 East
Richfield, Utah

SAWTOOTH NATIONAL F.
Headquarters
1525 Addison Avenue East
Twin Falls, Idaho

UINTA NATIONAL FOREST
Headquarters
88 West 100 North
Provo, Utah

Heber Ranger District
125 East 100 North
Heber City, Utah

Nephi Ranger Station
Nephi, Utah

Pleasant Grove Ranger District
390 North 100 East
Pleasant Grove, Utah

Spanish Fork Ranger District
44 West 400 North
Spanish Fork, Utah

WASATCH NATIONAL FOREST
Headquarters
8226 Federal Building
125 South State Street
Salt Lake City, Utah

Evanston Ranger District
Federal Building
221 10th Street
Evanston, Wyoming

Kamas Ranger District
50 East Center Street
Kamas Utah

Logan Ranger District
910 South Highway 89-91
Logan, Utah

Mountain View Ranger District
Lone Tree Road, Highway 44
Mountain View, Wyoming

Ogden Ranger District
Federal Building
324 25th Street
Ogden, Utah

Salt Lake Ranger District
6944 South 3000 East
Salt Lake City, Utah

Bureau Of Land Management (BLM)
Offices And Ranger Stations

BLM UTAH HEADQUARTERS
University Club Building
324 S. State Street
Salt Lake City, Utah

CEDAR CITY DISTRICT
Headquarters
1579 North Main Street
Cedar City, Utah

Beaver River Resource Area
44 South Main
Cedar City, Utah

Dixie Resource Area
24 East, St. George Blvd.
St. George, Utah

Escalante Resource Area
Escalante, Utah

Kanab Resource Area
320 North First East
Kanab, Utah

MOAB DISTRICT
Headquarters
82 E. Dogwood
Moab, Utah

Grand Resource Area
Sand Flats Road
Moab, Utah

Price River Resource Area
900 North, 7th East
Price, Utah

San Juan Resource Area
284 South, 1st West
Monticello, Utah

San Rafael Resource Area
900 North, 7th East
Price, Utah

RICHFIELD DISTRICT
Headquarters
150 East, 900 North
Richfield, Utah

Henry Mountain Resource Area
Hanksville, Utah

House Range Resource Area
Fillmore, Utah

Sevier River Resource Area
180 North, 100 East
Richfield, Utah

Warm Springs Resource Area
Fillmore, Utah

VERNAL DISTRICT
Headquarters
170 South 500 East
Vernal, Utah

Bookcliffs Resource Area
170 South 500 East
Vernal, Utah

Diamond Mtn. Resource Area
170 South 500 East
Vernal, Utah

SALT LAKE DISTRICT
Headquarters
2370 South 2300 West
Salt Lake City, Utah

Bear River Resource Area
2370 South 2300 West
Salt Lake City, Utah

Pony Express Resource Area
2370 South 2300 West
Salt Lake City, Utah

National Parks and Monuments of Utah
(HEADQUARTERS OFFICES)

Arches National Park
125 W. 200 S.
Moab, Utah

Bryce Canyon National Park
Bryce Canyon, Utah

Canyonlands National Park
125 W. 200 S.
Moab, Utah

Capitol Reef National Park
Torrey, Utah

Cedar Breaks National Monument
82 North, 100 East
Cedar City, Utah

Dinosaur National Monument
Dinosaur, Utah

Glen Canyon National
Recreation Area
Page, Arizona

Natural Bridges National Monument
125 W. 200 S.
Moab, Utah

Rainbow Bridge National Monument
Page, Arizona

Zion National Park
Springdale, Utah

Mt. Ellsworth in far background, from the ruins of Star Ranch (50mm lens).

Further Reading

History

Canyon Country Prehistoric Indians, Barnes and Pendleton, Wasatch Publishers, Inc., 4647 Idlewild Road, Salt Lake City, Utah.

Canyon Country Geology, F.A. Barnes, Wasatch Publishers, Inc., 4647 Idlewild Road, Salt Lake City, Utah.

Geologic History of Utah, Hintze, Brigham Young University, Provo, Utah

Incredible Passage (Through the Hole-in-the-Rock), Lee Reay, Meadow Lane Publications, Provo, Utah.

Millard and Nearby, Frank Beckwith (1947), Art City Publishing Co., Springville, Utah

Prehistoric Rock Art, F.A. Barns, Wasatch Publishers, Inc., 4647 Idlewild Road, Salt Lake City, Utah

Origin of Quaternary Basalts from the Black Rock Desert Region, Utah, Condie and Barsky, **Geological Society of America Bulletin**, v. 83, p. 333-352, Feb., 1972.

The Archeology of Eastern Utah (emphasis on the Fremont Culture), J. Eldon Dorman, College of Eastern Utah Prehistoric Museum, Price, Utah

Guide Books

Canyon Country Hiking, Fran A. Barnes, Wasatch Publishers, Inc., 4647 Idlewild Road, Salt Lake City, Utah.

Cache Trails (Revised Edition), Davis and Schimpf, Wasatch Publishers, Inc., 4647 Idlewild Road, Salt Lake City, Utah

Capitol Reef National Park — A Guide to the Roads and Trails, Ward J. Roylance, Wasatch Publishers, Inc., 4647 Idlewild Road, Salt Lake City, Utah.

Guide to the Trails of Zion National Park, Zion Natural History Association, Springdale, Utah.

High Uinta Trails, Mel Davis, Wasatch Publishers, 4647 Idlewild Road, Salt Lake City, Utah.

Hikers Guide to Utah, Dave Hall, Falcon Press Publishing Co., Inc., Billings and Helena, Montana.

Hiking the Escalante, Rudi Lambrechtse, Wasatch Publishers, Inc., 4647 Idlewild Road, Salt Lake City, Utah

Utah Valley Trails, The Paxmans and Taylors, Wasatch Publishers, Inc., 4647 Idlewild Road, Salt Lake City, Utah

Wasatch Trails — Volume I, Betty Bottcher, Wasatch Mountain Club, Salt Lake City, Utah.

Wasatch Trails — Volume II, Daniel Geery, Wasatch Mountain Club, Salt Lake City, Utah.

Wasatch Quartzite, John W. Gottman, Wasatch Mountain Club, Salt Lake City, Utah

Other Books by the Author

From Kelsey Publishing, 310 E. 950 S., Springville, Utah, USA, 84663, tele 801-489-6666

Climbers and Hikers Guide to the Worlds Mountains (2nd Ed.), Kelsey, 800 pages, 377 maps, 380 fotos, waterproof color cover, 14cm × 21cm × 4cm (5½" × 8" × 1½"), ISBN 0-9605824-2-8. **US$19.95** (Mail orders US$20.95).

China on Your Own, and the Hiking Guide to China's Nine Sacred Mountains (3rd Ed.), Jennings—Kelsey, 240 pages, 110 maps, 16 hikes or climbs, waterproof color cover, 14cm × 21cm) 5½" × 8½"), ISBN 0-9691363-1-5, **US$9.95** (Mail orders US$10.95).

Canyon Hiking Guide to the Colorado Plateau, Kelsey, 256 pages, 120 maps, 130 fotos, waterproof color cover, 15cm × 23cm (6" × 9"), ISBN 0-9605824-3-6, **US$9.95** (Mail orders US$10.95).

Hiking Utah's San Rafael Swell, Kelsey, 144 pages, 30 mapped hikes, plus History, 104 fotos, waterproof color cover, 15cm × 23cm (6" × 9"), ISBN 0-9605824-4-4. **US$7.95** (Mail orders US$8.95).